STEPHAN BALKENHOL, GANZ GROSSER KOPF, 1992,

Wawaholz gefasst, H. 380 cm mit Sockel / VERY BIG HEAD, 1992, polychromed wawa wood, h. 12' 6" with ba...

(INSTALLATION BLACKFRIARS BRIDGE, EXHIBITION DOUBLETAKE)

SOPHIE CALLE, WEDDING / HOCHZEIT, JUNE 20, 1992.

INHALT / CONTENTS

MOndrian vor MAtisse im MOMA gesichtet

Als hätte ein Bild aus der Sammlung des Museum of Modern Art sich von der Wand gelöst und kurzfristig personifiziert, geht eine Dame in einem Mondrian-Mantel durch die Matisse-Ausstellung im MOMA – das klassische Kunstereignis im vergangenen Winter – und stiehlt sich auf diesem Weg in die Schau des Maler-Kollegen.

Man erinnert sich an Sophie Calles GHOSTS (Fantômes) 1991/92 in der Ausstellung *DisLocations* ebenfalls im MOMA, in welcher die Künstlerin quer durch die gesamte Belegschaft, vom Direktor bis zum Aufsichts- und Reinigungspersonal, sich gerade jene Bilder beschreiben liess, die sie vorher temporär von den Wänden hatte entfernen lassen. Durch die evozierten Kommentare bekannte sie das Interesse für die persönlichen Konnotationen, für die andere Erinnerung und Wahrnehmung als diejenige der Kunstgeschichte.

Sowohl Sophie Calle als auch Stephan Balkenhol, unsere beiden Collaboration-Künstler in dieser Nummer, entwickeln ihre Arbeiten wie von einem Aussen her in die Kunst hinein, indem sie unpathetisch, aber mit Nachdruck auf den Menschen verweisen. Doch könnte man sagen: Was er ausspart, erweckt gerade ihre besondere Beachtung. Bleiben wir bei den Kleidern. Während Balkenhols Aufmerksamkeit für die Bekleidung seiner Figuren zwar liebevoll das Individuelle typisierend sich möglichst auf das Einfache, das Alltägliche richtet, steuert Sophie Calle gerade mit Akribie auf die Details zu. Ihre Edition für *Parkett* (s. S. 72) stellt eines jener intensiv phantasierten Kleidungsstücke dar, die sie sich von einem unbekannten, von ihr beobachteten Mann getragen wünscht.

SOPHIE CALLE, *Magritte: The Menaced Assassin from GHOSTS / FANTOMES, 1991 / Margritte: Der bedrohte Attentäter, aus GEISTER / FANTOMES, 1991.*

(INSTALLATION: MUSEUM OF MODERN ART, NEW YORK)

Menschen, Tiere, Fabelwesen bevölkern Stephan Balkenhols Figurenwelt – aber keine Kinder, denn die Skulpturen entstehen in einer Art Nachvollzug des kindlichen Blicks auf Elementares. Dieser gleicht jenem «taktilen Blick», wie ihn Joseph Grigely bezüglich Sophie Calles Arbeit LES AVEUGLES beschreibt, der hier zum Befreiungsakt von der Last der verlorenen Unschuld wird. Es ist wie auf dem gestellten Hochzeitsbild von Sophie Calle auf der vorangehenden Seite, welches den *Rite de passage* auf einer höheren Ebene vollzieht.

Bice Curiger

MOndrian sighted in front of MAtisse at MOMA

As if it had suddenly stepped off the wall of the museum, a Mondrian—in the form of a coat worn by a woman—strolls through the Matisse exhibition at MOMA (the classic art event of the past winter): Thus does Mondrian steal his way into the show of his colleague.

We are reminded of Sophie Calle's GHOSTS (1991/92), appearing in the same museum at the exhibition *DisLocations.* The artist asked the entire museum staff—from director to guards and cleaners—for descriptions of paintings that she had removed from the walls. Through the commentaries thus garnered, she professed her interest in personal connotations, in recollection and perception on the opposite shore of art history.

Both Sophie Calle and Stephan Balkenhol—our collaborating artists in this issue—develop their works as if to bring the outside world into art through the emphatic yet impassive involvement of other human beings. However one might say that the focus of Calle's interest is actually that terrain which Balkenhol assiduously avoids.

Take dress, for instance: Balkenhol, though lovingly typifying the individuality of his figures' garb, seeks utmost simplicity and ordinariness; Calle, on the other hand, pays meticulous attention to detail. Her edition for *Parkett* (see p. 72) represents the first of the tastefully selected articles of clothing that she has been sending to a badly dressed but attractive man whose image she intends to remold according to her fantasy.

People, animals, and mythical beasts populate Stephan Balkenhol's world of figures—but no children as the sculptures themselves might be regarded as an implementation of the child's gaze upon the elementary. This resembles the "tactile gaze" that Joseph Grigely introduces in reference to Sophie Calle's work THE BLIND. Here it has become an act of liberation from the burden of lost innocence, as in Sophie Calle's "wedding picture" on the preceding page which enacts the *rite de passage* on a higher level.

(Translation: Catherine Schelbert)

Bice Curiger

URSULA PANHANS-BÜHLER

«LERNE ZAPLN TOD»* EVA HESSE

(1936–1970)

WEIBLICHER TRICKSTER

Mitten in der Vorbereitung ihrer ersten Einzelausstellung von Skulpturen (New York, November/Dezember 68) notiert Eva Hesse in ihr Tagebuch:

> ◆ *Dream.*
> *top center left.*
> *bottom center left*
> *felt them loosen*
> *felt them fall out*
> *at same time*
> *loosen*
> *I panicked totally*
> *dependent on others*
> *helpless*[1] ◆

Mit einer minimalen, kaum merklichen anagrammatischen Inversion lenkt die poetische Verarbeitung des Traumgeschehens die katastrophische Erfahrung um in einen Prozess mit Eigenregie. Aus dem aussichtslosen doppelten «left» am Ende von Zeile 2 und 3 wird zu Beginn der nächsten beiden Zeilen ein «felt». Fühlend müssen die Extreme nun nicht mehr unbedingt entgleiten, und der Verlaufsform von

Traum und Traumbericht setzt das Anagramm seine gegenläufige Steuerungsenergie entgegen.

Die Ausstellung in der Fischbach Gallery wurde ein Erfolg. In knapp einem Jahr hatte Eva Hesse eine ganze Reihe grosser serieller Arbeiten aus Fiberglas, sachkundig beraten von Doug Johns, fertiggestellt, so unter anderem die zehn Meter überspannende, an der Wand befestigte Skulptur SANS II, die 50 Röhren von ACCRETION, deren luminoser Schimmer und zarte Schattenverdoppelungen die Galeriewand in einen medialen Grenzbereich verwandelten, die rätselhaft übergrossen «Eimer» von REPETITION NINETEEN III, ausserdem Latexarbeiten, Probestücke, Zeichnungen ihrer Accessionboxes, deren eine im Zentrum des Hauptraums stand.

Mit dieser Fiberglasbox ACCESSION III war Eva Hesse nicht zufrieden. Sie schien ihr zu schön in ihrer verklärenden Helligkeit, und so schob sie noch im selben Jahr zwei weitere kleinere Boxen hinterher, diesmal wie die ersten beiden mit dunklen Röhrchen, ACCESSION IV und ACCESSION V. Zählt man einmal die Löcher der vorfabrizierten Kisten, die sie in den Jahren 67/68 bearbeitete, so kommt man auf über siebzigtausend, durch die Eva Hesse, nur teilweise mit fremder Hilfe, etwa 35 000, auf gleiche

*Aus: Ulrike Scholvin, *Berlin Anagramm*, edition norden, Berlin 1992.

URSULA PANHANS-BÜHLER ist Dozentin für Kunstgeschichte an der Universität Trier und arbeitet an einer Studie zum Schatten.

EVA HESSE, SANS II, 1968,
fiberglass and polyester resin, 5 units,
each: 38 x 36 x 6½" / 5teilig,
je 96,5 x 91,4 x 16,5 cm.
(WHITNEY MUSEUM, NEW YORK)

Länge selbst geschnittene Plastik- oder Gummiröhrchen zog. Was als der Gipfel einer absurd repetitiven Tätigkeit erscheinen mag – aufseufzend erinnert man sich der wenigen Klebestriche, mit denen seinerzeit Meret Oppenheim ihre Tasse rundum zügig verpelzte –, hat dennoch ein verblüffend ökonomisches Resultat bewirkt. Das optische Gewirr der Schläuche, gleichsam nach eigenem Belieben ihren Platz im Gedränge der Boxen suchend, erweckt den Wunsch, die Schläuche einfach von innen nach aussen durchzuziehen – und trotz der Härte der Kistengerüste mag man sie, zumindest in der Phantasie, wie einen Handschuh einmal umgestülpt haben. Umgekehrt ist jedoch so, in einem scheinbar aberwitzigen Prozess, eine Energie nach innen gedrängt und gebündelt worden, konzentriert und gesammelt.

Mit komplizenhaftem Grinsen taucht Eva Hesse in Dorothy Beskinds im Winter 67/68 entstandenen Atelierfilm ihren Kopf in eine der Accessionboxes. Betrachter, die im musealen Milieu ihren Blick in eine der Kisten versenken, werden über das Kunststück der Herstellung eines allerfremdesten Innern staunen, trotz naheliegender symbolischer Konnotation, trotz offenem Einblick. Durch diesen paradoxen Vorgang entsteht also ein unantastbarer Kern. Einer solchen Box können nun Werke entströmen, die den mythographischen Rekurs auf Pandora ebenso wie eine selbstreferentielle Nabelschau längst hinter sich gelassen haben, Werke, die «detached but intimate personal» (zurückhaltend, aber intim-persönlich, Eva Hesse 1967) zugleich, aus der Hand gelassen, ein buchstäblich emanzipiertes Eigenleben entfalten.

«We are left ultimately with a visual presence» (Zum Schluss bleibt uns nur eine visuelle Präsenz), schrieb Eva Hesse in einem Text für Sol LeWitt, und offenbar gehörte dazu für sie die Einbeziehung eines «big nothing», dem sie in verschiedenen Werken näherückt, indem sie vexierbildhaft die Leere und das Luminose miteinander ins Spiel brachte. Nähert man sich, verführt durch den Lichtschein, gleichsam besitzergreifend der grossen Fiberglasarbeit SANS II, so sitzt man in einer Falle fest: man sieht sich einer Serie gleichförmiger Hohlraumkästen gegenüber; erst in der Distanz verwandelt sich das Gebilde in ein schwingend nuanciertes optisches Relief. Und ebenso mag einen aus der Nähe die Leere der übergrossen Eimer von REPETITION NINETEEN III erschrecken, was die Wahrnehmung des sublimen Scheinens, die man aus der Ferne hatte, beeinträchtigt. Die Leere «füllt» sich also in einem Wechsel des Blickpunkts auf die Objekte, dem Einnehmen einer

Distanz. Das bestürzend Hohle von REPETITION NINETEEN III faltete Eva Hesse übrigens wenig später ganz selbstverständlich zu einem konkreten Teil auseinander, indem sie die Formmodelle aus Maschendraht als Trägergerüste für eine Latexarbeit benutzte. Das im emotionalen Sinn latente, bodenlos Hohle wird so trickreich zum Massstab eines begrenzten «Felds», AREA (1968).

Wer möchte nicht sich lösen im reinen Licht! Als paradiesisches Versprechen hat die malerische Tradition zuweilen es am Ende langer dunkler Tunnels lokalisiert. Die Konstruktion von Distanz wird daher zur Voraussetzung einer Beziehung zum Sublimen; die taktile Unfassbarkeit des Lichts kann dem entgegenkommen. Unter diesem Aspekt wird ein Rückblick auf Eva Hesses Selbstportraits aus der Zeit um 1960 aufschlussreich. Zumeist im prekären Quadratformat, ziehen gleichmässige Lichtvaleurs in die Fläche zurück, der sich jähe Konturen einer Figur widersetzen. Joseph Albers, ihr Lehrer an der Universität Yale, muss von diesen Eigentümlichkeiten beeindruckt gewesen sein, denn seine Farbquadrate galten nicht nur am Rande dem Limes des Lichts.

Als Eva Hesse später in Latex und Fiberglas die ihr kongenialen Materialien entdeckt hatte, konnte sie dem Sichlösen im Schein distanzierend begegnen. Unter diesem Aspekt ist ihr 1969 mit CONTINGENT ein souveräner Wurf geglückt. Acht aufgehängte Bahnen, die Enden aus Fiberglas, die Mittelstücke aus dünnem Latex, schimmern dem Betrachter entgegen. Geht man auf die Arbeit zu und um sie herum, so wird man, wie Rosalind Krauss formuliert hat, einer anamorphotischen Erfahrung ausgesetzt: die Flächen schnurren auf schmale Stege zusammen, dazwischen der Schauder der Leere. Utopische Fülle und pures Nichts tauschen die Plätze. Repetition, Wiederholung, ehemals ihre eigene obsessive Tätigkeit, rutscht nun auf die Seite des Betrachters. Das In-der-Schwebe-Halten von «Malerei», «Skulptur» und Realem (der Raum seiner Existenz) provoziert die Wiederholung. Die Leere zu erfahren, sie auszuhalten, kann auch Lust machen, und so mag dem Betrachter in Wiederholungen das paradoxe Zugleich des Werkes nicht mehr auseinanderfallen. Das big nothing, ein kontingentes Moment des Gebildes, wird Teil der Erfahrung des Werks, für den Betrachter ein rite de passage, eine Annahme der Sterblichkeit.

Mit Schwerkraft als Moment der puren Physikalität der Dinge – ein zentrales Stichwort in der künstlerischen Praxis der 60er Jahre in New York – ist Eva Hesse nur ein einziges Mal direkt konfrontiert worden,

EVA HESSE, REPETITION 19 III, 1968, fiberglass, 19 units, each: 20 x 12” / 19teilig, 50,8 x 30,5 cm. (MOMA, NEW YORK)

EVA HESSE, ACCESSION V, 1968, galvanized steel and rubber tubing, 10 x 10 x 10" /
ANNÄHERUNG V, 1968, galvanisierter Stahl und Gummischläuche, 25,4 x 25,4 x 25,4 cm.

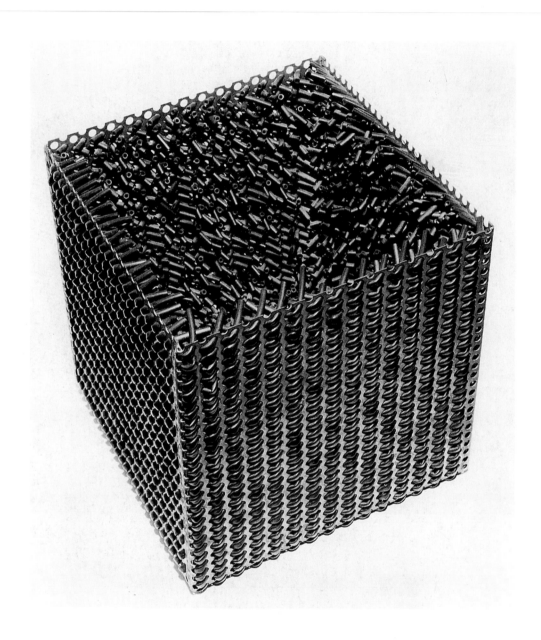

EVA HESSE, ACCESSION II, 1969, galvanized steel and plastic tubing, 30¾ x 30¾ x 30¾" /
ANNÄHERUNG II, 1969, galvanisierter Stahl und Plastikschläuche, 78 x 78 x 78 cm. (DETROIT INSTITUTE OF ARTS)

als nämlich 1966 METRONOMIC IRREGULARITY II in der Fischbach Gallery plötzlich herunterkrachte, während sie die Schnüre durch die an der Wand hängenden Platten zog. Freilich liess sich, was gefallen war, wieder aufheben – und so mag der traumatische Zwischenfall zur ätherisch gewitzten Arbeit von 1967, ADDENDUM, beigetragen haben. Im simplen Akt des Anhebens eines schmalen Schafts auf Überfigurenhöhe an die Wand wird das weite Feld darunter mit einem zarten Relief besetzt, indem Halbkugeln, in progressiv erweiterter Reihe auf dem Schaft sitzend, Schnüre mitgezogen haben, deren träg sich ringelnde Enden auf dem Boden verbleiben. Das feine Gespinst aktiviert die Leere der Zwischenräume und macht überdeutlich, wohinein die Schnüre in früheren Arbeiten baumelten.

Denkt man an den Flächensog der Malereien zurück, so erscheinen die mit schwarz glänzenden Schnüren umgarnten Ballons von 1966 als Eva Hesses höchstpersönliche Weise, zu einem Gewicht der Dinge im Medium der Skulptur zu gelangen. Dort, wo sie einmal wirklich mit Gewichten hantiert, versenkt in Netze, an deren Ziehen Schwere spürbar wird, fügt deren Umwicklung mit schwarz glänzendem Papiermaché, und noch mehr mit unsubstantiell hell glänzendem Polyäthylen, ein paradoxes «Ungewicht» ein. Die Schönheit von NOT YET (1966) vertrug sich offenbar nur schwer mit dem Gefühl für Gewicht.

Auf clowneske Weise wird schliesslich die Formstrenge minimalistischer Serialität unterlaufen. In einer Reihe von Reliefs in dumpfem Grau, durch die sie kurze, am Ende verknotete Schnüre gleicher Farbe nach strengem Rasterplan zieht, wird die schöne geometrische Ordnung dadurch torpediert, dass die herunterhängenden Schnüre, etwa bei COMPART (1967), sanftmütig alles durcheinanderbringen. Ein wahrer Slapstick dieser Art schliesslich bei STRATUM (1967): ein Latexlappen mit weisser Pigmentbeimischung hängt, sobald er mit Nieten an der Wand befestigt ist, zu einem flexiblen Relief durch, und die regelmässig durchgezogenen kurzen Schnüre scheinen nun in alle erdenklichen Richtungen «Nasen zu drehen».

Das Gesetz lacht nicht. – Nun ging es Eva Hesse um alles andere als eine Ironisierung des Minimalis-

mus. Dem widersprechen schon ihre eigenen Arbeiten von 1966/67, gerasterte Reliefs mit Dichtungsringen, überzogen mit Modelliermetall, und gerasterte Kreiszeichnungen, laviert mit Tusche. Andererseits wäre es zu einfach, sie zu einer Schlüsselfigur der «Wiederkehr des Körpers» zu stilisieren – zu einer Zeit, als man sich mit guten Gründen und viel Risiko am Nonanthropomorphen, Abstrakten abarbeitete – und dadurch zu erklären, dass das Sensible, Körperliche, Emotive einfach einer abstrakten Ordnung hinzugeschlagen wird, quasi als prophetische Vorwegnahme einer neuen, postminimalistischen Weiblichkeit. Ihr Verfahren ist weit komplizierter und, wie mir scheint, gefährdender.

Das «Sensible» entsteht im Paradox zwischen rigoroser Ordnung und Zufall; zur Formstrenge untaugliche Materialien – und Verfahrensweisen – geben letzterem seine Chance. Indem sie so die Gesetze der Ordnung ein wenig distanziert, entwickelt sie ihre eigne «abstrakte Groteske» (Robert Storr). Der «Körper» verdankt seine Präsenz nicht einem (weiblichen) Apriori – als solcher war er Zitat, ikonographisches, im Frühwerk –, sondern einer trickster-haften Verschiebung «left-felt». Material und Verfahrensweisen werden zum Medium der Erfahrung des Sensiblen. Latex lässt sich auch in perfekte Formen giessen; sie benutzt es wie Malmaterie auf unterschiedlichen Trägern, vom feinsten Nessel bis zu Maschendraht, gewinnt ihm dadurch groteske Qualitäten ab. Fiberglas und Polyesterharz formt sie «impure» (so voller Bewunderung Sol LeWitt), über «unreinen» Drahtgerüsten. Mit Papier umwickelte Gussformen für die Kästen von SANS II erlauben zufällig unebene Begrenzungen, indem die Kanten des ausgehärteten Materials abgeschlagen werden; mühsam abzuschälende Trennfolien lassen die Ränder der Latexbahnen von EXPANDED EXPANSION (1969) wie nachlässig ausgerissen zurück. Hängende Latexbahnen geben launisch dem eignen Gewicht nach.

«Can cloth go through form?» (Kann Stoff durch Form gehen?) Eva Hesses Frage zum Entwurf von EXPANDED EXPANSION, die Verbindung der Latexbahnen mit den Fiberglasstützen meinend, liesse sich notfalls auch metaphorisch lesen, nämlich wie nachgiebig widerstandsloser Stoff – das Amorphe, was Rosalind Krauss als Herausforderung der Ordnung gespürt hat – durch starre Formen hindurchgehen kann. Es scheint so – im die Starre erschütternden Gelächter, was zunächst dem Werk gilt; Eva Hesse hat andererseits immer betont, «my life and my art are inseparable»(mein Leben und meine Kunst sind untrennbar). In der starren Ordnung, die in absurder Komik verzogen wird, steckt aber auch wie im Spiegel eine verhärtete Realität.

Was steckt in einem Namen? Direkt ins Bild, unter ein Sujet, auf eine Schwelle, den Rand einer Linie setzt Eva Hesse den ihren im Frühwerk. Gleichbleibend handschriftliche Züge, nun an neutralen Stellen angebracht, zeigen die Signaturen seit 1966. Eine Studie zu ihrer letzten Skulptur SEVEN POLES trägt wie zufällig eine Verwandtschaft zur Signatur, in wacklig steilen Balken, schrägem Aufwärts, verbindenden Schlaufen. Kurz vor ihrem frühen Tod, 1970 mit 34 Jahren, hat sie dem Vorschlag ihrer Assistenten zur heutigen Form des Werks, ohne verbindende Schlaufen – vielleicht eine Notlösung – zugestimmt. Ihr traumatisches Schicksal, die Flucht der jüdischen Familie aus Nazideutschland, hat sicherlich ihren Sinn für den in anonymen Terror umschlagenden Fluchtpunkt der Ordnung geschärft.

Eine Retrospektive wird zur Zeit von Yale und Washington nach Valencia und Paris übernommen. Die mit intuitiver Sicherheit gewählten «unmöglichen» Formate ihrer Werke lassen in Reproduktionen nur schwer sich einfangen. Dass deren Wahrnehmung vom Grotesken zum Schönen hin sich verschoben hat (Lucy Lippard), kann auch eine Chance der Zustimmung sein. Hat sie dem doch selbst mit «weird humor» (schrägem Humor) vorgearbeitet, als sie ihr ROPE PIECE (1970) mit hintergründiger Inversion als «very ordered» beschrieb. Dies, das strukturierte Netzwerkchaos, sieht man inzwischen möglicherweise mit verwirrendem Vergnügen.

1) Traum. Oben Mitte weg. Unten Mitte weg. Fühlte, wie sie sich lösten. Fühlte, wie sie wegfielen. Zugleich sich lösten. Ich geriet in Panik ganz und gar. Abhängig von anderen. Hilflos. (Schreibweise von «paniced» gemäss Eva Hesses Tagebuch. Anm. d. Red.)

EVA HESSE, SEVEN POLES, 1970, reinforced fiberglass over polyethylene, aluminum wire, 7 units, each: 74–111 x 10–16” /
SIEBEN PFÄHLE, 1970, verstärktes Fiberglas über Polyethylen, Aluminiumdraht, 7teilig, je 188–282 x 25,4–40,6 cm.

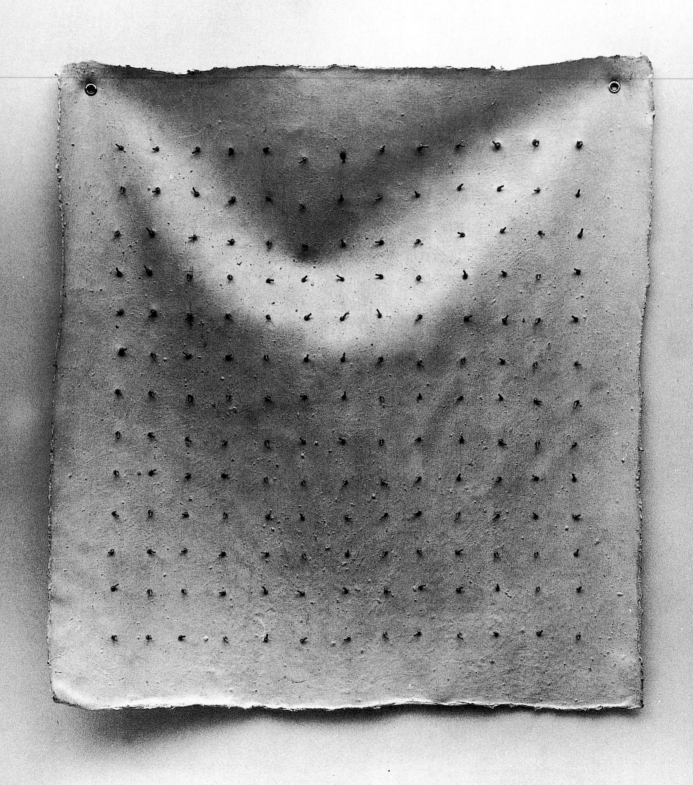

URSULA PANHANS-BÜHLER

LEARN TO WRIGGLE, DEATH

TRICKSTER EVA HESSE

(1936–1970)

In the midst of preparations for her first one-woman sculpture exhibition (in New York, November/December 1968), Eva Hesse noted in her journal,

> ◆ *Dream.*
> *top center left.*
> *bottom center left*
> *felt them loosen*
> *felt them fall out*
> *at the same time*
> *loosen*
> *I paniced [sic!] totally*
> *dependent on others*
> *helpless* ◆

The poetic device of minimal, almost inconspicuous anagrammatic inversion diverts the catastrophic experience of dreamt events into a process with a choreography of its own. The futile "left" that ends the second and third lines becomes a beginning "felt" in the following pair of lines: through feeling, the extremes no longer glide inevitably out of sight,

and the anagram exerts an energy that runs counter to the progress of the dream and the tale it tells.

The show, at the Fischbach Gallery, was a success. In barely a year and with the expert advice of Doug Johns, Eva Hesse had completed a whole collection of large, serial works in fiberglass. One such was the sculpture SANS II, spanning some ten meters of wall space to which it was attached; or the fifty tubes of ACCRETION which transformed the gallery walls into a medial border zone with their luminous haze and soft double shadows. There were also the enigmatic, oversized "buckets" of REPETITION NINETEEN III, the latex works, the trial pieces, and the drawings of her fiberglass boxes, one of which, ACCESSION III, stood at the center of the main exhibiting space.

But Eva Hesse was not content with ACCESSION III. She felt it was too aesthetic in its visionary radiance, and so she followed it in the same year with two smaller boxes, ACCESSION IV and ACCESSION V, this time, as in the first two, with somber little tubes. If one pauses to count the holes in the prefabricated boxes produced by Hesse in 1967/68, one would find that they number over seventy thousand. Hesse cut

URSULA PANHANS-BÜHLER teaches art history at the University of Trier, Germany, and is working on a study on shadow.

thin rubber or plastic tubes to about equal lengths and pulled them through half of the holes, that is, some thirty-five thousand, with little outside assistance. It may strike one as the ultimate in absurdly repetitive activity—think of the casual efficiency with which Meret Oppenheim glued a layer of fur onto a cup and saucer—but the outcome is surprisingly economical in effect. On seeing the visual tangle of tubes, each seeming to look for a spot of its own in the crowded boxes, one is tempted simply to pull them all from the inside out. Despite the rigidity of the box, one might thus imagine turning it inside out, like stripping off a glove. By some bizarre process, however, the bundled energy has instead come from outside in, penetrating the box in concentrated and accumulated form.

In Dorothy Beskind's film, shot in Hesse's studio in the winter of 1967/68, the artist is seen sticking her head into one of her accession boxes with a conspiratorial grin. Viewers gazing into one of the boxes in a museum environment will marvel at the complex artifice of its most strange interior, despite the patent symbolic connotations, despite the openness of the view. Through this paradoxical process, an inviolable core has been formed. The works issuing from these boxes have obviously outstripped the need for mythographic recourse to Pandora, or indeed, self-referential introspection. "Detached but intimate, personal" (E. H. 1967) in one, they develop a literally emancipated life of their own.

When she wrote in a text for Sol LeWitt that "we are ultimately left with a visual presence," Eva Hesse was evidently also referring to the "big nothing" that she comes close to in a number of pieces in which illusive optics mark the relationship between void and luminosity. Attracted by the aura of light emanating from the large fiberglass piece, SANS II, viewers approach in order to take visual possession of it only to find they have been tricked. It is nothing but a series of identical hollow boxes. Only from a distance does the configuration become a vibrating, subtle optical relief. Similarly, the shock of the void discovered in the close-up view of REPETITION NINETEEN III rather stints the perception of the sublime aura conveyed from a distance. Thus, a change in vantage point, a distanced stance, "fills" the emptiness. It was not long after she had finished this piece with its disturbing hollowness that Eva Hesse simply unfolded the wire-mesh matrices used in its making to serve as the skeleton framework for a latex piece. The latent hollowness, emotionally perceived as unfathomable, has thus been converted by a conceit into defining the scale of a delimited field, in AREA (1968).

Who would not wish to dissolve in pure light! It has materialized occasionally in the history of painting as a promise of paradise at the end of dark tunnels. The construction of distance is, in fact, essential to a relationship with the sublime; what better means of approach than the tactile intangibility of light! A survey of Eva Hesse's self-portraits of about 1960 are illuminating in this context. Done mostly in the challenging square format, they show the stark contours of a figure set off against even light values receding into the surface. This idiosyncratic treatment of light must have impressed her teacher at Yale, Josef Albers, whose squares of color were themselves dedicated to the very subtlest reaches of light.

Later, when Eva Hesse discovered her ideal materials, latex and fiberglass, she was able to confront the idea of self-dissolution in light with detachment. She pulled off a masterful stroke of this kind in a work of 1969, CONTINGENT. Viewers walking around the eight glowing, suspended swathes—the ends made of fiberglass, the middle sections of latex—are subjected, as Rosalind Krauss puts it, to an anamorphotic experience. The humming surfaces converge into slender straps; between them, the shudder of nothingness. Utopian profusion and pure void change places. Repetition, once Hesse's own obsessive activity, has now shifted to the part of the beholder. The suspension of boundaries between "painting," "sculpture," and reality as the place of their existence, provokes repetition. To experience and endure emptiness can also induce pleasure, so that the paradoxical simultaneity of the work no longer falls apart in repetition. The "big nothing," a contingent factor in the overall structure, becomes part of the experience of the work, for the beholder a "rite of passage," an acceptance of mortality.

Only once was Eva Hesse directly confronted with the pure physical gravity of things—an issue crucial to the artistic practice of 1960s New York. While she was pulling strings through plates suspended on the wall to mount METRONOMIC IRREGULARITY III at the Fischbach Gallery in 1966, the work came crashing to the floor. Though the work was easily retrieved, the traumatic incident may well have contributed to the ethereal, witty piece of 1967, ADDENDUM. Through the simple act of placing a slender shaft higher than human height on the wall, the wide area beneath has been covered by a delicate relief consisting of strings proceeding from progressively expanding hemispheres attached to the shaft above. The curled ends of the strings are left dragging on the floor below. The fine web of cords intensifies the emptiness of the interstices and clearly indicates the destination of the dangling strings in earlier works.

Recalling the inward pull of her painted surfaces, Eva Hesse's balloons of 1966 girthed with gleaming black string illustrate her extremely personal means of generating weight in the medium of sculpture.

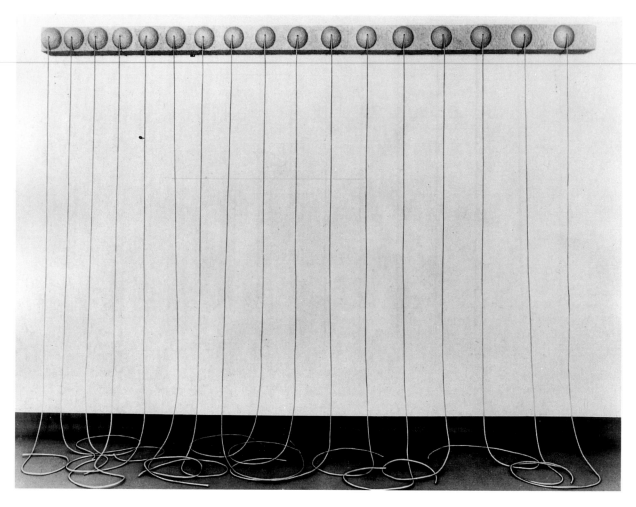

EVA HESSE, ADDENDUM, 1967, painted papier-maché, wood and cord, 4⅞ x 119¼ x 5⅞–8⅛" /
ZUSATZ, 1967, 12,4 x 303 x 15–20,6 cm. (TATE GALLERY, LONDON)

Where she does operate with real weight, heaviness becomes visibly tangible through the pull on the nets in which the weights have been placed. But wrapped in gleaming black papier maché and a layer of insubstantial, brightly shining polyethylene, they have, in fact, been converted into a paradoxical "unweight." The beauty of NOT YET (1966) was evidently difficult to reconcile with a sense of weight.

Finally, there is Hesse's clownish subversion of minimalism's austere seriality of form. In a series of reliefs (for example COMPART, 1967) executed in dull gray, short strings of the same color have been drawn through an exact grid and tied in a knot at the ends, but the sacrosanct geometric order is sabotaged by the gentle muddle of the dangling strings. This turns to slapstick of the first order in STRATUM, 1967. There, a swatch of latex into which white pigment has been blended is loosely riveted to the wall so that it sags into a flexible relief, and the short pieces of string woven through it now seem to be thumbing their noses in every direction.

The Law brooks no humor. Eva Hesse certainly had no intention of having a laugh at the expense of minimalism. This is plain from her works of 1966/67, the gridwork reliefs with sealing rings coated in modeling metal and the ink-washed, gridwork circle

EVA HESSE, AREA, 1968, Latex on wire mesh and metal wire, 240 x 36" /
FELD, 1968, Latex auf Maschendraht und Metalldraht, 610 x 92 cm. (WEXNER CENTER, OHIO STATE)

drawings. Conversely, it would be simplistic to cast her as a key protagonist of the "return of the body" at a time when, for good reason and at great risk, artists were working away at the non-anthropomorphic and abstract; or to claim that sensitivity, physicality, and emotion have simply been coupled with an abstract order, prophetically anticipating a new, post-minimalist femininity. Hesse's procedure is much more complex, and, it seems to me, more explosive.

"Sensitivity" is a product of the paradoxical association of rigorous order and chance. Materials and techniques unsuited to formal rigor give scope to chance. By thus neutralizing the laws of order, Hesse develops her own "abstract grotesquerie" (Robert Storr). The "body" owes its presence not to some (female) apriority—a form adopted, in fact, as iconographic quotation in her early work—but to artifice as in the shift from "left" to "felt." Materials and techniques become the medium through which sensitivity is experienced. Latex can be cast in perfect molds. By using it like a painting medium on various supports, ranging from the finest cotton duck to wire mesh, Hesse manages to wrest grotesque qualities from it. Sol LeWitt admiringly describes her application of fiberglass and polyester resin to wire-mesh frameworks as "impure." By wrapping the molds in

21

EVA HESSE, UNTITLED OR NOT YET, 1966,
9 dyed bags filled with weights wrapped in clear polyethylene, 72 x 24 x 14" /
OHNE TITEL ODER NOCH OHNE, 1966, 9 gefärbte Säcke, gefüllt mit in Plastik gehüllten Gewichten, 183 x 61 x 36 cm.

Hanging sheets of latex moodily yield to their own weight.

"Can cloth go through form?" Eva Hesse's question regarding EXPANDED EXPANSION, that is, the idea of combining latex sheets with fiberglass supports, could also be read metaphorically. Can yielding, unresisting cloth with its amorphous quality, which Rosalind Krauss read as a challenge to order, pass through rigid forms? It would seem so, at least in the laughter that rocks rigidity, which applies specifically to her work, although Hesse always insisted, "my life and my art are inseparable." However, in rigid order, which absurd comedy deforms, there resides a hardened reality as in a mirror.

What's in a name? In the early work, Eva Hesse places hers right in the picture, under a subject, on a sill, the edge of a line. From 1966 it is applied in a steady, constant hand, at neutral points now. A study for her last sculpture, SEVEN POLES, seems to resemble her signature, as if by chance, with wobbly, steep beams, an oblique upward thrust, and connecting loops. Not long before the artist's untimely death in 1970, aged 34, she approved her assistants' proposal for the present form of the piece, without the connecting loops—perhaps a temporary expedient. Her traumatic history, the escape of the Jewish family from Nazi Germany, surely honed her instinct for the vanishing point at which order precipitates into an anonymous reign of terror.

Valencia and Paris have taken over a retrospective, following Yale and Washington. The "impossible" formats of her work, chosen with unerring intuition, are difficult to capture in reproduction. The fact that perception of them has shifted from the grotesque to the aesthetic (Lucy Lippard) may also be indicative of affirmation—considering how she prepared the ground for it with "weird humor" by subtly inverting the impact of her ROPE PIECE (1970) through a description of it as "very ordered." By now, chaos as structured mesh-work has possibly come to be regarded with perplexing pleasure.

(Translation: Stephen Reader)

paper to make the boxes for SANS II, she comes up with randomly uneven edges produced by simply knocking off the edges of the hardened material. Hard-to-peel separating film leaves the edges of the latex sheets in EXPANDED EXPANSION of 1969 looking as if they had been casually torn out.

DOUGLAS BLAU

CLOCKWORK
(Jon Kessler)

It was a curious dream—and perhaps that accounts for the fact that I can recall it at all, as I rarely remember anything that I've seen while asleep:

I was in the city, standing on the southwest corner of Houston and Mercer, watching cars moving east, waiting for the light to change so that I could cross the street, when Jon Kessler pulled up in his 1965 Ford Comet Caliente, a cream-colored convertible with red leather bucket seats, a car he had sold at least four years before, but there it was, top down, chrome polished, looking sleek.

"What are you doing here?" I asked. "I thought you were supposed to be in Paris." "I am," he explained, "but I'm here, working on a piece. I'm on my way to Brooklyn now. Why don't you get in and come out there with me?"

Apparently I agreed, as the next scene I remember was set in a vast room, a hall of clutter, a depository for assemblages and disassembled machines. Parts and pieces were everywhere. A layer of dust covered every surface. Iridescent fabrics were draped over chairs and hung like curtains from the ceiling. The shelves running along the walls held a flea-mar-

ket assortment of curiosities, giving this space the look of a wunderkammer, something of a cross between a storage vault beneath a science and technology museum and a prop room in the attic of a theater. Trying to envision it now, I find myself picturing a still life of incredible variety and scale. But despite the clarity with which I recall the overall scene, I have only vague memories of its many details.

Perhaps the thing I remember most vividly is the collection of clocks that filled an entire section of the shelves. Every kind of timepiece was represented: from hourglasses and sundials to mechanisms that were extremely complex and detailed; stopwatches and intricately crafted pocket watches and the most commonplace digitals. I was looking at a metronome from the early part of this century when Kessler called my attention to another piece, which he lifted off the shelf and set down on a table next to me. "This is what I've been working on," he said, "this is what I wanted you to see." He offered a chair, and I sat down to examine the object more carefully.

A curious little box about the size of a small clock, it consisted of a number of interlocking parts, each of which had been constructed out of a different material. Covering the surface of the entire piece, a decorative pattern fashioned out of nickel, silicon, and zinc, framed by inlaid bands of aluminum, colored plastic, ebony, and rock crystal. Tiny fire opals

DOUGLAS BLAU, critic, curator, etc., lives in New York City. His exhibitions have included: *Fictions; The Observatory; The Times, the Chronicle & the Observer; The Library;* and, most recently, *The Naturalist Gathers.*

JON KESSLER, UNTITLED / OHNE TITEL, 1986,

mixed media, lights, motors,

39½ x 53 x 19¼ " / 100 x 134,6 x 48,9 cm.

and circles of imitation ocean pearl, set at regular intervals around the object's base, made it appear luminescent and created the illusion that it hovered slightly above the surface of the table. But, picking it up, I found the thing to be unexpectedly heavy, as if it contained something made of an unnaturally dense metal. I remember inspecting it for a length of time, marveling at its exquisite design, turning it over and over in my hands, searching in vain for some way to grasp it.

Seeing that I was completely baffled by his puzzle, that I had no clue as to how the thing worked or what it was meant to be, Kessler asked me to place it back down on the table—clearly, it was time for the secret to be revealed. He reached into his shirt pocket and pulled out something that resembled a miniature key, which he inserted into a nearly imperceptible opening at the base of the piece. Then he sat back with a strange smile on his face and said: "Watch carefully."

A low-pitched note, followed by another, then a series of beeps, each one slightly higher than the other: I assumed that this was the beginning of a melody, but before a tune took place, the sequence began to repeat, slowing after each round until the rhythm became a soft, constant tone, a pulsing drone that sounded less like a heartbeat than like breathing. Then the fire opals began to glow, not simultaneously, but, again, in sequence, as if a beam of light were circling clockwise within the device, going faster and growing more intense with every revolution. It was a beautiful effect, but I remained perplexed, impatient to see what would happen next, and curious to know where all of this was going. I was about to ask when the thing began unfolding.

The process took only a few moments to complete, but for those few moments I stared in a state of absolute disbelief as the piece transformed itself into an entirely different object: a small translucent cube that shimmered in the light as if it had been dusted with flecks of mica. Looking inside, through a blue-tinted glass that encased the entire structure, I saw what appeared to be a miniature room, reminiscent of both the interior of a space capsule and an alchemist's laboratory. It was lined with copper circuit boards and stainless steel consoles, all covered by geometric patterns formed by scores of flashing orange and yellow diodes. In each corner, there were at least a dozen crystal shafts with bubbling phosphorescent liquids flowing through them, and, at the center, something that resembled a bellows, making a discomforting but strangely soothing sound as it moved slowly up and down, its action setting countless metallic gears into motion. But the thing I found most curious at the time—and which no doubt led me to perceive the piece as a miniature interior—was the fact that it also contained two tiny reclining chairs and a doll's house version of a Persian carpet.

When it appeared that the device had reached the end of its cycle, I turned to Kessler and applauded, telling him that I had been amazed by his programming feats and by the range of effects he had mastered. I asked a few questions about the construction of the mechanism and was curious to know where and when he planned to show the piece. His reply took me by surprise, for he explained that the invention wasn't a work intended for exhibition, but was, instead, a working model of his time machine.

By way of explanation, Kessler offered some background information, though I remember only aspects of the narrative he told: while conducting research in the archives at the Conservatoire des Arts et Métiers, he had apparently stumbled across a manuscript; the plans were flawed and fragmented, but he had succeeded in filling in the gaps and making the necessary adjustments; after years of failed experiments and more than a few explosions, the machine now worked as intended.

As a prelude to the actual demonstration, Kessler, anticipating skepticism, suggested that I inspect the table so that I wouldn't suspect him of any sleight of hand. Seeing that I was satisfied, he asked me to take a seat and to watch carefully as he continued with his preparations. Once again, he reached into his pocket and pulled out a tiny key, which he somehow inserted into the blue glass sheath, causing the panel to lower like a car window. He pointed to a pair of levers that were placed between the chairs and in-

JON KESSLER, TAIWAN, 1987,
mixed media with lights and motors,
variable dimensions, detail.

vited me to select a destination: The silver one would send the machine into the future; the black would cast it back, into history. I can't recall what I said, or if, at that moment, I was capable of speaking; nonetheless, Kessler proceeded, touching buttons on the miniature panels with a tool that looked like a pin. When a number appeared on one of the consoles' screens, the sheath reappeared—as did the inventor's peculiar grin.

Whatever happened happened very quickly, so quickly that I'm not quite sure if I actually saw the thing disappear. I recall a brief, blinding flash, and by the time my eyes had readjusted, the surface of the table was bare. I've gone over the event countless times in my mind, playing it back frame by frame, trying to picture the action in slow motion; and perhaps this has confused me further as, by now, fact has been fused with speculation, and I can no longer distinguish between imagination and memory. At this point in time, all that remains is a list of unanswerable questions: Did the piece just fade into space, becoming progressively more transparent; or had it imploded in a series of folding motions, like some elaborate origami trick? What color had that ray of light really been: An array of the entire spec-

trum would be my guess; but then why do I still see it as a burst of black light that, for an instant, transformed every surface in the room into a soft, violet velvet? And the accompanying sound track: Did I actually hear that quick succession of inhaling sounds, or have I just invented them in order to see the piece being sucked, once again, into a whirlpool of light, into the idea of a perfect vacuum? In any case, one thing was clear: The time machine had vanished, and, if Kessler's calculations were correct, it was now somewhere between here and the distant future.

"Am I supposed to believe..." I wondered aloud before Kessler interrupted: "It should be returning in a minute or two; in the meantime, come with me into the other room, and I'll show you the larger version." I followed him through the piles of clutter, to a wall at the far end of the studio. There, he produced yet another key, and, after opening the door, pushed aside a series of curtains.

Before he activated the machine, I could see it clearly, sitting in the middle of a vast, empty room, glowing in the darkness. It was the color of a swimming pool illuminated at night, and, had I not just seen the model, my first impression might have been that the cube was an aquarium of some sort, or perhaps, an undersea tableau from a natural history museum. Using a remote-control device, Kessler switched on all the internal lights and lowered one of the blue-tinted panels, revealing the full-sized version of the familiar interior. The shift in dimensions was somewhat disorienting, but the vertigo passed quickly, and I started looking around, examining the details inside this bizarre contraption.

It was a curious space, at once Victorian and futuristic, as if the style belonged to no particular time at all, as if in any age it would have been anachronistic. Eclectic but nonetheless consistent, it was funkier than I had envisioned; the surfaces that I had expected to be made of burnished copper and stainless steel were, in fact, a patchwork of industrial scraps and corroded metals. Other variations accompanied the shift in scale: There were cabinets filled with Pyrex beakers; coils of fiber optic wire lined Plexiglas shelves; a stuffed bird was perched atop one of the consoles; and on dozens of small monitors were displays of colorful charts and graphs. The shafts of glass in each corner of the room were far more exquisite than I could ever have imagined; the multi-colored fluids flowing through them were more substantial than I'd supposed, now having the consistency of molten lava; and what I had taken to be bubbles were actually thousands of opalescent particles, each radiating a light less intense but just as bright as neon.

I was standing in the corner with my back to the room, staring at those slowly swirling liquids, completely immersed in their currents and rhythmic tides, when a loud gong sounded, cracking my concentration and snapping me out of my reverie. I turned around to see Kessler holding a silver object out to me: a cross between an old leather football helmet and an aviator's cap, just like the one he was wearing. "That signals that the machine is ready," he said. "Do you have time to go for a ride?" I looked at my watch to see if I needed to return to the city, and, realizing that I'd fallen for Kessler's joke, laughed.

"We'll be back in no time flat," he added, clearly unable to resist using the line.

We were already strapped into our seats—here, red leather bucket seats, not the reclining chairs that I had seen inside the model—when Kessler raised the sheath and asked whether I wanted to see the future or the past. I pointed to the silver lever, and then leaned back, still doubting that anything would happen and yet hoping that everything he had described would in fact come to pass. The room on the other side of the glass was disappearing when I saw a flash of light and heard another sound, an unpleasant noise, shriller and yet fainter than the previous gong. I took it to mean that the machine was working, but I was disturbed when I heard the ring again. The room on the other side had been dust for over a century when the telephone rang a third time and I realized I was in bed.

JON KESSLER, TAIWAN, 1987,
mixed media with lights and motors, detail:
16 x 22½ x 7" / 40,6 x 57 x 17,8 cm.

JON KESSLER, BIRDRUNNER, 1990, Detail.

JON KESSLER, AMERICAN LANDSCAPE I, 1989,
wood, steel, glass, mechanics, lights, 49½ x 67¾ x 29¼" /
AMERIKANISCHE LANDSCHAFT I, 1989,
Holz, Stahl, Glas, Mechanik, Licht, 125,7 x 172 x 74,3 cm.

JON KESSLER, EXODUS, 1988,
mixed media with knitting machine, variable dimensions /
Mischtechnik, Strickmaschine, Dimensionen variabel.

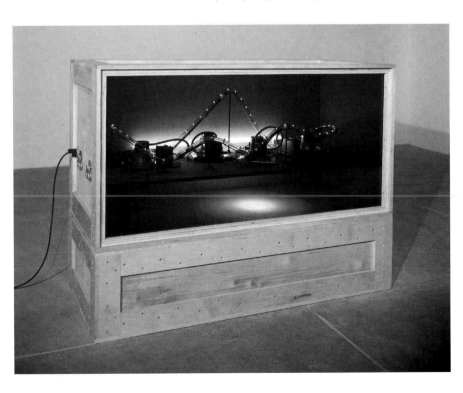

DOUGLAS BLAU

CLOCKWORK
(Jon Kessler)

Es war ein eigenartiger Traum, und vielleicht erklärt das die Tatsache, dass ich mich überhaupt an ihn erinnern kann, wo ich doch selten etwas in Erinnerung behalte, was ich im Traum gesehen habe.

Ich war in New York City, stand an der Südwestecke der Kreuzung Houston und Mercer. Während ich darauf wartete, dass die Ampel umschaltete, damit ich die Strasse überqueren konnte, sah ich den Autos zu, die ostwärts fuhren. Da fuhr Jon Kessler in seinem 1965er Ford Comet Caliente heran, einem cremefarbenen Kabriolett mit roten Ledersitzen; diesen Wagen hatte er vor mindestens vier Jahren verkauft, aber jetzt kam er damit an, Verdeck aufgeklappt und Chromteile poliert, einfach scharf.

«Was machst du denn hier?» fragte ich. «Ich dachte, du wärst eigentlich in Paris.» – «Bin ich auch», erklärte er, «aber ich arbeite hier gerade an einem Objekt. Bin gerade auf dem Weg nach Brooklyn. Steig doch ein und fahr mit mir raus!»

Ich muss wohl zugestimmt haben, denn die nächste Szene, an die ich mich erinnern kann, spielte in einem grossen Raum, der ein einziges Durcheinander war, eine Montagehalle mit lauter zerlegten

Maschinen. Ersatzteile und Stücke lagen überall herum. Eine Staubschicht bedeckte alles. Phosphoreszierende Stoffe waren über Stühle drapiert und hingen wie Vorhänge von der Decke. Auf den Regalen, die an den Wänden entlangliefen, hatte sich ein Flohmarkt der Kuriositäten angesammelt, was dem Raum das Aussehen einer Wunderkammer gab, eine Kreuzung zwischen dem Lagergewölbe des Museums für Technologie und Wissenschaft und dem Requisitenfundus auf dem Speicher eines Theaters. Bei dem Versuch, mir diesen Raum jetzt vorzustellen, merke ich, dass ich ein Stilleben voll unglaublich abwechslungsreicher Elemente in allen Grössen entwerfe. Doch trotz der Klarheit, mit der ich die ganze Szene vor mir sehe, sind mir die Einzelheiten nur vage in Erinnerung geblieben.

Am lebendigsten habe ich die Ansammlung von Uhren vor Augen, die eine eigene Abteilung auf den Regalen belegte. Jede Art von Zeitmesser war vertreten: von Stundengläsern und Sonnenuhren bis hin zu Mechanismen, die äusserst komplex und detailliert waren; Stoppuhren und knifflig konstruierte Taschenuhren und die ordinärsten Digitaluhren. Ich schaute mir gerade ein Metronom vom Anfang dieses Jahrhunderts an, als Kessler mich auf ein anderes Stück aufmerksam machte, das er aus dem Regal nahm und auf einem Tisch in meiner Nähe absetzte. «Daran habe ich die letzte Zeit gearbeitet», sagte er.

DOUGLAS BLAU, Kritiker, Kurator usw., lebt in New York. Seine Ausstellungen waren unter anderen: *Fictions; The Observatory; The Times, the Chronicle & the Observer; The Library;* zuletzt: *The Naturalist Gathers.*

JOHN KESSLER, UNTITLED / OHNE TITEL, 1986,
mixed media, lights, motors,
39½ x 53 x 19¼" / 100 x 134,6 x 48,9 cm.

«Das wollte ich dir zeigen.» Er bot mir einen Stuhl an, und ich setzte mich, um das Objekt sorgfältiger zu untersuchen.

Ein eigentümliches Kistchen, etwa in der Grösse einer kleinen Uhr. Es bestand aus diversen, ineinander verschachtelten Teilen, jedes aus einem anderen Material hergestellt. Die Oberfläche des Ganzen überzog ein dekoratives Muster aus Nickel, Silikon und Zink, eingerahmt von eingelegten Streifen aus Aluminium, farbigem Plastik und Bergkristall. Winzige Feueropale und Ringe aus imitiertem Perlmutt waren in regelmässigen Abständen in den Fuss des Objekts eingearbeitet. Sie liessen es aufschimmern und schufen die Illusion, es würde ganz leicht über der Tischplatte schweben. Als ich das Ding aufhob, entpuppte es sich als unerwartet schwer, so als enthielte es ein unnatürlich dichtes Material. Ich weiss noch, wie ich es ausgiebig inspizierte und seine erlesene Ausführung bewunderte, in meinen Händen drehte und wandte, vergeblich einen Schlüssel suchend, um es zu begreifen.

Als Kessler sah, dass sein Rätsel mich vollkommen verblüffte und ich keine Ahnung hatte, wie das Ding funktionierte oder was es überhaupt sein sollte, bat er mich, es wieder auf den Tisch zu stellen – offenbar war der Zeitpunkt gekommen, das Geheimnis zu lüften. Er holte etwas aus seiner Hemdtasche, das aussah wie ein Miniaturschlüssel. Er steckte ihn in eine fast nicht wahrnehmbare Öffnung am Fuss des Objekts. Dann lehnte er sich mit einem seltsamen Lächeln zurück und sagte: «Pass gut auf!»

Ein tiefer Ton, dann ein zweiter, dann eine Reihe Piepsignale, jedes etwas höher als das vorherige; ich nahm an, dass dies der Anfang eines Themas sei, doch bevor eine Melodie Gestalt annahm, wiederholte sich die Sequenz, bei jeder Runde langsamer, bis der Rhythmus in einen leisen Dauerton überging, ein pulsierendes Summen, das sich wie ein Herzschlag, nein, wie Atmen anhörte. Dann begannen die Feueropale zu leuchten, nicht gleichzeitig, sondern einer nach dem anderen, als drehte sich ein Lichtstrahl im Uhrzeigersinn im Innern des Appa-

rats, immer schneller und stärker mit jeder Umdrehung. Es war ein wunderschöner Effekt; ich blieb weiterhin sprachlos, konnte kaum abwarten, was als nächstes passieren würde, neugierig, wohin all dies führen würde. Ich wollte gerade fragen, als sich das Ding auffaltete.

Der Vorgang brauchte nur wenige Augenblicke, aber während dieser Sekunden starrte ich vollkommen ungläubig hin, denn das Objekt verwandelte sich in etwas völlig anderes: einen kleinen, durchscheinenden Kubus, der im Licht schillerte, als wäre er übersät von Glimmertüpfeln. Im Innern erkannte ich, durch ein blaugetöntes Glas, das die gesamte Struktur umhüllte, eine Art Miniaturzimmer, das zugleich an das Innere einer Raumkapsel und das Laboratorium eines Alchimisten erinnerte. An den Wänden kupferne Schalttafeln und Stahlkonsolen, allesamt überzogen von geometrischen Mustern aus Reihen blinkender Dioden, orangefarben und gelb. In jeder Ecke standen mindestens zwölf Kristallzylinder, durchströmt von blubbernden, phosphoreszierenden Flüssigkeiten. In der Mitte stand etwas, das aussah wie ein Blasebalg; es gab ein unangenehmes und doch seltsam beruhigendes Geräusch von sich, während es langsam auf und nieder pumpte und so zahllose Zahnräder in Gang setzte. Doch was ich in diesem Moment am merkwürdigsten fand – zweifellos auch der Grund, warum ich das Objekt als Miniaturzimmer wahrnahm –, waren die beiden winzigen Liegestühle und die Puppenhausversion eines Perserteppichs darin.

Es sah so aus, als hätte der Apparat seinen Zyklus beendet, und ich wandte mich Kessler zu und applaudierte. Ich sagte, ich sei verblüfft über seine Programmierkünste und über die vielfältigen Effekte, die er erzielt habe. Dann stellte ich ein paar Fragen über die Konstruktion des Mechanismus und erkundigte mich danach, wo und wann er vorhatte, das Stück auszustellen. Seine Antwort verschlug mir die Sprache. Er erklärte, seine Erfindung sei nicht für eine Ausstellung gedacht, sondern nur ein Arbeitsmodell seiner Zeitmaschine.

Damit ich ihn verstehen konnte, lieferte Kessler mir einige Hintergrundinformationen, auch wenn ich mich nur an einzelne Ausschnitte seines Berichts erinnere: Offenbar war er bei seiner Forschungsarbeit in den Archiven des Conservatoire des Arts et Métiers auf ein Manuskript gestossen, Fragmente von Bauplänen voller Fehler. Doch er schaffte es, die Lücken auszufüllen und die notwendigen Korrekturen vorzunehmen; nach jahrelangen vergeblichen Experimenten und mehr als nur ein paar Explosionen funktionierte die Maschine jetzt, wie sie sollte.

Als Vorspiel zu der eigentlichen Demonstration schlug Kessler, der mit Skepsis rechnete, vor, ich solle den Tisch untersuchen, so dass ich ihn nachher keinerlei manueller Tricks verdächtigen konnte. Als das zu meiner Zufriedenheit geschehen war, setzte er seine Vorbereitungen fort; ich sollte mich wieder hinsetzen und genau aufpassen. Wieder griff er in seine Hemdtasche und holte einen winzigen Schlüssel heraus, den er irgendwie in die blaue Glashülle einführte, wodurch die Scheibe versenkt wurde wie ein Autofenster. Er deutete auf zwei Hebel, die zwischen den Stühlen angebracht waren, und forderte mich auf, ein Ziel auszusuchen: der silberne würde die Maschine in die Zukunft schicken, der schwarze zurück in die Vergangenheit. Ich weiss nicht mehr, was ich sagte oder ob ich überhaupt einen Ton hervorbrachte; jedenfalls machte Kessler weiter, drückte Knöpfe auf den Mini-Tafeln mit einem Werkzeug, das wie eine Nadel aussah. Als auf einem Bildschirm der Konsolen eine Zahl erschien, tauchte die gläserne Hülle wieder auf – genau wie das seltsame Grinsen des Erfinders.

Was immer geschah, spielte sich blitzschnell ab, so schnell, dass ich nicht sicher bin, ob ich wirklich sah, wie das Ding verschwand. Ich erinnere mich an einen kurzen, blendenden Blitz, und bis sich meine Augen davon erholt hatten, war der Tisch leer. Unzählige Male bin ich das ganze Geschehen im Geiste durchgegangen, habe es Bild um Bild zurückgespult und versucht, mir den Vorgang in Zeitlupe vorzustellen; vielleicht hat mich das nur noch mehr verwirrt, weil sich nunmehr Tatsache und Spekulation vermischt haben und ich nicht mehr zwischen Phantasie und Erinnerung unterscheiden kann. Es bleibt nur eine Liste von Fragen, die nicht zu beantworten sind: War das Objekt einfach immer transparenter geworden, bis es im Raum aufging, oder war es implodiert, sich Schritt für Schritt nach innen faltend wie ein ausgeklügelter Origami-Trick? Welche

Farbe hatte der Lichtstrahl wirklich: eine Kombination aus dem gesamten Spektrum, würde ich tippen; doch warum sehe ich ihn dann immer noch als einen Ausbruch schwarzen Lichts vor mir, der einen Augenblick lang jede Fläche im Raum zu weichem, violettem Samt machte? Und die Begleitgeräusche: Habe ich das mehrfache, hektische Einatmen wirklich gehört, oder habe ich das nur erfunden, um mir vorstellen zu können, wie das Ding wieder in einen Strudel des Lichts gesogen wurde, den Inbegriff eines vollkommenen Vakuums? Eins war auf jeden Fall klar: Die Zeitmaschine blieb verschwunden, und, wenn Kesslers Berechnungen stimmten, befand sie sich jetzt irgendwo zwischen heute und der fernen Zukunft.

«Soll ich jetzt glauben…», dachte ich laut, doch Kessler unterbrach mich: «Es müsste in ein, zwei Minuten zurückkommen; in der Zwischenzeit kannst du mich ins Nebenzimmer begleiten, ich zeige dir die grössere Version.» Ich folgte ihm zwischen den Gerümpelhaufen hindurch zu einer Wand am äussersten Ende des Ateliers. Dort holte er den dritten Schlüssel hervor, öffnete die Tür und schob mehrere Vorhänge zur Seite.

Noch bevor er die Maschine aktivierte, konnte ich sie klar erkennen, wie sie in der Mitte eines ausgedehnten, leeren Raumes stand und in der Dunkelheit leuchtete. Sie hatte die Farbe eines nächtlich beleuchteten Swimmingpools, und wenn ich nicht gerade das Modell gesehen hätte, wäre mein erster Eindruck vielleicht der eines Aquariums gewesen oder eines Untersee-Tableaus aus einem Naturkunde-Museum. Mit einer Fernbedienung schaltete Kessler alle inneren Lichter ein und versenkte eine der blaugetönten Scheiben, hinter der sich in voller

Detail of JON KESSLER'S THE OTHER SIDE.

32

Lebensgrösse der nunmehr bekannte Raum auftat. Der Wechsel der Grössenordnung war etwas verwirrend, doch das Schwindelgefühl ging schnell vorbei, und ich schaute mich um, musterte die Details im Inneren dieser bizarren Apparatur.

Es war ein eigenartiger Raum, viktorianisch und futuristisch zugleich, als wäre sein Stil keiner bestimmten Epoche zuzuordnen, anachronistisch in jedem Zeitalter. Eklektizistisch und doch schlüssig, aber schäbiger, als ich mir vorgestellt hatte; die Flächen, die ich als poliertes Kupfer und rostfreien Stahl erwartete, waren in Wirklichkeit ein Flickenteppich aus Industrieschrott und verrosteten Metallen. Weitere Abwandlungen begleiteten die Massstabsverschiebung: Da waren Vitrinen mit Bechern aus Pyrexglas, Glasfaserkabel-Spulen standen in Reih und Glied auf Plexiglasregalen; ein ausgestopfter Vogel thronte auf einer der Konsolen; und auf Dutzenden kleiner Monitoren leuchteten farbige Tabellen und Schaubilder. Die gläsernen Zylinder in den Ecken waren erlesener, als ich mir je hätte vorstellen können; die vielfarbigen Flüssigkeiten waren dichtere Substanzen, als ich angenommen hatte, eher von der Konsistenz flüssiger Lava; und was ich für Blasen gehalten hatte, waren vielmehr Tausende irisierender Partikel, die ein Licht ausstrahlten, das ebenso hell war wie Neon, wenn auch nicht so intensiv.

Ich stand in der Ecke, mit dem Rücken zum Raum, und starrte diese langsam strudelnden Flüssigkeiten an, völlig versunken in ihre Strömungen und rhythmischen Gezeiten, als ein lauter Gong erscholl, der meine Konzentration durchbrach und mich aus meiner Träumerei riss. Ich fuhr herum und sah, wie Kessler mir einen silbernen Gegenstand hinhielt: eine Kreuzung aus einem alten, ledernen Football-Helm und einer Fliegerkappe. Er trug ebenfalls so etwas. «Das war das Zeichen, die Maschine ist bereit», sagte er, «hast du Zeit für eine Spritztour?» Ich schaute auf meine Armbanduhr, um zu sehen, ob ich schon in die City zurückmusste, und lachte, als ich merkte, dass ich auf Kesslers Scherz hereingefallen war. «Wir brauchen überhaupt keine Zeit», fügte er hinzu, «exakt». Offenkundig konnte er der Pointe nicht widerstehen.

Wir hatten uns schon auf unseren Sitzen angeschnallt – hier waren es rote Ledersitze, nicht die

JON KESSLER, THE OTHER SIDE, 1990,
fiberglass shower, glass, wood, toy polar bear, 89 x 60 x 38" /
DIE ANDERE SEITE, 1990, Fiberglas-Dusche, Glas, Holz,
Spielzeug-Eisbär, 226 x 152,4 x 96,5 cm.

Liegestühle, die ich im Modell gesehen hatte –, als Kessler die Scheibe wieder hochfuhr und mich fragte, ob ich die Zukunft oder die Vergangenheit sehen wollte. Ich deutete auf den silbernen Hebel und lehnte mich zurück, immer noch skeptisch, hoffend, dass alles, was er beschrieben hatte, sich tatsächlich ereignen würde. Der Raum auf der anderen Seite des Glases verschwand allmählich, als ich einen Lichtblitz wahrnahm und etwas Neues hörte, ein unangenehmeres Geräusch, schriller und zugleich dünner als der vorherige Gong. Ich nahm es als Indiz dafür, dass die Maschine arbeitete, aber es beunruhigte mich, als ich den Laut wieder hörte. Der Raum auf der anderen Seite war Staub und Asche seit über hundert Jahren, als das Telefon ein drittes Mal klingelte und ich begriff, dass ich im Bett lag.

(Übersetzung: Frank Heibert)

STEPHAN
BALKENHOL

SOPHIE
CALLE

STEPHAN BALKENHOLS ATELIER IN EDELBACH, 1991.

NEAL BENEZRA

STEPHAN BALKENHOL:
The Figure as Witness

During the last ten years, Stephan Balkenhol has created a surprising body of work devoted to the figure. His is an altogether unassuming cast of characters, figures nearly generic in their portrayal and distinguished only by their sex, their particular pose, or the color of their hair, eyes, and clothing. While his carved and painted wood sculpture is characteristically flat-footed and inexpressive, Balkenhol's work bespeaks a thoroughgoing knowledge of the venerable history of figurative sculpture and of its placement in public. In addition to sculptures made for temporary installation indoors, he has created figures for long-term or permanent placement outdoors, figures to be mounted in niches, on bridges, or carved in bas-relief into friezes. His growing body of work is currently the subject of considerable discussion and critique because, although the figure has reemerged as a subject for a broad range of artists working in widely divergent ways, Balkenhol's analysis of sculptural tradition strikes many as out of step, even anachronistic, in relation to current practice.

Growing up in Kassel through a number of *Documentas,* Balkenhol recalls, in particular, seeing the work of Rauschenberg and Warhol, and he deter-

mined at a very early age to become an artist and "to make my own pop art."[1] Like many young European artists maturing in the early 1980s, Balkenhol was schooled in and influenced by the discipline and rigor of Minimalism and Conceptualism while simultaneously seeking new possibilities and an independent direction. Frustrated by the "rather dispassionate, rational and very unsensuous art of the 70s,"[2] and feeling increasingly that abstract sculpture had run its course, he sought a way to make the figure a viable subject for contemporary work. He recognized that throughout history figurative sculptors have been laden with the obligations of religious or political narrative, and that the academic tradition in Germany and France produced a "monument industry"[3] in the last half of the 19th century. While Balkenhol possesses abundant respect for Lehmbruck, Giacometti, Gonzalez, and Picasso, he feels—perhaps correctly—that in our century "by and large the tendency toward abstraction predominated." Having determined that abstract sculpture had "thrown the baby out with the bath water,"[4] he set out to define a new purpose for figurative work, "to reinvent the figure."[5]

Since 1983, Balkenhol has developed the approach that has characterized his work of the past decade. Initially he made wood sculptures that were rough-

---

NEAL BENEZRA is Chief Curator at the Hirshhorn Museum and Sculpture Garden.

hewn depictions of nude Adam- and Eve-like men and women. He quickly abandoned the nude, however, making the prosaic but exceptionally indicative observation that since "you normally don't encounter people in the nude, I dress my figures in ordinary, everyday clothes."[6] He found that he could impart a degree of naturalism to his work that allowed the pieces to hover tantalizingly between traditional portraiture and a more generic depiction. In part this was due to the increased subtlety of his carving, which was precise but never too detailed, thereby permitting facial detail without introducing a mimetic likeness. Similarly, he began to paint his sculptures, with color added to the hair, eyes, clothing, and shoes—everything, that is, except the skin, which retains its natural wood color and accentuates the figures' subtle separateness from life. Although Balkenhol's sculptures are usually presented individually, even in those instances in which a single work is composed of a group of figures, any anecdotal or narrative reference is conspicuously absent, repressed by the artist. Finally, while his figures are easily distinguishable, one from another, they are uniformly young and ultimately suggest the artist's visualization of a generation of entirely ordinary young individuals.

Balkenhol's sculpture can be differentiated immediately from the tradition of German expressionist sculpture, ranging from E.L. Kirchner and Emil Nolde early in the century, to Georg Baselitz more recently. Indeed, he works in direct opposition to expressionism, demonstrating—perhaps self-consciously—that carved and painted sculpture in wood can be free of angst-ridden gesture. His work similarly diverges from the sculpture of George Segal, arguably the most important American figurative sculptor of the postwar period. Unlike Segal, who casts his figures from life in order to grant them a subtle psychological resonance, Balkenhol enters into a dialogue with life, but always from a distance. He wants his "figures to be as open as possible with regard to their character, to their expression… I wanted an expression from which one could imagine all other states of mind, which was a starting point for everything else. Gestures tend to harden the figure…"[7]

If Balkenhol's figures evidence a historical debt, it is to the Egyptian sculpture that he has studied extensively, admiring its "aura of eternity and tranquillity. They seem to combine both: they emanate transcendence as well as reality and presence."[8]

Balkenhol's sculpture occupies a fascinating position between tradition and contemporary thought. Catalogues accompanying his exhibitions often include the artist's own photographs of historical sculpture, both installed in museums and permanently out-of-doors. Clearly, the artist carefully studies the display of figurative sculpture: for example, he uses the base to great effect by carving both sculpture and pedestal from the same block, thereby determining from the outset both the height at which his work will be seen and, in many instances, the color as well. Issues of relative scale are also critical in Balkenhol's installations, as in his juxtaposing enormous Constantine-scaled heads alongside undersized busts or humorous little animals.

To many, Balkenhol's animal sculptures are particularly perplexing. He has made a full menagerie of animals, almost all of them diminutive: bears, giraffes, horses, lions, penguins, and snails. These animals recall the work of academic *animaliers*, sculptors who have traditionally specialized in the production of animals for the market or for public commissions. Animals have had virtually no role in modern art; indeed, they are among the most clichéd subjects imaginable: Balkenhol's animals evoke the carved wooden figurines that one can find in German toy shops, while self-consciously depicting an enduring sense of childlike wonder at natural phenomena.

Balkenhol's small-scale work suggests contemporary practice in surprising ways, but it may be public sculpture which provides the most compelling format for his vision. Although (or perhaps because) his subjects are so ordinary, Balkenhol prefers to place his sculpture in close proximity to architecture. Invited to contribute outdoor sculptures to the Stadelgarten in Frankfurt in 1991, he placed three figures on public view, two of them—a man and a woman—in small, tightly enclosed stone cells in the center of

STEPHAN BALKENHOL, LIEGENDE FRAU aus einer Gruppe von 10 Skulpturensäulen, 1992,
Wawaholz gefasst, ca. 150 cm / RECLINING WOMAN out of a group of 10 sculpture columns, 1992, polychromed wawa wood, ca. 59". (PHOTO: WIM COX)

STEPHAN BALKENHOL, MANN MIT SCHNECKE, 1991,
Nadelholz gefasst, 157 cm / MAN WITH SNAIL, 1991,
polychromed soft wood, 61⅞". (PHOTO: BOB NOEDEWAAGEN)

the garden, and the third—another man—in one of
four blank niches on the rear facade of the Städtische Galerie. Unencumbered by the age-old expecta-
tion that only celebrated historical figures—actors
on the world's stage—may be enshrined in promi-
nent public sculptures, Balkenhol's red-shirted man
in the street stands with characteristic modesty,
hands at his sides, a simple witness. The result is a fascinating combination: On the one hand, Balkenhol
engages in a lively dialogue with sculpture's history,
submitting himself and his work to this most time-
honored of sculptural tasks; on the other, he good-
naturedly retires the idea that figurative outdoor
sculpture must possess an active public purpose.[9]

All this is not to say that figurative sculpture has lost
its potential for public meaning and power. No
sculptor can consider placing a figurative work out-
of-doors without confronting the spectacle of a hasti-
ly constructed copy of the Statue of Liberty being
hoisted, albeit temporarily, in Tiananmen Square, or
the destruction of all public statuary devoted to
Lenin in the former Soviet Union. For Balkenhol,
working to date principally in a reunified and de-

ideologized Germany, the question must be framed
somewhat differently: What does it mean to make
public sculpture at a time when the ideologies that
have governed our recent history have dissipated
and when traditional social systems are in disarray?
In this sense, his work should be considered in the
context of a postconceptual artistic practice cen-
tered on private and public observation, rather than
in theory. What I am describing, however, is not a
rebirth of traditional humanism; Balkenhol is neither an activist nor an idealist, and just as overt ideo-
logical statements remain taboo, so too does excessive pathos. Ultimately, in an age of exceptional
public change, it is the very reticence of Balkenhol's
sculpture and our subsequent curiosity about these
figures as witnesses that marks their quiet power.

1) Quoted in *BiNationale: German Art of the Late 80s* (Boston:
The Institute of Contemporary Art and Museum of Fine Arts,
1988), p. 68.
2) In conversation with the author, November 1992.
3) Quoted in *Stephan Balkenhol: About Men and Sculpture* (Rotterdam: Witte de With Centre for Contemporary Art, 1991), p. 8,
supplement.
4) Quoted in *BiNationale*, p. 68. It should be noted that Balkenhol's phrase, "Nur ist meiner Ansicht nach vielleicht das Kind
mit dem Bade ausgeschüttet worden," was inaccurately translat-
ed in the Boston catalogue.
5) Quoted in *Stephan Balkenhol: About Men and Sculpture*, 1992,
p. 12, supplement.
6) Quoted in *Possible Worlds: Sculpture From Europe* (London:
Institute of Contemporary Art, 1990), p. 28.
7) Quoted in Stephan Balkenhol: *About Men and Sculpture*, p. 9,
supplement.
8) Quoted in *Possible Worlds*, p. 27.
9) Although the Städtische Galerie project originally involved
three figures, subsequently an additional sculpture was added to
a niche on one of the lateral facades of the museum. James Lingwood's fine essay, "Reluctant Monuments," in *Stephan Balkenhol:
About Men and Sculpture*, pp. 60–64, is devoted to the artist's
public sculpture.

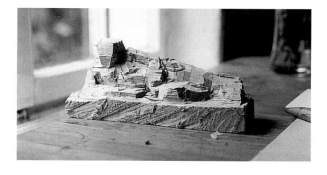

STEPHAN BALKENHOL, ZWEI GROSSE KÖPFE / TWO BIG HEADS, 1991. (INSTALLATION GALERIE LÖHRL, MÖNCHENGLADBACH)

NEAL BENEZRA

STEPHAN BALKENHOL:
Die Figur
als stummer Zeuge

Im Verlauf der letzten zehn Jahre hat Stephan Balkenhol der Figur ein erstaunliches bildhauerisches Œuvre gewidmet. Seine Figuren sind Exemplare einer überaus verhaltenen Spezies: fast allgemeintypisch in ihrer Darstellung und nur durch ihr Geschlecht, ihre jeweilige Pose oder die Farbe ihres Haars, ihrer Augen und ihrer Kleidung zu unterscheiden. So schlicht und ausdrucksleer seine geschnitzten und bemalten Holzskulpturen auch daherkommen mögen, so zeugt Balkenhols Schaffen doch von einer profunden Kenntnis der ehrwürdigen Geschichte der figürlichen Plastik und ihrer Plazierung im öffentlichen Raum. Neben Skulpturen, die zur vorübergehenden Aufstellung in Innenräumen bestimmt waren, hat er auch Figuren geschaffen, die langfristig oder auf Dauer zur Aufstellung im Freien vorgesehen waren, etwa in Nischen, auf Brücken oder in Flachrelief geschnitzt und angelegt als Fries. Sein wachsendes Œuvre ist heute Gegenstand lebhafter Diskussion und Kritik: Obgleich die Figur für ein breites Spektrum in unterschiedlicher Manier arbeitender Künstler als Motiv wieder in den Vordergrund gerückt ist, wirkt Balkenhols Analyse der bildhauerischen Tradition auf viele als diskordant, ja anachronistisch im Verhältnis zu den gegenwärtigen Gepflogenheiten.

NEAL BENEZRA ist leitender Konservator am Hirshhorn Museum and Sculpture Garden in Washington D.C.

Aufgewachsen in Kassel über einen Zeitraum von mehreren *documentas* hinweg, prägte sich Balkenhol insbesondere die Begegnung mit dem Werk Rauschenbergs und Warhols ein, und er beschloss in sehr frühen Jahren, Künstler zu werden und «meine eigene Pop art zu machen».[1] Wie viele junge europäische Künstler, die Anfang der 80er Jahre heranreiften, wurde Balkenhol an der Disziplin und Strenge des Minimalismus und der Konzeptkunst geschult, die ihn entsprechend nachhaltig beeinflussten, während er sich gleichzeitig um neue Möglichkeiten und eine eigene, unabhängige Richtung bemühte. Frustriert durch die «eher nüchterne, verstandesmässige und recht unsinnige Kunst der 70er Jahre»[2] und immer mehr der Überzeugung, dass die abstrakte Plastik ihre Entwicklung abgeschlossen habe, suchte Balkenhol nach einem Weg, die Figur zu einem lebensfähigen Sujet für heutige Kunst zu machen. Er erkannte, dass den Schöpfern figürlicher Plastik im Lauf der Geschichte stets die Pflichten religiöser oder politischer Darstellung aufgebürdet worden waren und dass die akademische Tradition in Deutschland und Frankreich in der zweiten Hälfte des 19. Jahrhunderts eine regelrechte «Denkmalindustrie» hervorgebracht hatte.[3] Bei all seiner Hochschätzung für Lehmbruck, Giacometti, Gonzalez und Picasso ist Balkenhol doch – wohl zu Recht – der Ansicht, dass in unserem Jahrhundert «im grossen und ganzen die Tendenz zur Abstraktion überwog». Nachdem er einmal festgestellt hatte, dass die abstrakte Plastik «das Kind mit dem Bade ausgeschüttet» hatte[4], machte er sich daran, eine neue Zielsetzung für figürliches Schaffen zu bestimmen, ja «die Figur neu zu erfinden».[5]

Seit 1983 hat Balkenhol den Ansatz, der sein Werk des vergangenen Jahrzehnts geprägt hat, weiterentwickelt. Anfangs machte er grobgeschnitzte Holzskulpturen, die nackte, in den paradiesischen Zustand zurückversetzte Männer und Frauen darstellten. Es kam jedoch bald zu einer Abkehr vom

STEPHAN BALKENHOL, SKULPTUR-KREUZ, 1991,
Pappelholz gefasst, 157 x 60 x 60 cm /
SCULPTURE CROSS, 1991, polychromed poplar wood, 61¾ x 23⅝".

Akt, nachdem er zu der prosaischen, aber für ihn überaus symptomatischen Erkenntnis gelangt war, dass «man normalerweise keinen nackten Menschen begegnet: Deshalb kleide ich meine Figuren in einfache, alltägliche Kleider».[6] Er stellte fest, dass er seinem Werk ein bestimmtes Mass an Naturalismus verleihen konnte, das es den einzelnen Arbeiten erlaubte, sich auf provozierende Weise zwischen traditioneller Porträtkunst und einer mehr allgemeintypischen Darstellung zu bewegen. Dies war teilweise der gesteigerten Subtilität seiner bildhauerischen Arbeit zu verdanken, die präzise, aber niemals allzu detailverliebt war und so zwar eine gewisse Detailzeichnung des Gesichts zuliess, jedoch ohne eine mimetische Ähnlichkeit hineinzubringen. In ähnlicher Weise begann er seine Skulpturen zu bemalen und Haare, Augen, Kleidung und Schuhe farbig zu fassen, alles, mit anderen Worten, bis auf die Haut, die ihre natürliche Holzfarbe behält und die subtile Abgegrenztheit der Figur vom Leben unterstreicht. Obgleich Balkenhols Skulpturen in der Regel als Einzelfiguren daherkommen, wird selbst in den Fällen, in denen sich eine bestimmte Arbeit aus mehreren Figuren zusammensetzt, jeder anekdotische oder narrative Zusammenhang vom Künstler unterdrückt, eine Aussparung, die ins Auge fällt. Schliesslich sind seine Figuren, obgleich relativ leicht voneinander zu unterscheiden, alle gleichermassen jung, was letztlich den Eindruck erweckt, hier werde vom Künstler eine Generation ganz und gar durchschnittlicher junger Individuen porträtiert.

Balkenhols Bildhauerkunst lässt sich unmissverständlich von zwei tonangebenden bildhauerischen Strömungen des 20. Jahrhunderts unterscheiden, insbesondere von der Tradition deutscher expressionistischer Plastik, die von Ernst Ludwig Kirchner und Emil Nolde zu Beginn dieses Jahrhunderts bis hin zu einem Gegenwartskünstler wie Georg Baselitz reicht. Ja, er setzt sich – möglicherweise ganz bewusst – vom Expressionismus ab, indem er aufzeigt, dass geschnitzte und farbig gefasste Holzskulpturen auch ohne die ausdrucksvolle Gestik einer angstbeladenen Befindlichkeit auskommen. Ebenso unterscheidet sich sein Werk vom plastischen Schaffen des wohl wichtigsten amerikanischen figurativen Bild-

hauers der Nachkriegszeit, George Segal. Anders als
Segal, der seine Figuren nach dem lebenden Modell
formt, um ihnen eine subtile psychologische Aus-
strahlung zu verleihen, tritt Balkenhol in einen Dialog mit dem Leben ein, allerdings immer aus einer
Distanz heraus. Nach seiner Vorstellung sollen seine
«Figuren im Hinblick auf ihren Charakter, ihren
Ausdruck möglichst offen sein. ... Mir war an einem
Ausdruck gelegen, von dem ausgehend jeder andere
Gemützustand vorstellbar wäre. Gesten neigen
dazu, die Figur zu versteinern...»[7] Wenn an Balkenhols Figuren der Einfluss eines historischen Vorbil-
des abzulesen ist, so der der ägyptischen Plastik, mit
der er sich intensiv befasst hat. Er bewundert «ihre
Aura der Ewigkeit und ruhige Gelassenheit. Sie
scheinen beides miteinander zu verbinden: sie strah-
len sowohl eine Transzendenz wie auch Realität und
Präsenz aus».[8]

Die Plastik Stephan Balkenhols nimmt eine faszi-
nierende Zwischenstellung zwischen Tradition und
heutiger Denkweise ein. In den Katalogen, die zu
Ausstellungen seiner Werke erscheinen, finden sich
häufig auch vom Künstler selbst gemachte Photos
historischer Werke der Bildhauerkunst, sowohl solcher, die im Museum, wie auch solcher, die auf Dauer
im Freien aufgestellt sind. Offensichtlich setzt sich
der Künstler sehr genau mit der Präsentationsweise
figürlicher Plastik auseinander. So bezieht er in überaus effektvoller Weise den Sockel mit ein dadurch,
dass er Skulptur und Postament aus ein und demselben Block schnitzt, wodurch er wiederum gleich
von Anfang an die Höhe festlegt, in der sein Werk zu
sehen sein wird, wie auch in vielen Fällen dessen Farbigkeit. Auch Massstabrelationen kommt in Balkenhols Installationen eine entscheidende Bedeutung
zu, etwa wenn er überdimensionale Köpfe in kon-
stantinischer Grösse mit Büsten oder humoristischen
kleinen Tieren kombiniert.

Balkenhols Tierskulpturen wirken auf viele besonders verstörend. Er hat eine ganze Menagerie fast
ausschliesslich miniaturisierter Tiere geschaffen:
Bären, Giraffen, Pferde, Löwen, Pinguine und
Schnecken. Balkenhols Tiere erinnern an das Schaffen akademischer animaliers, Bildhauer, die sich

STEPHAN BALKENHOL, 10 SKULPTURENSÄULEN, 1992,

Wawaholz gefasst, 130 – 150 cm / 10 SCULPTURE COLUMNS, 1992, polychromed wawa wood, 51 – 59".

traditionell auf die Produktion von Tierfiguren für den Markt oder in öffentlichem Auftrag spezialisiert hatten. In der modernen Kunst haben Tiere so gut wie keine Rolle gespielt, sie zählen, um genau zu sein, sogar zu den denkbar klischeehaftesten Sujets. Balkenhols Tiere erinnern an die geschnitzten Holzfigurinen, die man in deutschen Spielwarenhandlungen findet, während sie zugleich bewusst und überaus plastisch einen bleibenden Eindruck kindlichen Staunens angesichts von Naturerscheinungen verkörpern.

Auch wenn Balkenhols kleinformatige Werke auf sehr überraschende Weise Bezug nehmen auf die gegenwärtige Kunstpraxis, so ist doch wohl die öffentliche Skulptur das wohl zwingendste Format für seine künstlerische Vision. Obgleich (oder vielleicht gerade weil) seine Sujets so trivial sind, setzt Balkenhol seine Skulpturen mit Vorliebe in einen engen Zusammenhang zu Architektur. Als man ihn 1991 einlud, im Rahmen einer Ausstellung Aussenskulpturen für den Frankfurter Städelgarten beizutragen, präsentierte er drei Figuren, zwei davon, ein Mann und eine Frau, in kleinen, engen Steinkammern in der Mitte des Gartens, und die dritte, ein weiterer Mann, in einer von vier leeren Nischen auf der Rückseite des Städel. Völlig unbelastet von dem altüberlieferten Gedanken, dass es nur berühmten historischen Persönlichkeiten – Akteuren des Welttheaters – zustehe, in Form augenfälliger öffentlicher Skulpturen glorifiziert zu werden, steht Balkenhols Mann von der Strasse mit charakteristischer Bescheidenheit da, die Hände in die Seite gestemmt, ein schlichter Zeuge. Das Ergebnis ist faszinierend mehrdeutig: auf der einen Seite führt der Künstler einen lebhaften Dialog mit der Geschichte der Bildhauerei, indem er sich und sein Werk dieser altehrwürdigsten aller bildhauerischen Aufgaben widmet; auf der anderen verabschiedet er auf liebenswürdige Weise die Vorstellung, figürlicher Aussenplastik müsse ein ganz bestimmter öffentlicher Zweck eignen.[9]

Das alles soll nicht heissen, die figürliche Plastik habe jegliches öffentliche Bedeutungs- oder Wirkungspotential eingebüsst. Kein Bildhauer kann heute die Idee ins Auge fassen, eine figürliche Arbeit im Freien aufzustellen, ohne sich gedanklich etwa mit dem Geschehen auf dem Platz des himmlischen Friedens in Beijing auseinanderzusetzen, als dort, freilich nur für kurze Zeit, eine in Eile angefertigte Kopie der Freiheitsstatue errichtet wurde, oder mit der Zerstörung sämtlicher Leninstatuen in der ehemaligen Sowjetunion. Für Balkenhol, der heute hauptsächlich in einem wiedervereinten und entideologisierten Deutschland arbeitet, muss die Frage anders gestellt werden: was bedeutet es, öffentliche Skulpturen zu schaffen in einer Zeit, in der die Ideologien, die unsere jüngere und jüngste Vergangenheit bestimmt haben, verschwunden sind und gewachsene Gesellschaftssysteme in einem Prozess der Auflösung begriffen sind? In diesem Sinne sollte Balkenhols Werk im Kontext einer postkonzeptuellen künstlerischen Praxis gesehen werden, deren Schwerpunkt nicht in der Theorie, sondern in der privaten und öffentlichen Wahrnehmung liegt. Was hier beschrieben wird, ist jedoch keine Wiedergeburt eines traditionellen Humanismus: Balkenhol ist weder ein Aktivist noch ein Idealist, und explizite ideologische Aussagen bleiben ebenso tabu wie übermässiges Pathos. Letzten Endes ist es – in einer Zeit exzeptionellen öffentlichen Wandels – gerade die Schweigsamkeit und Verhaltenheit der Skulpturen Balkenhols und die Neugier, die sie daraufhin in uns wecken, die ihre stille Eindringlichkeit ausmachen.

(Übersetzung: Magda Moses, Bram Opstelten)

1) Im Gespräch mit dem Autor, November 1992.
2) Zit. in *BiNationale*, Ausstellungskatalog, Kunstsammlung Nordrhein-Westfalen, Düsseldorf 1988, S. 68.
3) Zit. in Stephan Balkenhol: *Über Menschen und Skulpturen*, Stuttgart 1993, S. 73.
4) Zit. in *BiNationale* (wie Anm. 2), S. 68.
5) Zit. in Stephan Balkenhol: *Über Menschen und Skulpturen* (wie Anm. 3), S. 77.
6) Zit. in *Possible Worlds: Sculpture From Europe*, Ausstellungskatalog, Institute of Contemporary Arts, London 1990, S. 28.
7) Zit. in Stephan Balkenhol: *Über Menschen und Skulpturen* (wie Anm. 3), S. 74.
8) Zit. in *Possible Worlds* (wie Anm. 6), S. 27.
9) Das Projekt für den Städelgarten umfasste ursprünglich drei Figuren, nachträglich wurde jedoch eine weitere Skulptur in einer der Nischen an der seitlichen Fassade des Museums aufgestellt. In einem vorzüglichen Beitrag zu dem Katalog *Stephan Balkenhol: Über Menschen und Skulpturen* (wie Anm. 3), S. 60–64, setzt sich James Lingwood mit der öffentlichen Plastik des Künstlers auseinander.

VIK MUNIZ

As time goes by

"Salomon saith: there is no new thing upon the earth. So that as Plato had an imagination, all knowledge was but remembrance. So Salomon giveth this sentence, that all novelty is but oblivion." (FRANCIS BACON, *Essays* LVIII)

It's 1993. While most art production is engaged in the process of scavenging the carcass of modernism in search for novelty, Stephan Balkenhol is carving living beings out of wood.

"It seemed an obvious thing to do. I think if anybody begins to make art, they perhaps start by drawing a figure or sculpting a head." (STEPHAN BALKENHOL)[1]

Here the obvious becomes the richest possible source of antagonism. And yet obvious it remains. Balkenhol plays between mimesis and ana-mimesis, between mimicry and memory. But his figures are less about recognition than they are about apprehension. "Apprehension" means to arrest, to fix, to bring into presence, to behold as well as to withhold. But "apprehension" may also mean anxiety, discomfiture, dread.

Within the framework of the modernist problematic, sculpture "takes place." That is to say, it advances a claim to presence while at the same time—with regard to statuary—it takes the place of the (represented) body. Modernism's abhorrence of the figural and suppression of the body as representation produces an anxious search on the spectator's part for his/her body in every object.

Balkenhol's artistic education occurred during the 1970s under the tutelage of Ulrich Rückriem. One

STEPHAN BALKENHOL, ZWEI VOLUMEN-RELIEFS, 1992,
Pappelholz gefasst, 221 x 114 x 114 cm /
TWO RELIEFS VOLUMES, 1992, *polychromed poplar wood,*
87 x 44⅞ x 44⅞".

can clearly discern in both student and teacher ideas of reduction and simplification. In Balkenhol's case, however, minimalism is simplified beyond the closure of modernism and its abhorrence of the figure. Both Rückriem and Balkenhol overcame the prejudice towards carving, a technique that by lacking

VIK MUNIZ is an artist and writer living in New York City.

STEPHAN BALKENHOL, VIER MOOREICHENSÄULEN, 1990, ca. 136 cm / FOUR COLUMNS IN OAK, 1990, ca. 53½".

the appeal of serial replication was, at the beginning of the century, denigrated to the category of craft.

Carving works by means of subtraction. The removal of layered substance from a desired "essence." As an archeologist systematically sifts meaningless matter from what is not yet historical, the sculptor removes material from what is not yet semantically transcendental to that particular material.

The unfinished look of Balkenhol's carvings and the admitted speed at which he works marks a relationship between labor and anxiety. When something is done fast, it is often the case that it is done because that something can be easily lost or missed. The presence does not come from a real subject but from an idea, or memory, or a peripheral trace of that particular subject.

Just as Phydias made athletes from models and gods from memory, Pygmalion had to forget all women in order to create Galatea. Balkenhol makes both man and beasts without reference. He makes them as if for the first time.

When, in the case of public monuments, a recourse to constant referentiality precludes the necessity to memorize, things become virtually invisible. Balkenhol's figures play with this temporality; they always look as if they are caught either before or after an action they don't accomplish. Arrested in this way, they simply are.

"Don't smile, don't squint, avoid expressions, just be yourself." Guideline for passport portraiture, Consulate General of Brazil.

Although Balkenhol's works appear to be done after a photograph, it is more likely that they occupy a position of one before being photographed. Like extras on a film set, his "characters" carry no subjectivity, no narrative, they are not there to do anything, they simply reiterate their presence, punctuate and fill space. Yet at the same time, they are charged, loaded with potential and hope for action. They are proleptic markers—they pose, they do not act, they pose in place of act.

Posture, counterposed to gesture, is a stasis, a duration or persistence of the body in time. Gesture, on the other hand, is a photographically decisive moment, a rupture in time of movement or spectacle. Balkenhol's figures arrest the viewer's attention with the opaque reflection of presence in shared time. In sculpture, a figure has to attain a certain identity before being granted the privilege of resting. Only the famous are allowed to be at rest. Anonymous or symbolic bodies always have to be doing something, engaged in some sort of activity.

Obsessed with posterity, Juárez ordered hundreds of busts of himself to be made and placed in every single small Mexican village. Due to the still-precarious state of photography at the time, and to the unavailability of the subject for posing, the artisans who made the bust had to rely on every possible bit of information in order to be able to complete their monuments: single and collective memory, quick sketches of brief apparitions or copies from previously executed works. As a result, each bust has unique facial characteristics; yet all "represent" Juárez.

For all we know, Juárez always wore a bow tie.

The delinquent removal of the plaques bearing the name of Juárez from these monuments brings them to a state of complete anonymity. The man with the bow tie has accidentally entered the world of Balkenhol's characters where one can only be differentiated by the color of his/her clothes. The impossible placing of the generic into the ideal; monuments of oblivion, yet remarkably unforgettable.

"We easily retain a sensible, visible, imaginable statue, we commend easily to the work of memory fabulous fictions; therefore (through them) we shall be able without difficulty to consider and retain mysteries, doctrines, and disciplinary intentions…as in nature we see vicissitudes of light and darkness, so also there are vicissitudes of different kinds of philosophies. Since there is nothing new…it is necessary to return to these opinions after so many centuries."

(GIORDANO BRUNO, *Lampas triginta statuarum padua*, 1591)

1) From the exhibition catalogue, *Possible Worlds* (London: ICA and Serpentine Gallery, 1992).

STEPHAN BALKENHOL, MANN MIT SCHWARZER HOSE, 1987,
Rotbuche gefasst, 205 cm / MAN IN BLACK TROUSERS, 1987, polychromed red beech wood, 80¾". (PHOTO: HELGE MUNDT)

VIK MUNIZ

Salomo sagt: «Es geschieht nichts Neues unter der Sonne»;
während Plato den Gedanken ausspricht, dass alles Wissen
nur Erinnerung sei, meint Salomo, dass alle Neuheit auf
Vergessen beruhe.

FRANCIS BACON, *Essays LVIII (Über die Wandelbarkeit der Dinge)*

Wir schreiben das Jahr 1993. Während der Grossteil
des Kunstschaffens damit befasst ist, den Kadaver der
Moderne auf der Suche nach Neuem auszuweiden,
schnitzt Stephan Balkenhol lebendige Geschöpfe aus
Holz.

«Es war etwas, das nahezuliegen schien. Ich glaube,
jeder, der anfängt, Kunst zu machen, zeichnet vielleicht zuerst eine Figur oder schnitzt einen Kopf.»

(STEPHAN BALKENHOL[1])

Im Lauf der Zeit

Das Naheliegende wird hier zur denkbar reichsten
Quelle des Widerstreits. Und dennoch bleibt es
naheliegend. Balkenhols Kunst oszilliert zwischen
Mimesis und Anamimesis, zwischen Nachahmung
und Erinnerung. Allerdings geht es bei seinen Figuren weniger um das Wiedererkennen als vielmehr
um das Erfassen. Erfassen heisst festhalten, fixieren,
vergegenwärtigen, wahrnehmen wie auch in sich aufnehmen. Zugleich spielt in dieses Erfassen bei Balkenhol ein Moment der Verwirrung, der Besorgnis,
ja der Angst hinein.

Im Rahmen der Problemstellung der Moderne ist die
Skulptur etwas, das «Statt findet», das heisst, sie
macht einen Anspruch auf greifbare Präsenz gel-
tend, während sie zugleich – mit Blick auf figürliche
Plastik – an die Stelle des (dargestellten) Körpers
tritt. Die Antipathie der Moderne gegen das Figürliche und ihre Verdrängung des Körpers als vergegen-
wärtigender Darstellung führen auf seiten des
Betrachters zu einer besorgten Suche nach seinem
Körper in jedem Gegenstand.

VIK MUNIZ ist bildender Künstler und Schriftsteller und lebt in
New York.

Balkenhols künstlerische Ausbildung erfolgte in den
70er Jahren unter Ulrich Rückriem. Bei Schüler wie
Lehrer sind Tendenzen der Reduktion und Vereinfa-
chung unübersehbar. In Balkenhols Fall jedoch wird
der Minimalismus jenseits des geschlossenen Systems
der Moderne und ihrer Abneigung gegen die Figur
vereinfacht. Rückriem wie Balkenhol überwanden
das Vorurteil gegen das Meisseln und Schnitzen, eine
Technik, die, weil ihr der Reiz der seriellen Verviel-
fältigung abging, zu Beginn des Jahrhunderts zum
blossen Handwerk degradiert wurde.

Meisseln und Schnitzen sind subtraktive Techniken:
Durch die Entfernung überlagernder Schichten von
Materie wird ein ersehnter Kern herausgeschält. So,
wie der Archäologe systematisch bedeutungslose
Materie vom noch nicht Historischen scheidet, so
entfernt der Bildhauer Material von dem, was noch
keine über das spezifische Material hinausweisende
Bedeutung birgt.

Das unfertige Erscheinungsbild der Schnitzereien
Balkenhols und seine eingestandenermassen schnelle Arbeitsweise markieren einen Zusammenhang zwischen Arbeit und Angst. Wenn etwas schnell gemacht

wird, so oft deshalb, weil die betreffende Sache leicht verlorengehen oder sich «entziehen» könnte. Die Präsenz entspringt nicht einem konkreten Gegenstand, sondern einer Vorstellung, einer Erinnerung

oder einem peripheren Eindruck vom betreffenden Gegenstand.

Genauso wie Phidias Athleten nach dem Modell und

Götter aus dem Gedächtnis schuf, so musste Pygmalion die Erinnerung an alle Frauen tilgen, um Galatea zu erschaffen. Balkenhol macht Menschen wie Tiere ohne jede Bezugnahme. Er erschafft sie wie zum ersten Mal.

Wenn, im Falle öffentlicher Denkmäler, ständig auf Referentialität gesetzt wird und die Notwendigkeit der Einprägung entfällt, werden die Dinge praktisch unsichtbar. Balkenhols Figuren treiben ein Spiel mit dieser Zeitweiligkeit: sie wirken immer wie unmittelbar vor oder auch nach einer Handlung eingefangen, die sie nicht zu Ende führen. In dieser Art festgehalten, tun sie nichts, als einfach da zu sein.

«Nicht lächeln, nicht blinzeln, das Gesicht möglichst ausdruckslos, ganz einfach man selbst sein.» Anleitung für das Aufnehmen von Passphotos, brasilianisches Generalkonsulat.

Obgleich Balkenhols Figuren so aussehen, als wären sie nach einer photographischen Vorlage entstanden, ist es vermutlich eher so, dass sie die Position einer oder eines zu Photographierenden einnehmen. Wie Statisten am Drehort eignet seinen Figuren keine Subjektivität, keine Geschichte; sie sind nicht da, um irgend etwas zu tun, sie bekräftigen nur immer wieder aufs neue ihre Präsenz, durchstellen und füllen den Raum. Zugleich jedoch sind sie spannungsgeladen, angefüllt mit Möglichkeiten der Bewegung oder Handlung. Sie sind vorwegnehmende Signifikate: sie posieren, sie handeln nicht, sie posieren anstatt zu handeln.

Die Pose ist, gegenüber der Geste, ein Stillstand, ein Anhalten oder Ausharren des Körpers in der Zeit. Die Geste dagegen ist ein haarscharf einschneidender Augenblick, eine Unterbrechung der Zeit in Form von Bewegung oder Erblicktem. Balkenhols Figuren fesseln die Aufmerksamkeit des Betrachters kraft des opaken Abglanzes der Gegenwart in einer gemeinsamen Zeit. In der Bildhauerei muss eine Figur einen Wiedererkennungswert erlangt haben, ehe ihr das Privileg einer ruhenden Stellung gewährt wird. Nur Berühmtheiten dürfen eine Ruhestellung einnehmen. Anonyme oder symbolische Körper müssen immer gerade etwas tun, in irgendeiner Art tätiger Bewegung begriffen sein.

Besessen von dem Gedanken an seinen Nachruhm, liess Benito Juárez Hunderte von Büsten von sich anfertigen und sie in jedem kleinen mexikanischen Dorf aufstellen. Da die Photographie damals immer noch in den Kinderschuhen steckte und weil der zu Porträtierende für eine Sitzung als Modell unabkömmlich war, waren die Bildhauer, die die Büsten anfertigten, auf jede nur denkbare Information angewiesen, um ihre Denkmäler vollenden zu können: auf individuelles und kollektives Gedächtnis, schnell hingeworfene Skizzen flüchtiger Auftritte oder Kopien früher entstandener Arbeiten. Infolgedessen besitzt jede Büste einzigartige Gesichtszüge, und dennoch «stellen» alle Juárez «dar».

Soweit uns bekannt ist, trug Juárez immer eine Fliege.

Die unter Strafe gestellte Entfernung der Plaketten mit Juárez' Namen versetzt diese Denkmäler in einen Status völliger Anonymität. Der Mann mit der Fliege hat sich somit unbeabsichtigt in der Welt der Figuren Balkenhols eingefunden, in der der einzelne nur durch die Farben seiner Kleidung zu unterscheiden ist. Die unmögliche Einordnung des Allgemein-Typischen in das Ideale: Monumente der Vergessenheit, doch ausserordentlich einprägsam.

«Wir prägen uns leicht eine wahrnehmbare, sichtbare, vorstellbare Statue ein, wir vertrauen ohne weiteres erdichtete Fabeln dem Wirken unseres Gedächtnisses an. Deshalb wird es uns (durch sie) ohne Schwierigkeiten möglich sein, über Mysterien, Lehren und erzieherische Absichten nachzudenken und sie uns einzuprägen... Ebenso wie wir in der Natur einen ewigen Wechsel von Licht und Dunkel beobachten, so gibt es auch einen ewigen Wechsel unterschiedlicher Philosophien. Da nichts neu ist, ... lässt es sich nicht umgehen, nach einigen Jahrhunderten immer wieder zu diesen Anschauungen zurückzukehren.»

GIORDANO BRUNO, *Lampas triginta statuarum padua,* 1591

1) Zitiert nach dem Ausstellungskatalog *Possible Worlds,* ICA und Serpentine Gallery, London 1992.

53

(Übersetzung: Magda Moses, Bram Opstelten)

MAX KATZ

Autonome Menschen

SACHLICHKEIT UND SINNLICHKEIT

Balkenhols Skulpturen beziehen ihre qualitative Neuartigkeit und Bedeutung aus ihrem Ursprung in zwei ganz entgegengesetzten Bereichen. Sie entstammen einerseits der verstandesbetonten Sachlichkeit, Anorganik und Serialität der Minimalkunst, andererseits einem unmittelbar sinnlichen Zugang zur Welt. Balkenhol gelingt es, beide Pole in seiner Arbeit zu verbinden. Der sinnliche, erotische Zugang zu allem Lebendigen zeigt sich in seiner Wiedereinführung des Körpers in die zeitgenössische Kunst und in seiner handwerklichen, körperbetonten Arbeitsweise. Ein wesentlicher Aspekt seiner Arbeit ist sein Talent, sinnliche Eindrücke unmittelbar durch schnelle und präzise Handgriffe in ästhetisch-formale Bilder umzusetzen. Die Fähigkeit zum schnellen, genauen Zugriff ist vereint mit der bei Ulrich Rückriem geschulten Disziplin im Umgang mit Form, Material und Raum. In den einfachen, manchmal fast steifen Haltungen der Figuren wirken sowohl das Wesen des Baumstammes wie auch das serielle, anorganische Moment der Minimalkunst nach, jedoch verwandelt in klassische Haltungen der Ruhe. Mit fast wissenschaftlicher Nüchternheit, die an die Portraits von Thomas Ruff erinnert, gelingt es Balkenhol, die sinnliche Lust des Realisten an der Welt mit der konzeptuellen Strenge der Minimalkunst, die ein ganz neues, offenes Verhältnis von Form, Material und Raum erschuf, zu verbinden.

MAX KATZ ist Kunstkritiker und lebt in Köln.

GRÖSSE UND ALLTÄGLICHKEIT

«Der Kouros ist Zeugnis des ersten Persönlichkeitskults in der Geschichte des Westens, ist eine Ikone des Kults um die Schönheit, Ausdruck eines Hierarchiedenkens». CAMILLE PAGLIA

Balkenhol übernimmt von der Minimalkunst die Auflösung des Hierarchischen und des Schönheitskults griechischer Plastik und ihrer langen Tradition, ohne jedoch den menschlichen Körper zu fragmentieren oder zu verzerren wie viele Künstler im 20. Jahrhundert.

Balkenhols Figuren sind ebensoweit entfernt von der Idealisierung und Heroisierung des Menschen wie von der Dominanz des künstlerischen Egos in expressionistischen Kunstrichtungen. Alles Herausragende und Monumentale wird vermieden zugunsten einer lebensnahen, profanen Alltäglichkeit. Kleidung und Frisuren sind auf einfachste Elemente reduziert und lassen sich keiner Mode oder gesellschaftlichen Stellung zuordnen. Es werden keine Ideen vergrössert, auch nicht die Idee des einfachen Menschen und Arbeiters wie im sozialistischen Realismus. So gelingt es Balkenhol, ein offenes, lebendiges Menschenbild zu schaffen, das noch frei ist von gesellschaftlichen Festlegungen.

KÖRPER UND GESCHWINDIGKEIT

Die Geschwindigkeit der Arbeit ist von grosser Bedeutung. Während andere Künstler heute ihre Bilder

durch den Einsatz von Technik wie etwa der Photographie oder industrieller Produktionsweisen hervorbringen, entstehen Balkenhols Figuren noch ganz traditionell durch den Einsatz von Körper und Hand. Doch er unterbindet jede nostalgische Reminiszenz durch die enorme Geschwindigkeit der Bearbeitung, die ihm sein

grosses handwerkliches Können erlaubt. Durch die Geschwindigkeit der Bearbeitung findet eine Umsetzung und Verallgemeinerung der realen Vorlage statt, die jedoch immer erkennbar bleibt. Es entsteht eine bewegte Oberfläche, die fein genug ist, wesentliche Details wie Hände, Nase oder Augen genau zu erfassen, die sich jedoch nicht in fixierende, hyperrealistische Details, die wenig Raum für alle anderen an der Arbeit beteiligten Faktoren lassen würden, verliert. So bleiben die Figuren stets in der Schwebe zwischen individueller Charakterisierung und Verallgemeinerung, jedoch nicht im Sinne idealisierender Abstraktion, sondern im Sinne einer prozessualen Offenheit durch die leicht unfertig und roh belassene Oberfläche.

Nichts wird nachträglich verbessert oder korrigiert. Jeder Handgriff muss präzise sitzen, der Künstler muss schnell auf die Zufallsstrukturen des Holzes reagieren. Balkenhol verliert sich nicht in die Kleinförmigkeit von Details, sondern die genaue Beschreibung beschränkt sich auf das Wesentliche, das der Schnelligkeit der Wahrnehmung und des Schaffens entspricht. Das Studium der Menschen und Tiere kann lange dauern, der Schaffensprozess unterliegt der Forderung nach grösster Schnelligkeit, so wie es auf der Rennstrecke kein Zögern mehr geben darf. Formale Konzeption, Körper und Sinne werden dadurch zu einer Einheit. In der Geschwindigkeit der Arbeit müssen sich alle an der Arbeit beteiligten Faktoren beweisen.

MATERIAL UND SYMBOLIK

Das Holz als Werkstoff ist in mehrerer Hinsicht von grosser Bedeutung. Es ist zuerst ein Abwenden von Stein und Bronze, deren anorganische Härte und Dauerhaftigkeit sich zu sehr mit den Vorstellungen von Idealen, ewigen Werten und Wahrheiten traditioneller Skulptur verbindet. Holz ist ein organisches, weiches Material, das sich dem Bildhauer als Herausforderung entgegenstellt und sich dennoch bei handwerklichem Können schnell bearbeiten lässt. Es steht dem lebendigen menschlichen Körper näher als geglätteten Idealisierungen oder intellektuellen Abstraktionen. Der Baum bietet vielerlei Vergleiche mit dem Menschen an: das Zeitmass seines Wachstums, sein Blühen und das Fallen seiner Blätter, seine Verwurzelung in der Erde und seine in den Himmel reichenden Äste bis hin zur romantischen Symbolik des einsamen Baumes. Die warme Farbigkeit des Holzes erinnert an die Farbe der

Detail zweier Skulpturen
von Stephan Balkenhol aus dem Jahr 1983 /
details of two sculptures
by Stephan Balkenhol from 1983.

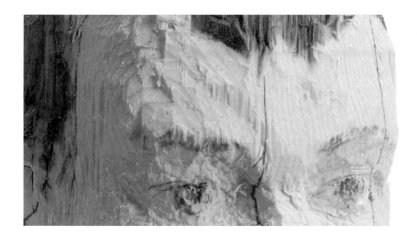

Details zweier Skulpturen /
details of two sculptures, 1987 and 1983.

Haut, und die statuarische Ruhe der Bäume findet sich wieder in den gelassenen, stillen Haltungen der Figuren.

Die Bemalung erfolgt ebenso schnell wie die Bearbeitung des Holzes, sie verstärkt den Realismus der Figur und nimmt den Materialcharakter des Holzes zurück. Balkenhol beschränkt sich meist auf zwei bis drei Farben, wodurch die Figuren eine grössere Klarheit und Einfachheit erhalten.

KÄLTE UND BESEELTHEIT

In Balkenhols Arbeit verbindet sich die Kälte strenger, anorganischer Form mit dem Abbild des Körpers und einer Beseeltheit des Ausdrucks. Körper und Gesichter seiner Skulpturen entsprechen keinen Idealen von Schönheit. Es sind individuelle, alltägliche Gesichter, deren Charakter durch das Stehenlassen der Arbeitsspuren, leichte Ungenauigkeiten und die Art der Bemalung eine gewisse Verallgemeinerung erfährt. Die Maserung des Holzes und die rohe Oberfläche bilden zusammen mit den Farben, Formen und Linien eine neue, ästhetische Ebene, und dennoch scheinen es lebendige Menschen zu sein, die uns gegenüberstehen.

Die Beseeltheit der Figuren entspringt der Freiheit, mit welcher sich der Künstler einer glatten, konventionellen Umsetzung entzieht. Er hält sich nicht sklavisch genau an das Modell. Dieses ist Vorlage für ein fast freies Spiel zwischen körperlicher Arbeit, Material, Formen und Farben. Nichts entspricht genau dem Modell, und dennoch ist es sofort wiederzuerkennen. Die realistische Wiedergabe der Person wird immer im Auge behalten, doch wichtiger als photographische Genauigkeit ist der lebendige, beseelte Ausdruck, welcher dem freien, allein von der sinnlichen Intuition geleiteten Umgang mit den Mitteln entspringt. Balkenhol erlaubt sich eine virtuose Ungenauigkeit, die die Dinge beschreibt, ohne sie zu fixieren, wodurch sie als Bildnisse lebendig und als Kunstwerk offen bleiben.

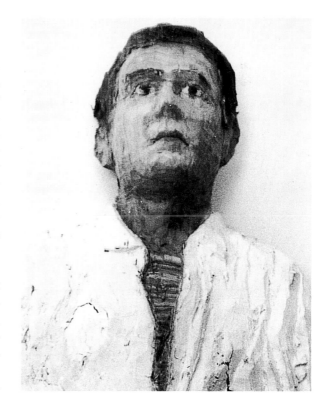

MAX KATZ

Autonomous People

SOBER AND SENSUAL

Balkenhol's sculptures derive their qualitative currency and significance from their origin in two diametrically opposed fields. They draw on the rational, sober, anorganic, and serial character of Minimal Art; yet they also provide immediate sensual access to the world. These two poles are successfully united in Balkenhol's work. His sensual, erotic approach to all living things is demonstrated by his reintroduction of the body to contemporary art and his explicitly physical craftsmanship. His talent for instantly converting sensual impressions into aesthetic, formal images with rapid and precise manipulations is an essential aspect of his work. Speed and precision are united with a disciplined treatment of form, space, and materials acquired under the tutelage of Ulrich Rückriem. The simple, almost stiff attitudes of the figures bring into play both the essence of the tree trunk and the serial, anorganic nature of Minimal Art—transmuted, however, into classical attitudes of balanced repose. With near scientific dispassion, in the vein of Thomas Ruff's portraits, Balkenhol succeeds in combining the sensual pleasure of the realist with the conceptual severity of Minimal Art, which had invented a new, undogmatic relationship between form, space, and material.

SUBLIME AND MUNDANE

"The kouros records the first cult of personality in western history. It is an icon of the worship of beauty, a hierarchism self-generated rather than dynastic." CAMILLE PAGLIA

Balkenhol has adopted Minimal Art's leveling of hierarchism and ancient Greek sculpture's cult of beauty,

without, however, fragmenting or distorting the human body, as many artists of the 20th century have done.

Balkenhol's figures are as far removed from the idealization and heroization of the human body as they are from the dominance of the artistic ego in Expressionist Art. All that is towering and monumental is waived in favor of the ordinary, the familiar, the mundane. Reduced to the simplest of elements, clothing and hairstyles cannot be ascribed to any particular fashion or social class. Ideas are not enlarged, not even the idea of the simple citizen and the value of work as in Socialist Realism. Thus Balkenhol succeeds in generating an open, lively image of human beings that transcends social definition.

BODY AND SPEED

The speed of working is of great significance. While other artists today produce their work with the help of such techniques as photography or industrial modes of production, Balkenhol still resorts to the age-old use of body and hands. However, he undercuts any nostalgic implications through the extreme speed of production made possible by his extraordinary craftsmanship. The speed of production transforms and generalizes the sitters—but not beyond recognition. The result is an agitated surface which is detailed enough to render essentials such as hands, nose, or eyes but not so detailed as to lose itself in dogmatic, hyperrealistic items such as fingernails or shoelaces, which would leave little leeway for the other factors involved in the work. The figures thus remain suspended between individual characterization and generalization—not in the sense of idealizing abstraction, but in the sense of a processual openness conveyed by the rough, unfinished surfaces.

MAX KATZ is an art critic living in Cologne.

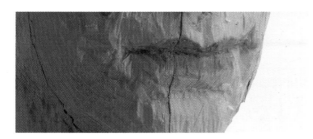

Detail von KLEINER KOPF / LITTLE HEAD, 1987.

Nothing is subsequently improved or corrected. Every move has to be right on the first try; the artist has to respond immediately to the chance structures of the wood. Balkenhol does not get bogged down in small-scale detail; instead, precise description rests on essentials as dictated by the speed of perception and production. The study of people and animals may be a prolonged undertaking, but—as on a racecourse—the speed imposed on the act of creation brooks no hesitation. Formal conception, body and senses thus become a unity. The speed of production puts all the factors involved in the work to the test.

MATERIAL AND SYMBOLISM

Wood as material is of significance in several respects. For a start, it is a repudiation of stone and bronze whose anorganic hardness and permanence are too closely associated with the ideals, eternal values and truths of traditional sculpture. Wood is a soft, organic substance that makes great demands on the sculptor although it can be quickly processed by the skilled craftsman. It is closer to the living human body than polished idealizations or intellectual abstractions. The tree shares many parallels with human beings: the measured time of its growth, its blossoming, the loss of its leaves, its roots in the soil, its branches that reach for the sky—and ultimately the romantic symbolism of the lonely tree. The warm colors of the wood evoke the color of skin, and the statuesque serenity of the tree is reflected in the self-contained, tranquil attitudes of the figures.

STEPHAN BALKENHOL, 1 von 10 Skulpturensäulen, 1992, Wawaholz gefasst, 145 cm / one of 10 sculpture columns, polychromed wawa wood, 57". (PHOTO: WIM COX)

The wood is painted as quickly as it is carved, in a fashion that heightens the realism of the figures and plays down the character of the wood. Moreover, by generally restricting himself to two or three colors, Balkenhol underscores the clarity and simplicity of his figures.

COOLNESS AND QUICKENING

Balkenhol's work combines the cold severity of anorganic forms with the representation of the body and a quickening of expression. The bodies and faces of his sculptures do not espouse an ideal of beauty. They are individual, ordinary faces, whose character is subtly generalized through visible gouges of carving, slight inaccuracies, and the manner in which they are painted. The grain of the wood and the rough surface in association with color, shape, and line form a new aesthetic plane, and yet the sculptures facing us seem to be real live people.

The quickening of the figures stems from the freedom with which the artist avoids smooth, conventional treatment. He is not slavishy bound to his models. Instead, they inspire almost free, spontaneous interaction between physical work, material, form, and color. Nothing is exact about the rendition of the sitters and yet they are unmistakable. Realistic representation is only one parameter. Essential is not photographic precision, but the dynamic, animated expression that springs from uninhibited treatment guided solely by sensual intuition. Balkenhol takes the liberty of indulging in a brilliant lack of precision that describes things without categorizing them. The result: likenesses that remain dynamic and works of art that remain open.

(Translation: Catherine Schelbert)

JEAN-CHRISTOPHE AMMANN

Stephan Balkenhol
57 PINGUINE

«Das Missliche bei den Pinguingeschichten ist, dass sie immer aus demselben Blickwinkel erzählt werden, nämlich dem menschlichen. Der unerschöpflichen Phantasie und Neugierde der Pinguine stülpen wir das, was zu uns gehört, auf und verändern so den Sinn. Deshalb glaubte man auch nicht, was der Seeräuber Francis Drake, der erste, der Pinguine gesehen hatte, als er am Ende des sechzehnten Jahrhunderts während eines Sturms zu weit nach Süden getrieben wurde, von ihnen berichtete. Er beschrieb sie seiner Königin, worauf diese heftig lachte, da sie glaubte, es handle sich um die Possen eines närrischen Piraten.»
DANIELE DEL GIUDICE

Die Zahl 57 ergibt sich aus dem Geburtsjahr des Künstlers: Er ist 1957 geboren. Im Frühjahr 1991 schlug er die Pinguine aus dem obersten Teil von 57 Vierkanthölzern heraus (farbig gefasst, je ca. 150 x 35 x 35 cm). In zehn Tagen und Nächten hatte er die Arbeit vollendet. Zum einen, weil das tropische Wawa-Holz relativ weich ist, zum anderen, weil sich durch das konzentrierte Arbeiten die eigene Bewegung gewissermassen auf jene der Tiere übertrug. Jede dieser Skulpturen ist ein Einzelwesen, drückt eine bestimmte Körperhaltung aus und ist dennoch Teil einer Gemeinschaft, die als Gesamtes das Besondere des einzelnen Tieres nachweislich hervorhebt. Das rasche Arbeiten entspricht einem plastischen «Skizzieren», als ginge es darum, die Pinguine in ihrer Bewegungsfreiheit nicht einzuschränken.

Ich verstehe diese Arbeit wie eine Steinkreisfläche von Richard Long, ausgeführt von einem Bildhauer, der, rund eine Künstlergeneration später geboren, dem Konzept des Ähnlichen und Verschiedenen, der Ordnung und der Unordnung ein figürliches, der Natur immanentes Gepräge verliehen hat.

Weshalb Pinguine? Ja, das ist so eine Frage, die Daniele Del Giudice bereits eingangs beantwortet hat. «Mit einer verzweifelten Geschwindigkeit ziehen sie nach Süden», beschreibt er eine kleine Gruppe von Adélie-Pinguinen. «Die Stummflügel erhoben, den Schnabel nach vorne gereckt, die Füsschen nach links und rechts gerichtet, mit dem Schwanz das Gleichgewicht ausbalancierend wie kleine dreibeinige Stative und mit ihrer aufmerksamen besorgten Miene wirken sie komisch. Es ist als wollten sie sagen: ‹I'm late, I'm late for a very important date›, wie im Buch von Alice im Wunderland.»

Natürlich sind Pinguine hochgradig konsensfähige Tiere. Sie sind possierlich, höflich, zivilisiert. All diese Eigenschaften mögen Stephan Balkenhol faszi-

---

JEAN-CHRISTOPHE AMMANN ist Leiter des Museums für Moderne Kunst, Frankfurt/Main.

niert, aber auch herausgefordert haben. Ich denke, es ist ihm auf eine wundersame Weise gelungen, diesen Konsens auf höchstem Niveau einzulösen.

Ich weiss, es gibt immer wieder skeptische Stimmen, die diesem von Balkenhol angestrebten Konsens misstrauen. Balkenhol kennt die Problematik des Konsenses sehr genau. Man darf nie vergessen, dass er nicht nur Student, sondern auch Assistent von Ulrich Rückriem gewesen ist. Der Vollblutbildhauer Balkenhol konfrontiert uns kontinuierlich mit dem, was den Holzschnitzer vom Bildhauer unterscheidet. Ich möchte fast sagen, er tut es bewusst, im Sinne einer Thematisierung. Er «zeigt» uns, dass ein Schnitzer die Regeln des Schnitzens befolgt, während ein Bildhauer diese Regeln stets von neuem bestimmt.

Zwei Momente zeichnen sein Schaffen besonders aus:

a) Seine unvoreingenommene Sicht: eine Art von Plötzlichkeit des Sehens und Wahrnehmens.

Ich möchte dies an einem Beispiel verdeutlichen. Im Museum für Moderne Kunst in Frankfurt/Main ist neben anderen Werken des Künstlers auch ein Strauss von Osterglocken zu sehen, die er aus einem Vierkantholz herausgeschlagen hat. Ein Vater erklärte dieses Vorgehen seinem 7jährigen Sohn, worauf der Bub den Vater fragte: «Weshalb wusste der Künstler, dass sich in dem Holz Osterglocken befanden?»

Ich glaube tatsächlich, dass dieser Bub die Sicht von Balkenhol nachvollzogen hat, als dieser 1991, zur Zeit der Osterglocken, im hessischen Kleinkahl-Edelbach den Wunsch des Holzes, sich in Form von Frühlingsblumen zu präsentieren, erspürte.

b) Sein Instinkt für räumliche Situationen. Zwei Beispiele: Als Balkenhol 1987 für die Ausstellung *Skulptur Projekte* in Münster, Westfalen, auf dem sieben Meter hohen Kaminvorsprung einer Brandmauer aus Ziegelsteinen einen «Mann mit grünem Hemd und weisser Hose» plazierte, wurde zu Beginn verschiedentlich die Polizei alarmiert, weil der Eindruck entstand, hier handle es sich um einen Selbstmörder. Später, während der Dauer der Ausstellung, wurde die lässig über das Platzgeschehen blickende Figur, die eine Hand locker auf die Hüfte gestützt, zu einem Identifikationsmoment.

Anlässlich der Ausstellung *Doubletake* 1992 in London hatte Balkenhol einen stehenden Mann auf eine kleinflächige Boje mitten in die Themse gesetzt. Nicht nur stürzte sich ein Mensch in die eiskalten Fluten, um – erneut – einen «Selbstmörder» zu retten, sondern die Polizei wurde auch von unzähligen Telefonaten genervt.

Ich habe bewusst diese anekdotischen Momente hervorgehoben, um deutlich zu machen, wie stark Balkenhol auf räumliche Situationen reagiert, stellen sich diese doch als seine eigentliche Herausforderung dar, ob im öffentlichen Aussen- oder Innenraum.

Als ich 1991 die 57 Pinguine erstmals sah, ausgestellt im Sommer bei Jörg Johnen in Köln, verspürte ich den dringenden Wunsch, dieses Werk für unser Museum zu erwerben. Da die Mittel fehlten, blieb mir nichts anderes übrig, als diesen Wunsch anderen zu erzählen. Er gelangte Horst Schmitter in Frankfurt zu Ohren, der die geniale

STEPHAN BALKENHOL, OSTERGLOCKEN, 1989, Zedernholz, Höhe 48 cm / DAFFODILS, 1989, cedar wood, 18⅞". (PHOTO: HELGE MUNDT)

Idee entwickelte, für jeden der 57 Pinguine eine Patenschaft ins Leben zu rufen. Gedacht, getan! Wir schrieben potentielle Patentanten und Patenonkel an, die *Frankfurter Allgemeine Zeitung* sponserte ein grossformatiges Inserat, und bereits nach drei Monaten hatten wir die Pinguine unter Dach und Fach. Wir hätten auch für 10 oder 15 weitere Pinguine Patenschaften finden können. Es waren bewegende Tage und Wochen: Zum einen gab es Menschen, auch Studenten, die bereit waren, kleinere Beträge für einen einzelnen Pinguin zu spenden; zum anderen war die Enttäuschung

gross, wenn wir sagen mussten, dass alle Pinguine bereits für das Museum erworben
worden seien. Es gab Momente, in denen ich innigst den Wunsch verspürte, ein Zau-
berer zu sein, der aus dem Zylinder, statt der weissen Tauben, Pinguine hätte zaubern
können. – Wenn immer die Pinguine von Stephan Balkenhol ausgestellt werden, zeigen wir sie in Verbindung mit der Donatorenliste. Diesen Hinweis möge man richtig
verstehen: Eine Patentante oder ein Patenonkel ist für «Kinder» ein biographischer
Anknüpfungspunkt. *STEPHAN BALKENHOL, 57 PINGUINE, 1991, Wawaholz gefasst / polychromed wawa wood.*

(MUSEUM FÜR MODERNE KUNST, FRANKFURT A. M.)

JEAN-CHRISTOPHE AMMANN

Stephan Balkenhol
57 PENGUINS

"Unhappily, penguin stories are always told from the same point of view, namely a human one. We superimpose what belongs to us on the inexhaustible imaginativeness and curiosity of penguins, thereby changing the message. That explains why no one believed what pirate Francis Drake, the first person ever to sight a penguin, had to say about them at the end of the sixteenth century, when he was driven too far south by a storm. He described them to his queen, who broke into peals of laughter, under the impression that he was spinning a pirate's yarn."

DANIELE DEL GIUDICE

The figure 57 stems from 1957, the year Stephan Balkenhol was born. The artist carved the penguins out of the top of 57 squared timbers in the spring of 1991 (each in color and measuring ca. 150 x 35 x 35 cm / 58½ x 13⅜ x 13⅜"). It took him only ten days and nights to complete the task, because, for one thing, tropical Wawa wood is relatively soft, and for another, the concentrated effort gradually transmitted his own movements to those of the animals. Each of these sculptures is an individual being with its own specific physical attitude. Together they form a community, a whole that reputably underscores the particularity of each individual animal. The speed of production in creating these penguins might be viewed as an act of sculptural "sketching," as if to avoid restricting the penguin's freedom of movement.

To me the piece is like one of Richard Long's stone circles, executed by a sculptor born approximately one artist's generation later, who has lent the concepts of sameness and difference, of order and disorder a figurative shape immanent in nature.

Why penguins? Daniele Del Giudice, quoted above, has already answered that question. "With desperate speed they move south," he says of a group of Adélie penguins. "They look very comical with their wings stretched, their beaks thrust forward, their little webbed feet pointing left and right, their tails used for balance like the third leg of a tripod, and with attentive, worried expressions, as if to say—like the rabbit in *Alice in Wonderland*—'I'm late, I'm late for a very important date.'"

Naturally penguins are masters of consensus. They are droll, polite, civilized. These traits probably fascinated but also challenged Stephan Balkenhol. I would

---

JEAN-CHRISTOPHE AMMANN is the director of the Museum of Modern Art in Frankfurt/Main.

STEPHAN BALKENHOL, MANN AUF BOJE, 1992,
Installation auf der Themse / MAN ON A BUOY, 1992,
installation on River Thames, exhibition Doubletake.

STEPHAN BALKENHOL, GROSSES KOPFRELIEF, 1993,
Pappelholz gefasst, Installation im Giebel der Deichtorhallen,
Hamburg / BIG HEAD RELIEF, 1993, polychromed poplar wood,
installation in the gable, Deichtorhallen, Hamburg,
exhibition Post Human. (PHOTO: WOLFGANG NEEB)

venture to say that he has succeeded in rendering this consensus with an excellence that borders on the miraculous.

I know there are skeptical voices, suspicious of the consensus Balkenhol seeks to convey. The artist is perfectly aware of its pitfalls. He was, after all, not only Ulrich Rückriem's student but also his assistant. As a full-blooded sculptor, Balkenhol consistently confronts us with the distinction between the wood-carver and the sculptor. I am inclined to believe he does so with intent, perhaps even as a statement. He "shows" us that a carver obeys the rules of carving, while a sculptor redefines the rules as he goes along.

Two features of his oeuvre deserve special attention:

a) His unprejudiced eye: a kind of suddenness of seeing and perceiving.
Let me illustrate. The Balkenhol works on view at the Museum of Modern Art in Frankfurt include a bouquet of daffodils carved out of a squared beam. A father was explaining the procedure to his seven-year-old son, who then inquired, "How did the artist know that there were daffodils in the wood?"

I actually believe this child felt the same impulse that moved Balkenhol in 1991, when the daffodils were in bloom in Kleinkahl-Edelbach, to respond to the desire of the wood to appear in the form of spring flowers.

b) His instinct for effective spatial situations. Two examples: In 1987 for the exhibition *Skulptur Projekte Münster,* Balkenhol placed MAN IN GREEN SHIRT AND WHITE TROUSERS on the projecting ledge of a brick fire wall seven meters (23 feet) high. At first the police were alerted several times by people mistaking the figure for someone trying to commit suicide. During the course of the show, however, the figure became an identifying landmark, coolly surveying the square below, one hand casually resting on his hip.

At the *Doubletake* exhibition in London in 1992, Balkenhol set the figure of a standing man on a buoy in the middle of the Thames. Not only were the police hounded by telephone calls, but people actually jumped into the freezing water to rescue the man from "killing himself."

I have intentionally focused on these anecdotes to demonstrate the intensity of Balkenhol's reaction to the spatial situations that he finds so challenging both indoors and out.

When I first saw 57 PENGUINS in the summer of 1991 at Jörg Johnen's gallery in Cologne, I knew immediately that I wanted to acquire them for our museum. Since I did not have the means, I had to make the best of it by telling others about my wish. When Horst Schmitter in Frankfurt heard about it, he came up with the ingenious idea of finding a godparent for each of the 57 penguins. No sooner said than done! We wrote to potential godfathers and godmothers, the newspaper *Frankfurter Allgemeine* sponsored a large-format ad, and within three months we had backing for all 57 penguins. We could in fact have found sponsors for an additional ten to fifteen animals. It was a very exciting time. For one thing, many people, even students, were prepared to make a smaller contribution for one penguin; however, the disappointment was great when we had to explain that all of the penguins had already been acquired for the museum. At times I would dearly have loved to be a magician in order to pull penguins instead of rabbits out of a hat! When the penguins are put on view, we show them along with the list of donors. This must be understood correctly: A godmother or a godfather is a biographical link for "children."

(Translation: Catherine Schelbert)

EDITION FOR PARKETT **STEPHAN BALKENHOL**

ZWEI ECHSEN MIT MANN, 1993
DREITEILIGE FIGURENGRUPPE,
GEGOSSEN IN BLEILEGIERUNG DURCH
GIESSEREI BÄRTSCHI, AEFLIGEN, SCHWEIZ.
JE CA. 30 x 13 x 4 CM, GEWICHT JE CA. 2 KG.
AUFLAGE: 85, SIGNIERT UND NUMERIERT.

TWO LIZARDS AND A MAN, 1993
GROUP OF THREE CAST LEAD FIGURINES,
PRODUCED AT THE BÄRTSCHI FOUNDRY,
AEFLIGEN, SWITZERLAND.
EACH FIGURE APPROX. $11^{7}/_{8}$ x $5^{1}/_{8}$ x $1^{1}/_{2}$",
WEIGHING APPROX. 4.5 LBS.
EDITION: 85, SIGNED AND NUMBERED.

Ich sah ihn zum ersten
Mal im Dezember 1985
bei einem Vortrag,
den er hielt. Ich fand ihn
attraktiv, doch etwas
störte mich: er trug eine
hässliche Krawatte.
Am nächsten Tag schick-
te ich ihm anonym
eine schmale braune
Krawatte. Später sah ich
ihn in einem Restaurant;

er trug sie. Dummer-
weise passte sie über-
haupt nicht zu seinem
Hemd. So entschied ich
mich, ihn von Kopf bis
Fuss neu einzukleiden:
Jährlich schickte ich
ihm zu Weihnachten
ein Kleidungsstück.
1986 erhielt er ein Paar
graue Seidensocken;
1987 einen schwarzen

Alpaka-Pullover;
1988 ein weisses Hemd;
1989 ein Paar vergoldete
Manschettenknöpfe;
1990 Boxer-Shorts mit
einem Weihnachtsbaum-
Muster; 1991, nichts; und
1992 eine graue Hose.
Irgendwann, wenn er
ganz von mir eingekleidet
sein wird, möchte ich
ihm vorgestellt werden.

EDITION FOR PARKETT **SOPHIE CALLE**

THE TIE, 1993
KRAWATTE MIT AUFGEDRUCKTER KURZGESCHICHTE «I SAW HIM»
SEIDE, CRÊPE DE CHINE, BRAUN MIT BLAUEM TEXT.
HERGESTELLT DURCH FABRIC FRONTLINE, ZÜRICH.
AUFLAGE: 150, SIGNIERT UND NUMERIERT.

THE TIE, 1993
PURE SILK CRÊPE-DE-CHINE MAN'S TIE.
PRINTED WITH AN AUTOBIOGRAPHICAL STORY.
PRODUCED BY FABRIC FRONTLINE, ZURICH.
EDITION: 150, SIGNED AND NUMBERED.

PHOTO: MANCIA/BODMER

LUC SANTE

SOPHIE CALLE'S UNCERTAINTY PRINCIPLE

Like a sculptor of a past century, Sophie Calle in her art manipulates and reconfigures a commodity central to the economy of her time. This commodity does not happen to be bronze or marble, however, but information, the elusive stuff that circulates incessantly between consciousness, document, and cyberspace. It is a maddeningly imprecise and unquantifiable commodity, hovering somewhere on the border between objective and subjective, public and private, hot and cold. It is farmed in huge quantities, fought over, stolen, adulterated, and negotiated by credit bureaus, intelligence agencies, polling organizations, market-research firms, and yet its value resides in minute specifics and fugitive shades of meaning. Its pursuit thus resembles experimental science—vast quantities of printouts are generated for every nit that can be seized upon and exploited—as well as art: It is at every point along its process so immaterial, so woozily figurative or abstract, that its commodity status seems like a bit of legerdemain, and its manufacture and trade a kind of parody.

Calle is not the first artist to work this medium, of course. The Surrealists probably were the pioneers, notably in their fascination with opinion polls. The aphorist and suicide Jacques Rigaut put his own spin on the matter: He carried on his person a tiny pair of scissors with which he used to remove surreptitiously a button from the garment of every person he met; this he insisted was a form of art collecting. The novelist Philippe Soupault once staged a version of a highway robbery: He stopped a bus on the Avenue de l'Opéra late at night by extending a chain across its path; then entered it and ordered all the passengers to tell him their birth dates (the combination of violence and trivia present in this act does not seem very far from Calle's concerns). Trivia devoid of violence, data accumulated for their own sake, the relentless documentation of

On Monday, February 16, 1981, after a year of trying and waiting, I was finally hired as a temporary chambermaid for three weeks, in a Venetian hotel: Hotel C.
I was assigned twelve bedrooms on the fourth floor.
In the course of my cleaning duties, I examined the personal belongings of the hotel guests and the way this succession of people staying in the same room set up their temporary homes. I observed through details lives which remained unknown to me.
On Friday, March 6, the job came to an end.

■

Am Montag, den 16. Februar 1981, nach einem Jahr von Versuchen und Warten, wurde ich schliesslich als Aushilfszimmermädchen für drei Wochen in einem venezianischen Hotel eingestellt: Hotel C.
Mir wurden zwölf Zimmer im vierten Stock zugeteilt.
Im Verlaufe meiner Reinemachtätigkeiten untersuchte ich die persönlichen Effekten der Hotelgäste und die Art, wie eine Reihe von Leuten, die jeweils im gleichen Zimmer übernachteten, sich vorübergehend heimisch einrichteten. Anhand der Details beobachtete ich ihr Leben, das mir unbekannt blieb.
Am Freitag, den 6. März war diese Arbeit beendet.

LUC SANTE is a writer who lives in New York City. He is the author of *Low Life* (Vintage, 1991) and *Evidence* (Farrar Straus Giroux, 1992).

Wednesday, March 4, 1981. 11:20 a.m. I go into room 30. Only one bed has been slept in, the one on the right. There is a small bag on the luggage stand. A beautifully ironed silk nightgown lies on the chair that has been pulled up near the bed: it clearly has never been worn. Everything else is still in the traveling bag. All I see there is men's clothing: grey trousers, a grey striped shirt, a pair of socks, a toilet kit (razor, shaving cream, comb, aftershave lotion), a dog-eared photograph of a group of young people surrounding an older woman, a passport in the name of M. L., male sex, Italian nationality, born in 1946 in Rome, his place of residence, five foot seven, blue eyes. The bathroom is empty, so is the closet, but in the drawer of the night table I find a box of Panter cigars, a fountain pen, airmail stationery, a leather box with the initials M. L. On a piece of paper is the address of a Mr. and Mrs. B. in Florence, a wallet with five identical photographs of a blond woman and a wedding photograph showing the man in a tuxedo and the blond woman in a wedding gown. There is also an old bill from the Hotel C., dated March 4, 1979, in the name of Mr. and Mrs. L. for the same room, number 30. Exactly two years ago, M. L. spent the night in the Hotel C. with his wife. He has come back alone. With the embroidered nightgown in his suitcase. His reservation was for last night only. He is leaving today. I'll do his room later.

■

Mittwoch, 4. März 1981. 11.20 Uhr. Ich gehe ins Zimmer 30. Nur in einem Bett war geschlafen worden, dem auf der rechten Seite. Eine kleine Tasche steht auf dem Gepäckständer. Auf dem Stuhl, der zum Bett geschoben ist, liegt ein wunderschön gebügeltes seidenes Nachthemd. Es ist klar, dass es noch nie getragen worden ist. Sonst ist alles noch in der Reisetasche. Ich sehe nur Männerkleidung: graue Hosen, ein graues, gestreiftes Oberhemd, ein Paar Socken, ein Toilettenbeutel (Rasierer, Rasiercrème, Kamm, Aftershave), eine Photographie mit Eselsohren, die eine Gruppe junger Leute um eine ältere Frau geschart zeigt, ein Reisepass auf den Namen M. L., männlichen Geschlechts, italienischer Nationalität, 1946 in Rom geboren, sein Wohnort, 1,70 m gross, blaue Augen. Das Badezimmer ist leer, wie der Schrank auch, aber in der Nachttischschublade finde ich eine Schachtel Panter-Zigarren, einen Füllfederhalter, Luftpostpapier, ein Lederetui mit den Initialen M. L. Auf einem Stück Papier steht die Adresse von Herrn und Frau B. in Florenz. Weiterhin: eine Brieftasche mit fünf identischen Photographien einer blonden Frau und ein Hochzeitsbild, das den Mann aus dem Pass im Smoking und die blonde Frau im Hochzeitskleid zeigt. Da ist auch eine alte Rechnung des Hotels C, auf den 4. März 1979 datiert, ausgestellt auf die Namen von Herrn und Frau L. für das gleiche Zimmer, Nummer 30. Er ist allein zurückgekommen. Mit dem bestickten Nachthemd im Koffer. Seine Reservierung war nur für letzte Nacht. Er reist heute ab. Ich mache das Zimmer später.

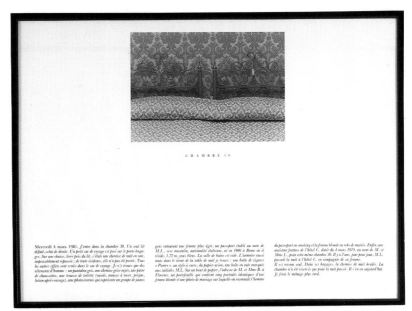

CHAMBRE 30

Mercredi 4 mars 1981. J'entre dans la chambre 30. Un seul lit défait, celui de droite. Un petit sac de voyage est posé sur le porte-bagages. Sur une chaise, tirée près du lit, s'étale une chemise de nuit en soie, impeccablement repassée ; de toute évidence, elle n'a pas été portée. Tous les autres effets sont restés dans le sac de voyage. Je n'y trouve que des vêtements d'homme : un pantalon gris, une chemise grise rayée, une paire de chaussettes, une trousse de toilette (rasoir, mousse à raser, peigne, lotion après-rasage), une photo écornée qui représente un groupe de jeunes gens entourant une femme plus âgée, un passeport établi au nom de M.L., sexe masculin, nationalité italienne, né en 1946 à Rome où il réside, 1,72 m, yeux bleus. La salle de bain est vide. L'armoire aussi mais dans le tiroir de la table de nuit je trouve : une boîte de cigares « Panter », un stylo à encre, du papier avion, une boîte en cuir marquée aux initiales M.L. Sur un bout de papier, l'adresse de M. et Mme B. à Florence, un portefeuille qui contient cinq portraits identiques d'une femme blonde et une photo de mariage sur laquelle on reconnaît l'homme du passeport en smoking et la femme blonde en robe de mariée. Enfin, une ancienne facture de l'hôtel C. datée du 4 mars 1979, au nom de M. et Mme L...pour cette même chambre 30. Il y a 2 ans, jour pour jour, M.L. passait la nuit à l'hôtel C. en compagnie de sa femme. Il est revenu seul. Dans ses bagages, la chemise de nuit brodée. La chambre n'a été réservée que pour la nuit passée. Il s'en va aujourd'hui. Je ferai le ménage plus tard.

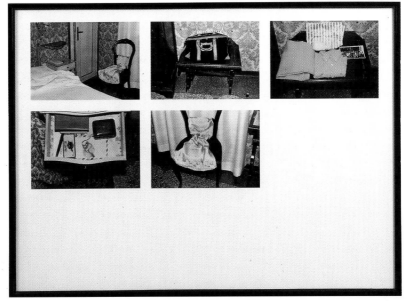

SOPHIE CALLE, ROOM 30, from
L'HÔTEL / THE HOTEL, 1981, diptychs
with color photos and texts, 40⅛ x 56" each /
ZIMMER 30 aus DAS HOTEL, 1981,
Diptychen mit Farbphotos und Texten,
je 102 x 142 cm.

the most apparently boring processes—these are traits associated with various phases of conceptual art, which pursued the sublime through several disciplines, one of them being busywork. The Surrealist and conceptual approaches to the management of information as a medium in itself could be said to represent in their very different ways the mingled fascination and horror inspired by the looming triumph of bureaucracy. The Surrealists responded with bemusement and savagery, the conceptualists with Zen, which is not identical to complacency.

The work of Sophie Calle appears at various times to display all of these qualities, at others only some. Her first work, THE SLEEPERS, resembles straightforward conceptual bookkeeping but with an added layer of sexual risk, at least by implication. Risk, as well as stealth, deception, and intrusion, dominates her most notorious works, SUITE VÉNITIENNE (Venetian Suite), THE SHADOW, THE HOTEL, and L'HOMME AU CARNET (The Man of the Address Book). The commanding metaphor here is espionage, with more than a suggestion of sadomasochism. ANA-

SOPHIE CALLE, LES DORMEURS
(THE SLEEPERS / DIE SCHLAFENDEN),
1979, b/w photos and texts, 199 pieces,
62 x 162" / s/w-Photos und Texte, 199teilig,
152 x 402 cm. (INSTALLATION LUHRING
AUGUSTINE GALLERY, NEW YORK)

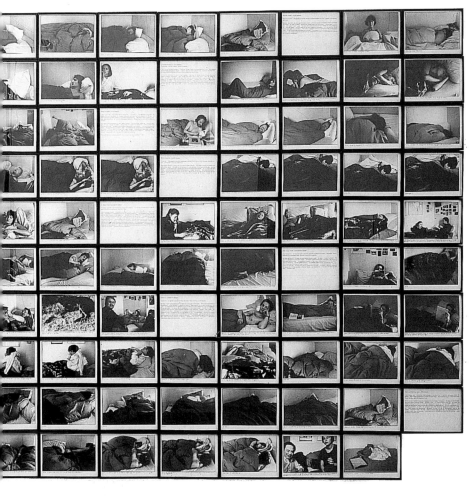

people to give me a few hours of their
o come sleep in my bed. To let them‐
e looked at and photographed. To an‐
estions. To each participant I suggested
hour stay, that of a normal sleep.

cted 45 persons by phone: people I
now and whose names were suggested
common acquaintances, a few friends,
dents of the neighborhood whose work
n them to sleep during the day: the
r instance. I intended my bedroom to
a constantly occupied space for eight
th sleepers succeeding one another at
intervals.

le finally accepted. Among these five
owed: an agency baby sitter and I took
aces. 16 people refused either because
d other commitments or the thing
gree with them. Some slept with part‐
st slept alone.

upation of the bed began on Sunday,
t, at 5 p.m. and ended on Monday, April
10 a.m. 28 sleepers succeeded one an‐
A few of them crossed each other.
st, lunch, or dinner were served to each
ng on the time of day. Clean bedsheets
ced at the disposition of each sleeper.

juestions to those who allowed me;
to do with knowledge or fact-gather‐
t rather to establish a neutral and
ontact.

hotographs every hour. I watched my
eep.

Leute, mir einige Stunden ihres Schla‐
eben. Zu mir zu kommen, um in mei‐
t zu schlafen. Zu gestatten, betrachtet
otographiert zu werden. Fragen zu
rten. Jedem Teilnehmer schlug ich
chtstündigen Aufenthalt vor, den eines
n Schlafes.

m mit 45 Personen telefonisch Kontakt
ate, die ich nicht kannte und deren
von gemeinsamen Bekannten vorge‐
schlagen worden waren, einige Freunde und
Leute aus der Umgebung, deren Arbeit von
ihnen verlangte, dass sie tagsüber schliefen,
der Bäcker zum Beispiel. Ich hatte vor, aus mei‐
nem Schlafzimmer acht Tage lang einen ständig
besetzten Raum zu machen, mit Schlafenden,
die sich zu regelmässigen Abständen ablösten.
Schliesslich sagten 29 Personen zu. Unter
ihnen waren fünf, die nie kamen, ein Baby‐
sitter von einer Agentur und ich sprangen für
sie ein. Sechzehn Personen weigerten sich, ent‐
weder weil sie andere Pläne hatten oder weil
die Sache ihnen nicht zusagte. Einige schliefen
mit Partnern, die meisten alleine.
Die Besetzung des Betts begann am Sonntag,
1. April, um 17 Uhr und endete am Montag,
9. April, um 10 Uhr. 28 Schlafende folgten auf‐
einander. Einige begegneten sich. Je nach
Tageszeit wurde ihnen Frühstück, Mittagessen
oder Abendessen serviert. Saubere Bettwäsche
stand jedem Schläfer zur Verfügung.
Ich befragte diejenigen, die es zuliessen; die
Fragen hatten nichts mit Wissen oder Recher‐
chen zu tun, sondern stellten einen neutralen
und distanzierten Kontakt her.
Ich photographierte stündlich. Ich beobach‐
tete meine Gäste im Schlaf.

TOLI is a portrait, sharing with her earlier works the fact of having been assembled not in spite of but through adverse conditions, in this case the lack of a common language. In its plainness it throws into relief this common thread, which we might name "the blind men and the elephant." Not surprisingly, her next piece is THE BLIND. This work, which connects as well to the earlier and more prosaic THE BRONX, employs hearsay in pursuit of the ineffable, in effect constructing a work of art that is only alluded to and not represented by the objects on the gallery wall, a pursuit taken up in GHOSTS, BLIND COLOR, and LAST SEEN.

There seems to be a rough split in Calle's career to date: Her earlier works are, broadly speaking, concerned with narrative, and the later ones with image. In both, the principal tool is language, with the visual component filling an illustrative role. In this way, her work suggests the forensic process during a police investigation: She assembles clues, descriptions, guesses, allusions, and pieces them together into an approximate rendering. In the earlier works, this rendering takes the form of a dossier; in the later ones it resembles an identikit sketch. CASH MACHINE might be a sort of pun on this idea, with its disembodied, almost ectoplastic surveillance-camera portraits. AUTOBIOGRAPHICAL STORIES and THE TOMBS extend the principle of the visual substitute or approximation in another direction, toward the iconic. The objects that stand in for epochal incidents in the artist's life and the laconic gravestones that reduce entire existences to a mere familial title possess a weight of their own; the referent is almost beside the point. If one were to hear or read a description of Calle's work and try to reconstruct it on that basis without actually seeing it, it is possible that one might imagine its theme to be the poverty of language or of image, the insufficiency of secondhand experience. Instead, her work continually stresses the beauty of imprecision, the poetry of gaps and lapses.

She is, in other words, a kind of impressionist. Uncertainty dapples her pictures the way the sun's rays spatter the leaves and splash the grassy swards in the Bois de Whatever. But that's not all there is to it. Uncertainty is an inevitability when it comes to information; information is uncertain in the same way that humans are mortal. But information nevertheless strives for certainty, or rather its purveyors do, whether quixotically or disingenuously. The police tipster, the industrial spy, the political clairvoyant, the highly placed source—all are in the business of pretending infallibility. And their commerce, once a small-time traffic, is in the process of becoming ever more institutionalized, increasingly central to the global economy as it moves from nocturnal alleys to glass-walled offices. Tremendous financial decisions are made on the basis of lore—consumer profiles, focus-group questionnaires, extrapolations of trend curves—that are about as reliable as the divination of bird entrails. This metaphor is not idly chosen: the commerce of information is descended in part from that of the augurers who advised military leaders in antiquity. It has merely been dressed up with technology and soft science for the benefit of contemporary rationalists.

Calle's work is to a certain degree a parody of this trade, and so could be said to be a parody of a parody, a simulacrum of a sham. But to the extent that her portraits—the address-book man, Anatoli, the occupants of the hotel rooms, herself even—are distortions, they are no more so than a Cubist head, say, would be as compared with a photographic likeness. Even when the deck appears stacked—the address-book scheme, viewed from one angle as a tin-pot *Citizen Kane*, might prompt questions about her motives—enough air is admitted in the form of indeterminacy to prevent any agent including Calle from having full control of the drift. Uncertainty, in short, is the footprint of truth. It is the only aspect of any piece of information that can always be relied upon, and, of course, it is the aspect that diminishes information's value as a commodity. It is nearly always inconvenient; it is unproductive and inefficient; it is often dangerous. And that is why it is so beautiful, as Calle repeatedly demonstrates in her work.

I had three cats. Félix died after having been accidentally locked in the fridge. Zoe was taken from me when my younger brother was born; I hated him from that moment on. Nina was strangled by a jealous man who had, some time before, given me the following ultimatum: to sleep, either with the cat or with him. I opted for the cat.

■

Ich hatte drei Katzen. Félix starb, nachdem er versehentlich im Kühlschrank eingeschlossen worden war. Zoe wurde mir weggenommen, als mein jüngerer Bruder zur Welt kam; von diesem Augenblick an habe ich ihn gehasst. Nina wurde von einem eifersüchtigen Mann erwürgt, der mir kurz vorher folgendes Ultimatum gestellt hatte: entweder mit der Katze oder mit ihm zu schlafen. Ich entschied mich für die Katze.

SOPHIE CALLE, FÉLIX,
from AUTOBIOGRAPHICAL STORIES,
1988, 6 b/w photos and texts 67 x 39½"
and 19¾ x 19¾" (text) /
AUTOBIOGRAPHISCHE GESCHICHTEN,
6 s/w-Photos und Text, 170 x 100 cm (Photo)
und 50 x 50 cm (Text).

Nächste Seite/following page
SOPHIE CALLE, THE SHADOW /
DER DETEKTIV, 1981, photos and text,
75 x 115" / 190 x 292 cm. (INSTALLATION
PAT HEARN GALLERY, NEW YORK)

At my request my mother went to the "Duluc" detective agency. She hired them to follow me, to report my daily activities, and to provide photographic evidence of my existence.

■

Auf meinen Wunsch ging meine Mutter zum Detektivbüro Duluc. Sie erteilte ihm den Auftrag, mir zu folgen, von meinen täglichen Tätigkeiten zu berichten und photographische Indizien meiner Existenz vorzulegen.

Thursday 16th of April, 10am. I am getting ready to go out. Outside, in the street, a man is waiting for me. He is a private detective. He is paid to follow me. I hired him to follow me, but he does not know that.

At 10:20am I go out. In the mailbox, a postcard from Mont Saint Michel. I read: "Sophie, I think of you often. Vacation...beautiful weather...vacation. Hugs and kisses. See you soon. Patrick". The weather is clear, sunny. It's cold. I am wearing grey suede sneakers, black tights, black shoes and a grey raincoat. Over my shoulder a bright yellow bag, a camera. I take rue Gassendi and buy marigolds for eight francs at the flower shop. I enter Montparnasse cemetery and lay the flowers on Pierre V's grave, b.1910 d.1981. I continue through the cemetery. Every day, for years, when I was going to school, I took that same route. It pleased me to imagine that there was a man hidden in R's family vault, and that he survived only because of my love and the food I scrupulously left on his gravestone. At the cemetery exit, on Boulevard Edgar Quinet, I buy "Le Monde" and "Pariscope".

At 10:40am, I get to "La Coupole", 102 Blvd. Montparnasse where I have an appointment with Nathalie M. I do not sit at our usual table, but closer to the window, and order a "café crème". At 10:45am, Nathalie M. joins me. I've known her for years. She always seems so fragile. She is beautiful, so I don't want to speak of "him", of the man who should be following me. I don't know if he is really here.

At 11:30am we leave "La Coupole". Nathalie walks with me to a hairdresser on rue Delambre. It is for "him" I am getting my hair done. To please him.

At 12:05pm I leave the hairdresser. My hair is electric; the young woman who hands me my raincoat is reassuring: "Outside, it will calm down". Then I walk towards Luxembourg Gardens. I want to show "him" the streets, the places I love. I want "him" to be with me as I go through the Luxembourg where I played as a child and where I received my first kiss in the spring of 1968. I keep my eyes lowered, am afraid to see "him".

12:30pm. I am waiting for Eugene B., publisher, beneath the statue of Danton at Odeon Square. We're supposed to talk about a book I would like to get published; five minutes go by. My eyes meet, on the other side of the boulevard St. Germain, those of a man about 22, 5'6", short straight light brown hair, who jumps suddenly and attempts a hasty and awkward retreat behind a car. It's "him". A stranger steps up to me and asks where I bought my raincoat. Eugene B. comes at 12:40pm. He kisses me and takes me to an outdoor café nearby. At 1:05pm we say goodbye, I head for the Pantheon. From a phone booth, I call Bernard F. whom I would very much like "him" to see. When I was 9, I was certain Bernard F. was my father. Going through my mother's letters, I found and stole a letter he wrote which began: "My darling, I hope you are seriously thinking of sending our Sophie to boarding school...". When he came to visit my mother, I would sit on his lap and stare expectantly at him. Then Bernard F's visits became less frequent. I stopped sitting on his lap, everyone told me how much I looked like my father. By the age of 12, I had forgotten this mistaken lineage. My call wakes him up. He tells me that he is not ready to cope with the street.

1:20pm. I get to my studio, located at 36 rue d'Ulm in the former

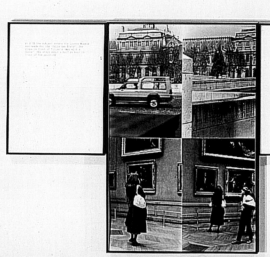

...of the convent of "Adoration Reparatrice". A short stop to ...me papers. At 1:30pm, I come out again. I decide to stroll ...ris. I take rue Soufflot, Blvd. St. Michel and St. Germain. ...I've lost "him". Since our "meeting" at Odeon, not once did ...resence. I walk in the middle of the streets.

...ing in front of 34 rue de Seine, Eric Fabre's Gallery, I try to ...the glass door, it does not budge. Further down the same ...front of #6, I wait for "Roger Viollet, Photographic ...to open. I walk in at 2pm and ask for the file on private ...I flip through the photographs: All the faces look older ...(I am reassured by his youth). I buy a portrait of Detective ...I raise my eyes, I notice through the window, sitting on a ...ss the street, the same young man I spotted at Odeon ...w I trust him. I'm not afraid of losing him anymore. I've ...part of the life of X., private detective. I structured his day, ...the 16th of April, in much the same way that he has ...mine.

...0pm, I move on. I cross the Pont Royal and head for the ...2:20pm, after walking quickly through the museum, I find ...ront of Titian's "Man with a Glove". I have always liked this ...The sad vacant eyes. The pouting mouth. The face as if ...resting on a lace collar. But above all, this hint of a

...0pm I leave the Louvre. In the garden of the Tuileries a ...her offers to take my picture with my camera. I accept. At ...stop at the Tuileries' outdoor cafe and order a beer. I take ...n watching "him" have his drink at the counter.

At 4pm, I leave the Tuileries, cross the Place de la Concorde. At 4:30pm, I enter the "Palais de la Decouverte" (Discovery Exhibition center) which seemed a propos. I have an appointment with Jacques M. I see his silhouette on the second floor. We meander from room to room. In a doorway "he" brushes past us. At 5:15pm we leave the "Palais de la Decouverte". I walk with Jacques M. to his car. I give him a kiss and continue my walk alone. I decide to rest in a movie theater. I walk up the Champs Elysees and after hesitating between Fassbinder's "Lili Marleen" and Lautner's "Is it Reasonable", a detective comedy, I opt for the first and enter the "Gaumont Colisee" at 5:25pm. Inside, I only think of "him". Is he enjoying this scattered, diffuse and ephemeral day I have offered him—our day. Half an hour later, at 6pm, I leave the theater. I walk towards Châtelet.

At 7pm, I arrive at Chantal Crousel's Gallery, 80 rue Quincampoix for the "Gilbert & George" opening. There, I meet my father and take him outside with me. I want "him" to see my father. Back at the Gallery I chat, forgetting "him" a little. At 8pm, friends take me by car to a party for George and Gilbert in an apartment at 120 Ave. de Wagram. At midnight I leave in the same car to "Le Palace" where we have been invited, still in honor of George and Gilbert. I get to know Dan J. better, whom I met a few months earlier.

At 2am a taxi takes us both to the "O.K. Bar" at Vavin. I eat spaghetti and drink whiskey.

At 5am we grab another taxi to go to his hotel, the "Hotel Tiquetonne". I am drunk and fall asleep. Before closing my eyes, I think of "him". I wonder if he liked me. Will he think of me tomorrow.

It was a young man, probably early thirties, facing the viewer, holding a glass of, I think, champagne, probably just writing out something, wearing a dark top hat and a dark jacket. On the left-hand upper corner, there was a view of the outside of the restaurant but little could be seen ♦ I don't remember it at all. Except, I remember there was a guy with a top hat and maybe a moustache ♦ He was a local writer that lunched in the café Tortoni everyday and always left his hat on. Manet used to eat there frequently and one day, he said: "Do you mind if I paint you?" ♦ It's kind of small and it's like a man, all dressed-up with a top hat, holding a pencil and drinking absinthe. I don't remember the background much because I used to just look at his eyes ♦ It was vibrant and the gentleman sitting there in the café looked at you with eyes of enjoyment and pleasure ♦ He had an inquisitive, questioning look in his eyes. This was not a man who was carrying major responsibility or authority. He was enjoying life but he was not just a pleasure seeker. There was also a mind at work there ♦ It seemed like he was looking far away. Looking out but not at you, as if in a dream more appealing and accessible. The mother, I hated her, she looked so domineering ♦ This dapper gentleman was so small in relation to Madame. I was more drawn to the solidity of the woman. I remember commenting to people about Madame Manet and then saying: "Oh! By the way, don't forget to

glance at this gentleman." ♦ Except for his very white skin, the colors were mostly rustic: dark browns, dark blues and a lot of black ♦ I remember a predominant russet tone apart from the pale rose colored face and hands ♦ It's a very moving work. It reminds me of something from a hundred years later, a poster called Café, on the walls of my dormitory at college by an artist who used the same kind of style ♦ It was signed Manet, at the foot, on the left.

■

Es war ein junger Mann, wahrscheinlich Anfang Dreissig, mit dem Gesicht dem Betrachter zugewandt, er hielt ein Glas Champagner, glaube ich, wahrscheinlich schrieb er nur etwas, er trug einen schwarzen Zylinder und eine dunkle Jacke. In der linken oberen Ecke war ein Ausblick nach draussen, vor das Restaurant, aber man konnte nicht viel sehen ♦ Ich erinnere mich überhaupt nicht daran. Ausser, dass ich mich an einen Mann mit einem Zylinder erinnere und vielleicht mit einem Schnauzbart ♦ Er war ein Schriftsteller, der jeden Tag im Café Tortoni zu Mittag ass und der immer seinen Hut aufbehielt. Manet ass häufig dort, und eines Tages fragte er ihn: «Würde es Ihnen etwas ausmachen, wenn ich Sie male?» ♦ Es ist irgendwie klein und da ist irgendwie ein Mann, fein angezogen mit einem Zylinder, er hält einen Bleistift und trinkt Absinth. An den Hintergrund kann ich mich nicht recht erinnern, da ich eigentlich nur auf

die Augen schaute ♦ Es war lebhaft und der Herr im Café betrachtete einem mit Augen voller Spass und Vergnügen ♦ Er hatte einen fragenden, forschenden Blick in den Augen. Er war kein Mann, der grössere Verantwortung trug oder Autorität hatte. Er genoss sein Leben, aber er war kein Bonvivant. Er hatte auch Verstand ♦ Er schien weit weg zu blicken. Hinauszublicken aber nicht auf dich, wie in einem Traum ♦ Es hing gerade unter dem mächtigen Portrait von Manets Mutter, aber es war viel ansprechender und zugänglicher. Die Mutter, ich habe sie gehasst, sie sah so dominant aus ♦ Dieser adrette Herr war so klein im Vergleich zu Madame. Ich war eher von der kompakten Masse der Frau angezogen. Ich erinnere mich, wie ich mit Leuten über Madame Manet sprach und dann sagte: «Ach, übrigens, versäumen Sie nicht, einen Blick auf diesen Herrn zu werfen.» ♦ Mit Ausnahme seiner sehr weissen Haut waren die Farben vorwiegend ländlich: dunkle Braun- und Blautöne und viel Schwarz ♦ Ich erinnere mich an ein vorherrschendes Rostbraun, ausser dem sehr zarten Rosé auf Gesicht und Händen ♦ Es ist ein sehr bewegendes Werk. Dabei fällt mir etwas von hundert Jahren später ein, ein Poster mit der Bezeichnung Café, an der Wand in meinem Zimmer im Studentenwohnheim, von einem Künstler, der die gleiche Art von Stil verwendete ♦ Es war «Manet» signiert, am Fuss, auf der linken Seite.

LUC SANTE

SOPHIE CALLE: UNSCHÄRFE-RELATION

Gegenüberliegende Seite/opposite page
SOPHIE CALLE, CHEZ TORTONI BY
MANET, detail from LAST SEEN, 1991,
color photo, 66½ x 50¾" (photo),
16¼ x 19½" (text) / Farbphoto, 169 x 129 cm
(Photo), 41,3 x 50 cm.
(CARNEGIE INTERNATIONAL, PITTSBURGH)

Gleich dem Bildhauer vergangener Jahrhunderte manipuliert und verformt Sophie Calle in ihrer Kunst eine Ware, die in der Wirtschaft ihrer Zeit eine zentrale Rolle spielt. Jedoch nicht mit Bronze oder Marmor hantiert sie, sondern mit Information, jenem flüchtigen Stoff, der unablässig zwischen Bewusstsein, Dokument und Cyberspace changiert. Es ist eine aufreizend unpräzise und unwägbare Ware, die sich irgendwo auf der Grenze zwischen Objektivem und Subjektivem bewegt, zwischen Öffentlichem und Privatem, zwischen Heiss und Kalt. Von Kreditbüros, Sicherheitsdiensten, Meinungs- und Marktforschungsinstituten wird sie in grossen Mengen ausgestreut, umkämpft, gestohlen, verfälscht, und doch liegt ihr eigentlicher Wert in minutiösen Details und dem flüchtigen Schatten von Bedeutung. Der Umgang mit Information gleicht denn auch einer experimentellen Wissenschaft: Für jede greif- und verwertbare Nichtigkeit werden Unmengen von Papier bedruckt; und er gleicht der Kunst: Während des gesamten Entstehungsprozesses ist sie derart immateriell, ein solch undurchdringliches Geflecht aus Figurativem oder Abstraktem, dass ihr Warenstatus doch irgendwie nach Scharlatanerie aussieht und dass Produktion und Handel als eine Art Parodie erscheinen.

Natürlich haben vor Calle auch schon andere Künstler mit diesem Medium gearbeitet. Wegbereiter waren da wohl die Surrealisten, vor allem in ihrer Vorliebe für Meinungsumfragen. Der Aphoristiker und Selbstmörder Jacques Rigaut erfand dazu seine eigene Variante: er trug immer eine kleine Schere bei sich, mit der er jedem, den er traf, heimlich einen Knopf von der Kleidung abschnitt. Das bezeichnete er als eine Form des Kunstsammelns. Der Schriftsteller Philippe Soupault insze-

LUC SANTE lebt in New York. Er ist der Verfasser von *Low Life* (Vintage, New York 1991) und *Evidence* (Farrar Straus Giroux, New York 1992).

nierte einmal seinen ganz persönlichen Highway-Überfall: spät abends spannte er eine Kette quer über die Avenue de l'Opéra und hielt auf diese Weise einen Bus an. Dann stieg er ein und forderte alle Passagiere auf, ihm ihr Geburtsdatum zu sagen. (Die darin liegende Kombination von Gewalt und Trivialität scheint vergleichbar mit Calles Anliegen.) Triviales ohne jede Gewalttätigkeit, Fakten, die nur um ihrer selbst willen gesammelt werden, die sture Dokumentation von offensichtlich belanglosen Vorgängen – all diese Merkmale sind in den verschiedenen Phasen der Konzeptkunst wiederzufinden, die ja das Sublime auf unterschiedlichste Weise verfolgte, zum Beispiel auch durch emsige Betriebsamkeit. Surrealisten wie Konzeptualisten stellten in ihrem Verständnis vom Umgang mit Information als dem eigentlichen Medium jeder auf seine Weise die verschiedenen Arten jener Mischung aus Faszination und Schrecken dar, die der Siegeszug der Bürokratie auslöste. Die Surrealisten reagierten mit wildwuchernder Fantasie, die Konzeptualisten mit Zen, was nicht gleichbedeutend mit Selbstzufriedenheit ist.

Manchmal scheinen in Sophie Calles Arbeit alle diese Elemente vereinigt, zuweilen aber auch nur einige davon. THE SLEEPERS (Die Schlafenden), ihr erstes Werk, erinnert unmittelbar an konzeptuelle Buchhaltung, doch kommt – zumindest andeutungsweise – noch eine Schicht von sexuellem Risiko hinzu. Risiko, List, Täuschung und Einmischung

I asked blind people to describe what they see contrasting their sayings with descriptions by artists of monochrome paintings (Manzoni, Richter, Reinhardt, Klein, Rauschenberg, Malevich).

■
Ich bat blinde Menschen, zu beschreiben, was sie sehen, und dem stellte ich die Beschreibungen von Künstlern monochromer Bilder gegenüber (Manzoni, Richter, Reinhardt, Klein, Rauschenberg, Malewitsch).

beherrschen ihre berüchtigtsten Werke: SUITE VÉNITIENNE (Venezianische Suite), THE SHADOW (Der Schatten), THE HOTEL (Das Hotel) und L'HOMME AU CARNET (Der Mann aus dem Adressbuch). Spionage ist die zentrale Metapher, wobei Sadomasochismus nicht nur andeutungsweise mitschwingt. ANATOLI ist ein Portrait, das mit Calles früheren Arbeiten nicht nur darin übereinstimmt, dass es sich gerade aus seiner inneren Widersprüchlichkeit heraus definiert, in diesem Fall dem Fehlen einer gemeinsamen Sprache. In seiner Einfachheit arbeitet es eben jene Gemeinsamkeit scharf heraus, die wir unter dem Titel «Der Blinde und der Elefant» zusammenfassen könnten. So nimmt es nicht wunder, dass ihr nächstes Werk THE BLIND (Die Blinden) heisst. Es knüpft an das frühere, eher prosaische Werk THE BRONX an und zeichnet in Gerüchten das Unnennbare nach; so entsteht ein Kunstwerk, das sich in den Objekten an der Galeriewand nur andeutet, nicht aber darin selbst Gestalt annimmt. Die Werke GHOSTS (Geister), BLIND COLOR (Blinde Farbe) und LAST SEEN (Zuletzt gesehen) funktionieren auf die gleiche Weise.

In Calles bisheriger künstlerischer Entwicklung gibt es einen deutlichen Bruch: in ihren früheren Arbeiten steht, grob gesprochen, das narrative Element im Vordergrund, in den späteren das Bild. Beide Male ist Sprache das wesentliche Instrument, während die visuelle Komponente eine illustrative Rolle spielt. Ihre Arbeit erinnert damit an die forensische Prozedur bei der Polizeiarbeit: Sie sammelt Spuren, Beschreibungen, Vermutungen, Hinweise und setzt sie zu einer annähernden Rekonstruktion zusammen. Bei den früheren Arbeiten ist diese Rekonstruktion eine Auflistung, in den späteren dagegen handelt es sich eher um so etwas wie Phantombildzeichnungen. So ist CASH MACHINE mit seinen entkörperten, fast ektoplasmischen Portraits aus Überwachungskameras vielleicht ein Wortspiel über diese Idee. AUTOBIOGRAPHICAL STORIES (Autobiographische Geschichten) und THE TOMBS (Die Grabsteine) führen das Prinzip des visuellen Substituts oder der Annäherung eher ins Ikonenhafte. Die Objekte, die für epochale Ereignisse in Calles Leben stehen, und die lakonischen Grabsteine, die ganze Existenzen auf einen blossen Familiennamen reduzieren, haben ihr ganz eigenes Gewicht; es geht nicht um ihren Bezug. Würde man nur eine Beschreibung von Calles Arbeit hören oder lesen, ohne die Werke vor Augen zu haben, so könnte es passieren, dass man sich als deren Thema die Unzulänglichkeit der Sprache und des Bildes vorstellen würde, die Lückenhaftigkeit der vermittelten Erfahrung. Dabei preist ihr Werk ohne Unterlass die Schönheit des Unpräzisen, die Poesie der Auslassungen und Fehler.

Mit anderen Worten, sie ist eine Art Impressionistin. Ungewissheit sprenkelt ihre Bilder gleich den Sonnenstrahlen, die ihr Licht über Blätter und Wiesen des Bois de Sowieso ergiessen. Aber das ist noch nicht alles. Bei jeder Information ist Ungewissheit im Spiel; sie gehört zur Information wie der Tod zum Menschen. Trotzdem strebt Information

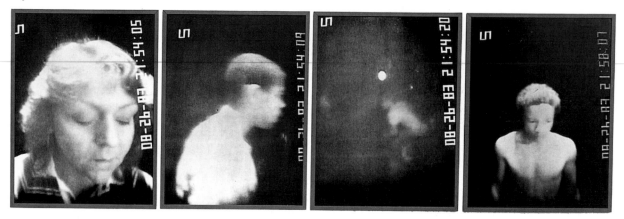

immer die Gesichertheit an, das heisst, ihre Lieferanten tun es, mag man es nun als Donquichotterie oder als Unredlichkeit bezeichnen. Der Polizei-Informant, der Industrie-Spion, der politische Beobachter, die zuverlässige Quelle – sie alle sind darauf aus, unfehlbar zu erscheinen. Und der einstmals unbedeutende Handel mit der Information entwickelt sich zusehends zu einer Institution von zentraler Bedeutung für die Weltwirtschaft, die ihren Sitz von düsteren Gängen in lichtdurchflutete Glaswandbüros verlagert hat. Immense Finanzentscheidungen werden auf der Grundlage eines Wissens getroffen (Konsumentenprofile, Zielgruppenbefragung, Trendforschung), das ungefähr so zuverlässig ist wie die Zukunftsvorhersage aus Vogelgedärm. Diese Metapher ist keineswegs an den Haaren herbeigezogen: Der Handel mit Informationen geht teilweise auf jene Wahrsager zurück, die in der Antike die Militärführer berieten. Er ist bloss technologisch und wissenschaftlich aufgerüstet worden, um die zeitgenössischen Rationalisten zufriedenzustellen.

Calles Arbeit ist gewissermassen eine Parodie auf diesen Handel beziehungsweise eine Parodie der Parodie, ein Scheinbild des Schwindels. Doch ihre Portraits sind Verzerrungen – der Mann aus dem Adressbuch, Anatoli, die Bewohner des Hotelzimmers, ja sogar sie selbst –, und eben deswegen sind sie keine Portraits mehr, genausowenig wie ein kubistischer Kopf zum Beispiel ein photographisches Abbild sein kann. Selbst wenn sie ein abgekartetes Spiel zu spielen scheint – und der Streich mit dem Adressbuch, der aus einem bestimmten Blickwinkel wie ein zweitklassiger Citizen Kane aussieht, mag durchaus Fragen zu ihren Motiven aufwerfen –, bleibt noch genug Luft in Form von Unbestimmtheit, um selbst Calle die vollständige Kontrolle über die Richtung ihrer Werke zu nehmen. Kurz gesagt, Ungewissheit ist das Markenzeichen der Wahrheit. Sie ist das einzige, worauf man sich bei jeder Information verlassen kann, und sie ist genau das, was den Warenwert der Information verringert. Sie ist fast immer störend; sie ist unproduktiv und uneffizient und oft sogar gefährlich. Und deshalb ist sie so schön, wie Calle in ihrem Werk immer wieder zeigt.

(Übersetzung: Nansen)

SOPHIE CALLE, CASH MACHINE SURVEILLANCE, THE ASSAULT ON PAMELA MAGNUSON, 26 AUGUST, 1983, AT 21 H 54 AND 20 SECONDS, 1991, b/w photo, 4 pieces, 37⅞ x 28¾" each / BANCOMAT-ÜBERWACHUNG, DER ÜBERFALL AUF PAMELA MAGNUSON AM 26. AUGUST 1983 UM 21 H 54 UND 20 SEKUNDEN, 1991, s/w-Photo, 4teilig, je 96 x 73 cm. (GALERIE BAMA CROUSEL-ROBELIN)

SOPHIE CALLE, FATHER, MOTHER, GRANDPA, GRANDMA, from LES TOMBES (THE TOMBS), 1990, b/w photos, 82⅞ x 15⅜" each / VATER, MUTTER, OPA, OMA, aus GRABSTEINE, 1990, 58,5 x 39 cm.

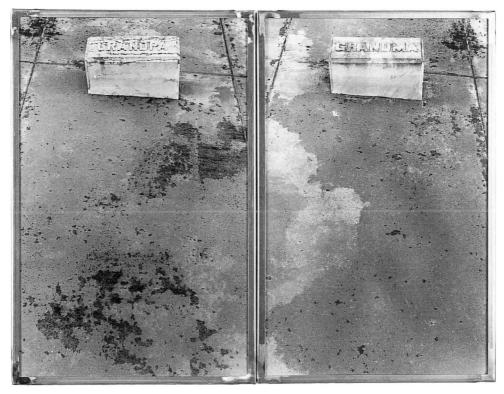

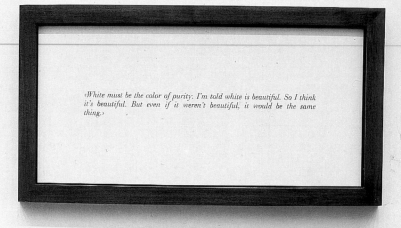

«White must be the color of purity. I'm told white is beautiful. So I think it's beautiful. But even if it weren't beautiful, it would be the same thing.»

Weiss muss die Farbe der Reinheit sein. Man sagt mir, Weiss sei schön. Deshalb glaube ich, es ist schön. Aber selbst wenn es nicht schön wäre, wäre es dasselbe.

White must be the color of purity. I'm told white is beautiful. So I think it's beautiful. But even if it weren't beautiful, it would be the same thing.

SOPHIE CALLE, LES AVEUGLES (THE BLIND / DIE BLINDEN), 1986, 23 photos and texts, 59 x 47¼" / 150 x 120 cm.

ON MY ARRIVAL IN NEW YORK THIS FEBRUARY I RECEIVED A MANUSCRIPT—THIRTY-FIVE "POSTCARDS"—FROM A MAN I DID NOT KNOW. HE HAD WRITTEN THEM ON THE OCCASION OF MY EXHIBITION AT LUHRING AUGUSTINE IN NEW YORK TWO YEARS AGO. A SELECTION OF THESE POSTCARDS APPEARS BELOW. *(Sophie Calle)*

POSTCARDS TO SOPHIE CALLE FROM JOSEPH GRIGELY

Dear Sophie,

I am writing to you about your New York show at Luhring Augustine in the spring of 1991, particularly about one installation: LES AVEUGLES (The Blind). My curiosity—or is it my concern?—is a reflection of anomalies and ambiguities: New York, with its unforgiving inaccessibility, is not a city of patience, nor is Luhring Augustine an art space where one expects the voice of an oppressed minority; and you, Sophie Calle, a professed voyeur of private lives, what is this installation you present to us?

On a small pedestal in the center of the room is a lectern on which is placed the conceptual locus of LES AVEUGLES: *"I met people who were born blind. Who had never seen. I asked them what their image of beauty was."*

Around the room framed texts record the responses of these people, brief, printed declarations of beauty. I—like others around me—am easily taken in by these voices and their resonance.

Yours,
Joseph

Dear Sophie,

My entrancement is mitigated by something troubling about these words, and what is troubling is that they are, shall we say, forthright. They do not apologize for the fact that it is the body, the engendered body particularly, that must be touched to be seen. This is the tactile gaze of the blind. It is a gaze unconditioned by whatever feminism and sexual politics have taught us about touching. The terms and conditions by which this tactile gaze exists thus cannot be judged by our own standard, where the actions of the blind become rendered—I use that word advisedly—into our vocabulary of tactile violence. This touching is not about feeling, not about touching even, but about seeing. Touching itself is elided; it is a semantic projection of our own physiology, not that of the blind. If everyone in the world were blind, perhaps touching would be called seeing.

Am I being too romantic? Quite possibly. But inasmuch as the Deaf do not see sign language as a pretty way of communicating—it's language, language pure and simple—I think the same can be said about this tactile gaze: It's about seeing, not about touching. This is the inevitable effect of an imposed transmodality: It reconfigures our physiological conventions and the language with which we describe these conventions. This room and the voices of the people in it require much patience, Sophie. I need to slow down here, we all need to slow down and begin to try to understand what is behind this tactile gaze—we need to rediscover the act of seeing, and should we freeze up at the sight—

JOSEPH GRIGELY is an artist who lives and works in New York City.

our sight—of this seeing-as-touching, it is our preconceptions that freeze us and our unwillingness—not inability, but unwillingness—to see what we are seeing.

And what are we seeing, Sophie?

Yours,
Joseph

Dear Sophie,

Beguiled now, I am almost afraid to face the photographs that supplement these texts, almost afraid to go past the honest audacity of this language to that which lies beyond: images that presume to be of the objects, people, places, and passions described. Yet, the most troubling part remains: your photographs of the faces of these blind people, their signatures. I am arrested by the fact that these images do not, because of their visual modality, return themselves to the blind. *Since your face is not available to me, why should my face be available to you?* An echo from somewhere, but I cannot pin it down. Something seems wrong to me: I am able to gaze, look, stare into the faces, into the eyes, of faces and eyes that cannot stare back. "Subjects," they are called. I feel I am in the presence of a social experiment. I feel I am being watched, feel as if I am a part of this experiment. Alone and not alone, I am uncomfortable.

Yours,
Joseph

Dear Sophie,

I hate myself here; yet I am taken in, seduced, drawn closer to this cultural keyhole. I struggle with my ambivalences—don't we all, don't you?—struggle with these images: hypostatization, the enscribed voice, and Sophie Calle's photographic interpretation of that voice. I look closer at the voices, try to listen, try to expunge the images that intervene—the faces, the photographs, the presence of Sophie Calle. It isn't easy. The photographs of the voices, your photographs, your interpretations, are resolutely hermeneutic: They crowd around me, crowd around the texts, impose themselves, and in the end reveal not so much the voices of the blind as the voice of Sophie Calle. I turn from the keyhole; I feel guilty, angry. Pushing away, I push myself closer.

Yours,
Joseph

Dear Sophie,

Language, which seems to be the locus here, keeps coming back to me: yours, mine, that of the blind. We mingle ourselves, our voices; this room doesn't know passivity. Perhaps unintentionally, language keeps intruding, asserting itself, taking control. It was Rousseau and Condillac who explained, with a sense of irresolvable resolve, the humanizing role of language in our lives, how it both makes and unmakes us, defines and de-defines what is around us—even, it seems, what one cannot see, what one cannot hear. It strikes me with a certain acuteness how a number of textual "images" of beauty begin as language and remain as language:

> *"…I'm told white is beautiful…"*
> *"Green is beautiful. Because every time I like something, I'm told it's green …"*
> *"…The sea must be beautiful too. They tell me it is blue and green and that when the sun reflects in it, it hurts your eyes…"*

It is easy to tell disabled people what they are missing; much more difficult to listen to, and understand, what they have. Deafness, as Victor Hugo said, is an illness of the mind, not of the ears.

Yours,
Joseph

Dear Sophie,

History is filled with examples of desire to relate to the other in some configuration: to experience the other possess it, control it. It is, almost ironically, a way of learning more about ourselves, of seeing how we fit into the grand scheme of being—the endless taxonomy of differences that we are forever trying to map, order, and organize into convenient compartments of knowledge. If it were only so simple, Sophie! But of course, it isn't. And it is not always quite the gesture of disinterested benevolence that it seems to be. Difference implies a degree of dispossession; it implies someone else is simultaneously what we want to be and what we fear to be. We want to touch this experience of difference, but we also want to do this from the safe distance of our own identity. We cannot quite forsake who we are to become someone else. We presume that to close our eyes is to experience blindness, or to sleep is to experience death—yet we know that we do not, cannot, abandon the sense of self in these endeavors; we cannot "unknow" ourselves as individuals. Empathy is an illusion, not a truth: The chameleon may change colors to blend in with its surroundings but it does not become those surroundings.

Yours,
Joseph

Dear Sophie,

I am beginning to think of you as a social archaeologist, as one who excavates the shards of human existence, makes notes, photographs, and so on. No scruples, no pettish qualms—truth only.

But whose truth?

Yours,
Joseph

Dear Sophie,

Saturday, March 23rd. I am here again in this room, here again among the blind and Sophie Calle. I am surrounded by your signature; yet I do not know who Sophie Calle really is, or who, for that matter, the author of this work really is. The advertisements read "Sophie Calle," but I am inclined to feel that the real artist in this room is not Sophie Calle but the blind themselves, for it is they who do what the artist must necessarily do: find beauty where others do not presume it to be. It is something not unique to the blind with whom Sophie Calle met and talked, but with all blind people, all disabled people, all of us, everyone—even, perhaps, Sophie Calle.

Art historians and contemporary critics are fond of saying that we now live in an age when the ontological distinctions between art and life are necessarily blurred; yet, at the same time, we seem unwilling to acknowledge art that makes no claim to itself as art, but modestly assumes the position of being whatever it finds itself being. Duchamp, it has been claimed, changed the rules by making the everyday object an object of art. The challenge today is to turn this around: to admire the everyday object or the ordinary person precisely because they are not art, and don't care to be. I'm afraid of my own voice. What, Sophie, have I said?

Yours,
Joseph

Dear Sophie,

There's something more than just a little bit engaging about how the idea of living can itself take on an aesthetic identity, how the a c t of living can supplant the mere object as an aesthetic ideal. At the present moment in cultural history we are facing the end of a century of objecthood, the end of a period in which (particularly during the 1980s) the art object became an object of physically and economically aggrandized proportions. To dismiss this art is not a sign of mere disaffection or residual Marxism; it is instead an act of turning, a gesture towards a certain kind of heretofore unacknowledged unpretentiousness where art is defined by a sincere sense of purpose, by a desire to be everything except this fiction we call art itself. It is, surely, not the only kind of art there is or will be, but it is an art germane, not ancillary, to our contemporary cultural consciousness. Perhaps this is what you yourself are trying to say in LES AVEUGLES. If so, it is a beautiful failure.

Yours,
Joseph

Dear Sophie,

April 30th. According to the New York *Gallery Guide*, LES AVEUGLES has closed, but according to the artworks on the walls of the gallery, it continues. The sixth week now. I do not stay long today: The comfort of familiar faces and familiar voices betrays my discomfort.

In the galleries I am genuinely surprised by the presence of traces of the lives of disabled people: enlarged braille texts, paintings that incorporate codified messages in the Deaf fingerspelling alphabet, sign language tattoos… The disabled seem to be everywhere in the galleries today, but only as subjects, the ordinariness of their lives framed and mounted for those who find it unordinary, "aesthetic," perhaps even strange.

To describe this activity as "appropriation" does not say enough. Couched within this quintessentially postmodern term is a desire to make something one's own, and the audacity to assume that we can transpose our selves to another state of being, or to some identity unique to another. The idea of theft is natural when it is unconsciously done within an intertextual matrix—every utterance necessarily steals something—but conscious theft is measured by its consequences, by those who are violated. The question is how far we can take the idea of appropriation, how willfully—or ruefully—we can make it serve our own needs at the expense of others. There is an unspoken line at which appropriation becomes a form of human violence, a point at which theft is transgressed by assault on the human psyche: the point at which appropriation becomes expropriation.

Yours,
Joseph

Dear Sophie,

My last postcard was perhaps a bit strong. Truth is rarely polite.

Part of the problem is related to representations of the disabled, and what are more generally discussed as "authentic" and "inauthentic" representations of racial and sexual difference. These are really difficult terms to qualify and they substantiate themselves only by virtue of the fact that they provide the grounds for an ongoing cultural debate, the tension by which culture necessarily sustains, perpetuates, and remakes itself. I may chastise you, Sophie, but I cannot correct you. In the realm of cultural exchanges everything that is right for somebody is wrong for somebody else.

It is not an ideology I am sending you in these postcards; there is no theoretical locus here, but only a theoretical tangle of frayed perceptions about the disabled as a part of the network of human differences. How, Sophie, can we measure and quantify something so abstract as difference? Why should we? We are all tangled in each other: Joseph, Sophie, LES AVEUGLES. All of us different, all of us equal in our differences.

A contradiction, yes. There are many of them, and that is my purpose here: to peel back the contradictions of ideology, not to create an ideology that represses contradictions. I would not be honest to you or to myself if what I said did not also reflect the chaos of who and what we are.

Yours,
Joseph

Dear Sophie,

The New Yorker has printed a brief description of your show in the gallery listings for April 8th. In part, it goes like this:

"Calle interviewed a number of people who were born blind, asking them to describe their images of beauty, then illustrating these definitions by taking pictures of the subjects and what they described. Some of these people look blind, some of them don't."

I stop at that last sentence, reread it: *Some of these people look blind, some of them don't.* I am not sure exactly what this means, how it is intended to mean; yet it somehow means much, in an unbearably predictable way. The very idea of looking blind, or bearing visible signs of identity, is somehow striking: One thinks of Paul Strand's photograph of a blind woman, a string with a signcard placed around her neck which reads BLIND. To what extent should otherness be a visible attribute? Would *The New Yorker* say of Robert Mapplethorpe's photographs: "Some of these people look homosexual, some of them don't?"

I look into a mirror at myself, search for my deafness, yet fail to find it. For some reason we have been conditioned to presume difference to be a visual phenomenon, the body as the locus of race and gender. Perhaps I need a hearing aid, not a flesh-colored one but a red one: a signifier that leaves little room for discursiveness, a signifier that ceremoniously announces itself. But I know, too, that the moment I open my mouth my nasal sibilants will give me away; I know that the moment you speak to me behind my back that you will think I am ignoring you. It is a scenario that is a cliché, yet is a cliché that is at times unbearably real. Once, at the Metropolitan Museum of Art, while sitting on the floor as I spent time with David's MARAT, a museum guard struck me on the shoulder and berated me for not getting up on my feet the first time he warned me.

Some of these people look blind, some of them don't.

Yours,
Joseph

Dear Sophie,

Can I tell you a story? It is not the sort of story that we describe as a tale with a moral, but a real story that is itself a moral.

One evening an acquaintance of mine, visiting New Orleans, went straight to the French Quarter for the sort of reasons people go to New Orleans: for the vibrations of jazz, the rhythms of blues, and the carnavalesque atmosphere that makes the French Quarter what it is. For her it was an inviting thing to do, and for a while at least it was inviting indeed. But then, early in the evening, something happened. A policeman had noticed her unsteady gait and stopped her to ask a few questions. She could not, however, understand him very well, nor did he understand her responses. He was a smart policeman and knew intoxication when he saw it.

She was arrested for public drunkenness. Her arrest record cites her "slurred speech," her "incomprehending behavior," and her "erratic movement." She spent a very long night alone in jail trying to understand why she was arrested for being everything she was, everything she could possibly be: a young deaf woman with cerebral palsy.

Some of these people look blind, some of them don't.

Yours,
Joseph

Dear Sophie,

A short recommended reading list in physiological otherness:

Harlan Lane, *The Mask of Benevolence*
John Hull, *Touching the Rock*
Georges Canguilhem, *The Normal and the Pathological*

Happy reading.

Yours,
Joseph

SOPHIE CALLE, LES AVEUGLES (THE BLIND / DIE BLINDEN), 1986. (INSTALLATION FRED HOFFMAN GALLERY, LOS ANGELES)

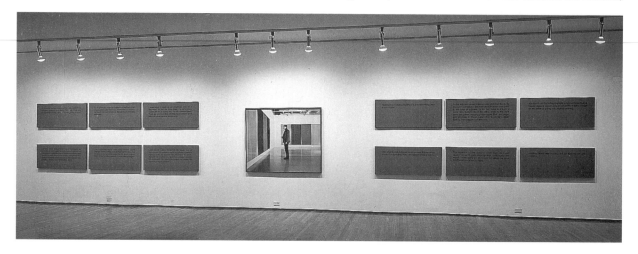

Dear Sophie,

I am getting closer to a theme now. Maybe I was wrong when I wrote to you and said I had no theoretical locus here. Perhaps there really is. I think it has to do with a topic that hasn't received serious critical discussion: the canonization of difference. Part of the problem, I think, is that we tend to define too much, categorize too much, and find ourselves trapped by our definitions and categories. If we really think about it, it's hard to define what a mother is. In Washington D.C. a series of posters promoting foster parenthood have recently appeared. They picture a middle-aged African-American man surrounded by three children, with the caption: "We need more mothers like him." The poster is an eloquent testimony to the fragility of our preconceptions about stereotyped social roles. What it does so well is get alterity out of theories, onto the streets, and into the public consciousness. We need more posters like that. More critical discourse. And more art.

Yours,
Joseph

Dear Sophie,

Never enough time, is there? Or space…

After eight visits to LES AVEUGLES perhaps it is time to come to an end of my monospondence.
I do not mean to imply that I have exhausted possibilities for continuing. You'll be hearing from me again. An ending is a mere formality, the point at which writing stops, the point at which the writer, as a character, exits from his text.
A friend encourages me to be blunt, straightforward, precise.

Since your face is not available to me, why should my face be available to you?

Perhaps, Sophie, you might someday return what you have taken, might someday undress your psyche in a room frequented by the blind and let them run their fingers over your body as you have run your eyes over theirs.

Yours,
Joseph

Postcards to Sophie Calle is a work in progress.

BEI MEINER ANKUNFT IN NEW YORK IM FEBRUAR DIESES JAHRES ERWARTETE MICH EIN MANUSKRIPT – 35 «POSTKARTEN» – VON EINEM MANN, DEN ICH NICHT KANNTE. ER HATTE SIE ANLÄSSLICH MEINER AUSSTELLUNG BEI LUHRING AUGUSTINE IN NEW YORK VOR ZWEI JAHREN GESCHRIEBEN. EINE AUSWAHL DIESER POSTKARTEN ERSCHEINT AN DIESER STELLE. *(Sophie Calle)*

POSTKARTEN AN SOPHIE CALLE VON JOSEPH GRIGELY

Liebe Sophie

Ich schreibe Dir über Deine Ausstellung bei Luhring Augustine vom Frühling 1991 in New York, über eine Installation im besonderen: LES AVEUGLES (Die Blinden). Meine Neugier – oder ist es meine Betroffenheit? – beruht auf Anomalien und Mehrdeutigkeiten: New York mit seiner gnadenlosen Unzugänglichkeit ist keine duldsame Stadt, noch ist die Galerie Luhring Augustine ein Kunstraum, in dem man auf die Stimme einer unterdrückten Minderheit gefasst wäre; und die Frage an Dich, Sophie Calle, erklärte Voyeurin des Privatlebens anderer: Was ist das für eine Installation, die Du uns zeigst?

Auf einem kleinen Podest in der Mitte des Raumes steht ein Lesepult, auf dem der konzeptuelle Ort von LES AVEUGLES eingetragen ist: *«Ich traf Menschen, die blind zur Welt gekommen waren. Die nie hatten sehen können. Ich fragte sie, was für ein Bild sie sich von der Schönheit machen.»* Überall im Raum sind ihre Antworten in eingerahmten Texten festgehalten: kurze, gedruckte Äusserungen darüber, was Schönheit ist. Ich erliege – wie andere um mich herum – diesen Stimmen und deren Resonanz fast widerstandslos.

Ich bin – wie soll ich sagen? – wie in Trance. Es passt kein anderes Wort.

Dein Joseph

Liebe Sophie

Mein Trancezustand wird von etwas Beunruhigendem, das jenen Aussagen anhaftet, abgeschwächt; das Beunruhigende daran ist, dass sie, sagen wir es so, g e r a d e h e r a u s kommen. Es wird nicht entschuldigend darum herumgeredet, dass es der Körper ist, der mit einem Geschlecht ausgestattete Körper insbesondere, der berührt werden muss, um gesehen zu werden. Das ist der taktile Blick der Blinden. Es ist ein Blick, der unbeeinflusst ist von all dem, was uns Feminismus und die Politisierung des Geschlechtes über das Berühren beigebracht haben. Die Voraussetzungen, unter denen dieser taktile Blick entsteht, lassen sich nicht nach unserem Massstab messen, bei dem das Verhalten der Blinden auf u n s e r Vokabular taktiler Gewalt zurückgeführt wird – ich setze mit Absicht dieses Wort. Dieses Tasten beinhaltet nicht das Fühlen, nicht einmal den Tastsinn, sondern das Sehen. Das Tasten selbst

JOSEPH GRIGELY ist ein Künstler, der in New York lebt und arbeitet.

wird ausgeklammert; es ist eine semantische Projektion unserer eigenen Physiologie, und nicht derjenigen der Blinden. Wenn alle Menschen blind wären, würde man vielleicht das Tasten Sehen nennen.

Klingt das jetzt zu romantisch? Schon möglich. Aber wenn man bedenkt, dass die Tauben die Zeichensprache nicht einfach als leidlich gutes Mittel zur Verständigung ansehen – sie ist Sprache, nicht mehr und nicht weniger –, dann kann man, meine ich, von diesem taktilen Blick gleichermassen sagen, dass er das Sehen, nicht das Tasten, zum Inhalt hat. Eine erzwungene Übertragungsweise hat unvermeidlich zur Folge, dass sie sowohl unsere physiologischen Verhaltensnormen als auch die Sprache nachbildet, mit der wir diese Normen beschreiben. Dieser Raum und die Stimmen der Menschen darin verlangen viel Geduld, Sophie. Ich muss hier bedächtiger werden, wir alle müssen bedächtiger werden und zu begreifen versuchen, was dieser taktile Blick durchscheinen lässt – wir müssen den Vorgang des Sehens wiederentdecken, und müssten wir beim sich u n s e r e m Auge darbietenden Anblick dieses Sehens-als-Tasten erstarren, so wären es unsere Vorurteile, die uns starr machen, und auch unsere Abneigung – Abneigung, nicht Unfähigkeit – zu sehen, was wir gerade sehen.

Und was sehen wir, Sophie?

Dein Joseph

Liebe Sophie

Der beunruhigendste Teil steht gleichwohl noch aus: Deine Photographien von den Gesichtern dieser blinden Menschen: ihre Signaturen. Die Tatsache, dass diese Bilder, weil sie dem visuellen Bereich angehören, sich den Blinden nicht offenbaren, hält mich gefangen. *Da ich dein Gesicht nicht zu sehen bekomme, weshalb solltest du dann mein Gesicht zu sehen bekommen?* Ein Echo von irgendwoher, ich weiss nicht mehr aus welcher Richtung. Da stimmt doch etwas nicht: Ich kann die Augen und Gesichter ansehen, anschauen, anstarren, Augen und Gesichter, die meinen Blick nicht erwidern können. «Subjekte» werden sie genannt. Ich spüre, dass ich einem sozialen Experiment beiwohne. Ich spüre, dass ich beobachtet werde, es ist mir, als ob ich Teil dieses Experiments wäre. Allein und nicht allein, mir ist unbehaglich zumute.

Dein Joseph

Liebe Sophie

Ich verabscheue mich hier selbst, und doch lasse ich mich überlisten, verführen, näher ans kulturelle Schlüsselloch heranlocken. Ich ringe mit meinen Ambivalenzen – tun wir das nicht alle, auch Du? –, ich ringe mit diesen Bildern: Hypostasierung, die eingeschriebene Stimme und Sophie Calles photographische Interpretation dieser Stimme. Ich sehe mir die Stimmen näher an, versuche hinzuhören, die hereindrängenden Bilder zu verscheuchen – die Gesichter, die Photographien, die Präsenz Sophie Calles. Es ist nicht einfach. Die Photographien der Stimmen, Deine Photographien, Deine Interpretationen, sind entschieden hermeneutisch: Sie umdrängen mich, umdrängen die Texte, behaupten ihren Platz und lassen letzten Endes nicht so sehr die Stimmen der Blinden als die Stimme Sophie Calles erkennen. Ich wende mich vom Schlüsselloch ab; ich fühle mich schuldig, bin verärgert. Indem ich zurückweiche, komme ich näher heran.

Dein Joseph

Liebe Sophie

Die Sprache, sie scheint hier die Grundlage zu bilden, kehrt fortwährend zu mir zurück: Deine, meine, diejenige der Blinden. Wir verschmelzen, unsere Stimmen gehen ineinander über; Passivität ist von diesem Raum ausgeschlossen. Es ist vielleicht nicht beabsichtigt, aber die Sprache dringt weiterhin ein, setzt sich weiterhin durch, übt immer noch Herrschaft aus. Es waren Rousseau und Condillac, die mit Sinn für unentschiedene Entschiedenheit die vermenschlichende Funktion erklärt hatten, die die Sprache auf unser Leben ausübt, wie sie uns sowohl hervorbringt als auch zu Fall bringt, wie sie unser Umfeld bestimmt und auflöst – sogar hinsichtlich dessen, so scheint es, was wir nicht sehen und nicht hören können. Es berührt mich recht stark, wie eine Anzahl textlich festgehaltener «Bilder» der Schönheit von der Sprache ausging und als Sprache weiterwirkt:

«*…Mir wird gesagt, Weiss sei schön…*»

«*Grün ist schön. Denn immer, wenn mir etwas gefällt, wird mir gesagt, es sei grün…*»

«*…Das Meer muss auch schön sein. Man sagt mir, es sei blau und grün und dass einem, wenn sich die Sonne darin spiegelt, die Augen schmerzen…*»

Es ist leicht, behinderten Menschen zu sagen, was sie sich entgehen lassen; bedeutend schwieriger ist, sich anzuhören, und zu begreifen, was sie besitzen. Taubheit ist, wie Victor Hugo sagte, eine seelische Erkrankung, keine Ohrenkrankheit.

Dein Joseph

Liebe Sophie

In der Geschichte lassen sich unzählige Beispiele anführen für den Wunsch, sich mit dem anderen einer gewissen Konstellation gemäss zu verbinden: das andere zu erfahren, zu besitzen, zu beherrschen. Es ist, fast ironischerweise, ein Mittel, mehr über uns selbst zu erfahren, zu erkennen, in welcher Weise wir in die grosse Seinsordnung eingefügt sind – die unaufhörliche Taxonomie der Verschiedenheit, die wir ständig zu kartographieren, klassifizieren und in die passenden Fächer unseres gesammelten Wissens einzuordnen versuchen. Wenn es nur so einfach wäre, Sophie! Aber so einfach ist es natürlich nicht. Und es ist auch nicht immer so ganz die Geste interesselosen Wohlwollens, die sich hier anzudeuten scheint. Die Differenz impliziert ein Stück Enteignung; sie impliziert, dass jemand anders gleichzeitig das ist, was wir sein wollen, und das, was wir zu sein fürchten. Wir wollen diese Erfahrung der Differenz zu greifen bekommen, aber wir wollen dies zugleich aus der sicheren Distanz tun, die uns unsere Identität gewährt. Wir können uns von dem, der wir sind, nicht ganz lösen, um jemand anders zu werden. Wir meinen, das Schliessen der Augen sei die Erfahrung der Blindheit, oder Schlafen sei die Erfahrung des Todes – und doch wissen wir, dass wir dabei das Bewusstsein von uns selbst nicht aufgeben (können); wir können uns selbst als Individuen nicht «verunkenntlichen». Empathie ist eine Illusion, keine Tatsache: Das Chamäleon mag wohl seine Hautfarbe ändern, um sich der Umgebung anzupassen, aber zur Umgebung selbst wird es dennoch nicht.

Dein Joseph

Liebe Sophie

Allmächlich betrachte ich Dich als eine soziale Archäologin, die Scherben der menschlichen Existenz ausgräbt, Notizen, Photographien macht usw. Keine Skrupel, keine launisch-missmutigen Bedenken – nur Wahrheit.

Aber wessen Wahrheit?

Dein Joseph

Liebe Sophie

Samstag, 23. März. Ich bin jetzt wieder in diesem Raum, wieder unter den Blinden und mit Sophie Calle. Rundherum sehe ich Deine Signatur, und doch weiss ich nicht, wer Sophie Calle wirklich ist, oder wer, in diesem Fall, das Werk wirklich hervorgebracht hat. In den Ankündigungen steht «Sophie Calle», aber mir will eher scheinen, dass der eigentliche Künstler in diesem Raum nicht Sophie Calle ist, sondern dass es die Blinden selbst sind, sind sie doch diejenigen, die das tun, was der Künstler notwendigerweise tun muss: Schönheit dort aufspüren, wo niemand sie vermutet. Dies zeichnet nicht nur die Blinden aus, mit denen sich Sophie Calle traf und unterhielt, sondern alle Blinden, alle Behinderten, uns alle, jeder und jede – sogar, vielleicht jedenfalls, Sophie Calle.

Kunsthistoriker und zeitgenössische Kritiker weisen gerne darauf hin, dass wir nun in einer Zeit leben, in der die ontologischen Unterscheidungen zwischen Kunst und Leben notwendigerweise verwischt sind; aber zugleich scheint man nicht willens zu sein, Kunst anzuerkennen, die sich nicht als Kunst ausgibt, sondern sich bescheiden daran hält, sich selbst zu sein, welche Form sie auch immer annimmt. Duchamp, so wird erklärt, änderte die Spielregeln, indem er den Gebrauchsgegenstand zu einem Gegenstand der Kunst machte. Heute gilt es dies umzukehren, also den Gebrauchsgegenstand oder den Alltagsmenschen gerade deshalb zu bewundern, weil beide nicht Kunst sind und es auch nicht sein wollen.

Ich fürchte mich vor meiner eigenen Stimme. Sophie, was habe ich gesagt?

Dein Joseph

Liebe Sophie

Wie der Begriff der Lebensweise selbst eine ästhetische Identität gewinnen kann, wie der Akt des Lebens den blossen Gegenstand als ästhetisches Ideal verdrängen kann, hat mehr als nur etwas leicht Verführerisches an sich. Zum jetzigen Zeitpunkt stehen wir kulturgeschichtlich am Ende eines Jahrhunderts der «Objektheit», am Ende einer Periode, in der (besonders in den 80er Jahren) das Kunstobjekt zu einem in physischer und ökonomischer Hinsicht übergrossen Gegenstand geworden war. Diese Kunst zu verwerfen, ist nicht ein Zeichen blosser Verdrossenheit oder ein Relikt des Marxismus; es ist vielmehr der Schritt zu einer Wende, eine Bewegung hin zu einer Art bisher nicht anerkannter Anspruchslosigkeit, wo Kunst wahrhaft unbeirrt ist, erfüllt vom Wunsch, alles ausser jener Fiktion zu sein, die wir Kunst nennen. Dies ist gewiss nicht die einzige Form von Kunst, die es gibt oder geben wird, aber es ist eine Kunst, die unserem jetzigen kulturellen Bewusstsein zugehört, also nicht nebensächlich ist. Vielleicht ist es das, was auch Du mit LES AVEUGLES sagen willst. Wenn ja, so ist es eine wunderbare Unterlassung.

Dein Joseph

Liebe Sophie

30. April. Gemäss dem New York *Gallery Guide* ist die Ausstellung von LES AVEUGLES zu Ende, aber gemäss den Installationen an den Wänden der Galerie geht sie weiter. Nun in der sechsten Woche. Heute bleibe ich nicht lange: Das Behagliche vertrauter Gesichter und vertrauter Stimmen verrät mein Unbehagen.

Dass in den Galerien Lebensspuren der Behinderten gegenwärtig sind, überrascht mich wirklich: erweiterte Braille-Texte, Bilder, die kodierte Botschaften mit der Fingersprache verknüpfen, Markierungen aus der Zeichensprache. Die Behinderten scheinen heute die Galerien zu bevölkern, aber nur als Objekte, ihr alltägliches Leben eingerahmt und inszeniert für jene, die es ungewöhnlich, «ästhetisch», vielleicht sogar fremdartig finden.

Diese Aktivität als «Appropriation» zu bezeichnen, sagt noch nicht alles. Diesem wesentlich postmodernen Begriff ist der Wunsch eingeschrieben, sich etwas zu eigen zu machen, die kühne Annahme, wir könnten unser Selbst in eine andere Seinsweise versetzen oder in die unverwechselbare Identität eines anderen schlüpfen. Der Begriff des Diebstahls hat nichts Ungewöhnliches an sich, wenn er innerhalb einer intertextuellen Matrix unbewusst abläuft – jede Äusserung entwendet notwendigerweise etwas –, bewusster Diebstahl jedoch wird auf seine Folgen hin eingeschätzt, von jenen, denen Leid zugefügt wird. Es fragt sich, wie weit wir die Idee der Appropriation führen, wie rücksichtslos – oder reuevoll – wir sie uns auf Kosten anderer zunutze machen dürfen. Es gibt eine unausgesprochene Grenze, jenseits derer Appropriation zu einer Form menschlicher Gewalt wird, einen Punkt, an dem Diebstahl sich zu einem Anschlag auf die menschliche Psyche steigert: der Punkt, an dem sich Appropriation in Expropriation verwandelt.

Dein Joseph

Liebe Sophie

Meine letzte Postkarte war vielleicht ein bisschen heftig. Wahrheit ist selten rücksichtsvoll.

Ein Teil des Problems hängt mit den Darstellungsweisen von Behinderten und damit zusammen, was in weiterem Sinne als «authentische» und «nicht authentische» Darstellungen der Differenz der Rassen und Geschlechter diskutiert wird. Diese Begriffe zu bestimmen, ist in der Tat schwierig, und sie haben allein deshalb Substanz, weil sie die Basis für eine gegenwärtige Kulturdebatte bilden, für jene Spannung, die für das Fortbestehen, Beharrungsvermögen und die Erneuerung einer Kultur notwendig ist. Ich kann Dich wohl tadeln, Sophie, aber ich kann Dich nicht korrigieren. Auf dem Gebiet kulturellen Austauschs ist alles, was dem einen richtig erscheint, falsch für den anderen.

Es ist keine Ideologie, die ich Dir mit diesen Postkarten übermitteln will; es gibt hier keinen theoretischen Ort, sondern einzig einen wirren theoretischen Knäuel, einen Knäuel zerfahrener Wahrnehmungen über die Behinderten als Teil im Netzwerk der menschlichen Differenz. Sophie, wie können wir so etwas Abstraktes wie die Differenz ausmessen und veranschlagen? Weshalb sollten wir? Wir alle sind ineinander verstrickt: Joseph, Sophie, LES AVEUGLES. Wir alle verschieden, wir alle ähnlich in unserer Verschiedenheit.

Ein Widerspruch, jawohl. Es gibt deren viele, und meine Absicht hier ist, die ideologischen Widersprüche herauszulösen und nicht eine Ideologie zu erzeugen, die Widersprüche unterdrückt. Es wäre mir selbst und Dir gegenüber nicht aufrichtig, wenn das, was ich gesagt habe, nicht auch das Chaos dessen spiegelte, wer und was wir sind.

Dein Joseph

Liebe Sophie

Der *New Yorker* hat im Galerienverzeichnis vom 8. April eine kurze Beschreibung Deiner Ausstellung abgedruckt. Eine Passage lautet wie folgt:

«Calle interviewte eine Anzahl Menschen, die blind zur Welt gekommen waren, und bat sie, ihr Bild von der Schönheit zu beschreiben; anschliessend illustrierte sie deren Definitionen, indem sie von den Versuchspersonen und dem, was sie beschrieben, Aufnahmen machte. Einige dieser Menschen sehen wie Blinde aus, einige hingegen nicht.»

Ich halte beim letzten Satz inne, lese ihn noch einmal: *Einige dieser Menschen sehen wie Blinde aus, einige hingegen nicht.* Ich weiss nicht recht, was dies genau bedeutet, welche Absicht dahintersteckt; jedenfalls hat es irgendwie viel zu bedeuten, in einer unerträglich schwer vorhersehbaren Weise. Allein die Idee, jemand sehe wie ein Blinder aus, trage ein sichtbares Kennzeichen, ist irgendwie bemerkenswert. Man denkt dabei an Paul Strands Photographie einer blinden Frau, die sich ein an einer Schnur befestigtes Schild mit der Aufschrift BLIND umgehängt hat. Bis zu welchem Grade sollte Anderssein ein sichtbares Attribut sein? Würde der *New Yorker* über Robert Mapplethorpes Photographien sagen: «Einige dieser Menschen sehen wie Homosexuelle aus, einige hingegen nicht.»?

Ich betrachte mich im Spiegel, suche nach Spuren meiner Taubheit, kann sie aber nicht finden. Aus irgendeinem Grund sind wir darauf programmiert, die Differenz als eine visuelle Erscheinung, und diese als Bezugspunkt im Hinblick auf Rasse und Geschlecht, vorauszusetzen. Vielleicht brauche ich ein Hörgerät, kein hautfarbenes, sondern ein rotes: einen Signifikanten, der sich feierlich zu erkennen gibt. Aber ich bin mir auch bewusst, dass in dem Augenblick, da ich den Mund auftue, mich meine nasalen Zischlaute verraten; ich bin mir bewusst, dass Du in dem Augenblick, da Du hinter meinem Rücken sprichst, annehmen wirst, ich ignoriere Dich. Diese Abfolge ist ein

Klischee, aber ein manchmal unerträglich reales Klischee. Einmal, es war im Metropolitan Museum of Art, ich sass auf dem Boden und widmete mich Davids MARAT, versetzte mir ein Museumswärter einen Schlag auf die Schulter und beschimpfte mich, weil ich nicht aufgestanden war, als er mich zum erstenmal gewarnt hatte.
Einige dieser Menschen sehen wie Blinde aus, einige hingegen nicht.

Dein Joseph

Liebe Sophie

Darf ich Dir eine Geschichte erzählen? Sie gehört nicht zu jener Art Geschichten, die wir als moralische Erzählung bezeichnen, sondern es ist eine reale Geschichte, die selbst eine Moral ist.

Eines Abends ging eine Bekannte, die sich in New Orleans aufhielt, geradewegs ins französische Viertel, und zwar aus denselben Gründen, aus denen auch andere Leute nach New Orleans gehen: die Vibrationen des Jazz, die Bluesrhythmen und die Karnevalsstimmung, die das französische Viertel zu dem macht, was es ist. Für sie war das ein verlockendes Vorhaben, und wenigstens für eine Weile blieb es auch tatsächlich verlockend. Doch dann, am frühen Abend, geschah etwas. Ein Polizist hatte ihren unsicheren Gang bemerkt und sie angehalten, um ihr ein paar Fragen zu stellen. Sie konnte ihn aber nicht eindeutig verstehen, und auch er verstand ihre Antworten nicht. Er war ein schlauer Polizist, der Betrunkenheit auf den ersten Blick erkannte.

Sie wurde wegen öffentlicher Trunkenheit festgenommen. Das polizeiliche Protokoll erwähnt ihre «undeutliche Aussprache», ihr «uneinsichtiges Verhalten» und ihre «unstete Fortbewegung». Sie verbrachte eine endlose Nacht allein in der Zelle und versuchte zu begreifen, weshalb sie für all das, was sie war, all das, was sie zu sein vermochte, verhaftet wurde: eine taube junge Frau mit einer Gehirnlähmung.
Einige dieser Menschen sehen wie Blinde aus, einige hingegen nicht.

Dein Joseph

Liebe Sophie

Eine kurze Bücherliste, die ich zum Thema physiologische Differenz empfehle:
  Harlan Lane, *Mit der Seele hören*, München 1988
  John Hull, *Im Dunkeln sehen*, München 1992
  Georges Canguilhem, *Das Normale und das Pathologische*, München 1974

Viel Vergnügen bei der Lektüre.

Dein Joseph

Liebe Sophie

Ich bin jetzt dabei, mich einem Leitmotif anzunähern. Vielleicht täuschte ich mich, als ich Dir schrieb und sagte, ich verfüge hier über keinen theoretischen Ort. Vielleicht gibt es tatsächlich einen. Ich glaube, er ist mit einem Thema verknüpft, das bis anhin keiner ernsthaften kritischen Diskussion unterzogen worden ist: die Kanonisation der Differenz. Das Problem liegt zum Teil darin begründet, dass wir die Tendenz haben, zuviel zu definieren und zu kategorisieren und uns in unseren eigenen Definitionen und Kategorien zu verheddern. Wenn wir wirklich darüber nachdenken, dann ist es schwierig zu definieren, was eine Mutter ist: In Washington D.C. sind seit kurzem Plakate angeschlagen, die für mehr Pflegeeltern werben. Sie zeigen einen Afroamerikaner mittleren Alters, der von drei Kindern umringt ist, dazu die Aufschrift «Wir brauchen mehr Mütter wie ihn». Das Plakat ist ein beredtes Zeugnis für die Brüchigkeit unserer Vorurteile in bezug auf stereotype soziale Rollen. Das richtig Gute daran ist, dass die

Andersheit so der Theorien enthoben und auf die Strasse und ins öffentliche Bewusstsein getragen wird. Wir brauchen mehr solche Plakate. Mehr kritische Diskurse. Und mehr Kunst.

Dein Joseph

Liebe Sophie

Nie genug Zeit, nicht wahr? Oder Platz…

Nach acht Besuchen bei LES AVEUGLES ist es jetzt vielleicht an der Zeit, meine Monospondenz abzuschliessen.

Das soll aber nicht heissen, dass ich damit die verschiedenen Möglichkeiten fortzufahren ausgeschöpft hätte. Du wirst wieder von mir hören. Ein Abschluss ist eine reine Formsache, der Punkt, an dem das Schreiben aussetzt, der Punkt, an dem der Schreibende, als Figur, aus dem Text heraustritt.

Ein Freund ermutigt mich, offen zu sein: geradeheraus, präzise.

Da ich dein Gesicht nicht zu sehen bekomme, weshalb solltest du dann mein Gesicht zu sehen bekommen?

Vielleicht könntest Du, Sophie, eines Tages zurückgeben, was Du genommen hast, könntest eines Tages Deine Psyche in einem von den Blinden häufig besuchten Raum entblössen und ihre Finger über Deinen Körper gleiten lassen, so wie Du mit Deinen Augen über ihre Augen gewandert bist.

Dein Joseph

Postkarten an Sophie Calle ist ein *work in progress.*

(Übersetzung: Thomas Aigner)

SOPHIE CALLE, LES AVEUGLES
(THE BLIND / DIE BLINDEN), 1986.

Morocco is beautiful. My house there is very pretty. Lost in the mountains, without electricity.

Marokko ist schön. Mein Haus dort ist sehr hübsch. Verloren in den Bergen, ohne Elektrizität.

PATRICK FREY

Grabsteine, Inschriften, Photographien und Legenden, Hyperfiktionen auf Leben und Tod

ZUM MOTIV DES

ABWESENDEN IN

ZWEI FRÜHEN

ARBEITEN VON

SOPHIE CALLE

PATRICK FREY ist Kabarettist, Kunstkritiker und Verleger in Zürich.

In Kunstwerken, gerade wenn sie scheinbar lebensnah und unmittelbar daherkommen – was für die Kunst der Photographie gewissermassen a priori gilt –, ist immer etwas ganz Entscheidendes enthalten, das nicht für, sondern gegen das Leben gerichtet ist, etwas Kaltes, Grausames, bei dem es um ein Sezieren oder Einfrieren von Leben geht.

1980 folgt Sophie Calle monatelang ihr unbekannten Leuten in den Strassen von Paris, aus reiner Freude am heimlichen Tun und nicht, «weil sie mich interessierten», wie sie selbst schreibt. Sie photographiert sie ohne deren Wissen, lässt sie dann wieder ziehen und wendet sich den nächsten zu. Zufällig wird sie eines Abends einem ihrer Opfer, Henri B., vorgestellt. Sie erfährt von ihm, dass er nach Venedig reisen will, und beschliesst, ihm zu folgen. Daraus entsteht SUITE VENITIENNE, ein ebenso hyperrealer wie hyperfiktionaler Bericht aus Texten, Photos und kartographischen Eintragungen der verschiedenen Verfolgungswege. Henri B.s gewöhnliche Existenz wird seltsam, mysteriös, und zwar nicht etwa, weil Sophie etwas entdeckt, das über einen banalen Ferienaufenthalt in Venedig hinausginge, nein, es ist ihre, Sophie Calles geheime Existenz selbst, die zum Geheimnis von Henri B.s Leben wird. Sophie Calle ist der Schatten, der auf sein Leben fällt. Am achten Tag der Suche, nachdem sie ihn endlich vor ihr Auge und ihre Kamera bekommt und nach einer Stunde wieder verliert, behauptet sie in ihren Aufzeichnungen, Henri B. habe ihr bei ihrer ersten kurzen Begegnung gesagt, dass er Friedhöfe liebe, das sei das einzige, was sie über ihn erfahren habe. Sie begibt sich deshalb zum alten jüdischen Friedhof des Lido und macht zwei Photos von halbverfallenen Grabsteinen. Henri B. ist nicht da. Sie notiert: «Es ist hier, wo er hätte sein müssen. Ich habe so sehr auf ihn gezählt.»

SOPHIE CALLE, SUITE VÉNITIENNE,
Collection Ecrits sur l'image, Editions de
l'Etoile, Paris 1983.

Monatelang folgte ich Fremden durch die
Strassen. Aus Spass am Verfolgen, nicht weil sie
mich besonders interessierten. Ich photographierte sie ohne ihr Wissen, beobachtete
ihre Bewegungen, schliesslich verlor ich sie
dann aus den Augen und vergass sie.
Ende Januar 1979 folgte ich einem Mann durch
die Strassen von Paris, den ich wenige Minuten
später aus den Augen verlor. Am gleichen
Abend machte ich zufällig an einer Vernissage
seine Bekanntschaft. Im Verlauf unserer Unter-
haltung erzählte er mir von einer geplanten
Reise nach Venedig. Da entschloss ich mich,
mich an seine Fersen zu heften und mich mit
seinem Leben bekanntzumachen.

Alle Kunst ist auch immer Kunst über die Lebenden hinaus, über das
Wirkliche hinaus, zu den Toten; Toten-Kunst gegen den Tod als ein blosses,
spurloses Verschwinden. Kunst als ein Versuch, den Tod zu beschwören, ihn
zu bannen mitten im Leben und ihn dadurch nicht zu erleiden. Kunst –
und dazu zählt in besonders intensivem Masse auch die Photographie – ist
immer auch Grabsteinkunst. Grabsteine sind primäre Kunst-Dinge. Sie stehen als versteinerte künstlerische Urgesten an einem Ort des Übergangs,
der Einmündung, dort, wo der je nachdem kurze oder lange Fluss des individuellen Lebens in den grossen Strom des Kollektiven mündet. Ihre Präsenz steht für Abwesende, für eine Abwesenheit. Als Sophie Calle im Juni
1983 in der Rue des Martyrs das Adressbuch des Pierre D. findet und
beschliesst, sich dem Unbekannten über Gespräche mit seinen im Adressbuch verzeichneten Bekannten zu nähern und diese Kolportagen und
Espionnagen während eines Monats in der Tageszeitung *Libération* zu publi-
zieren, so kündet schon der Name der Strasse von dem Schicksal, das die
Identität Pierre D.s dabei erleiden wird. Als sie ihn ein erstes Mal anruft,
spricht sein Anrufbeantworter die Wahrheit aus: «Ich bin abwesend. Ich bin
nicht da.» Dazu zeigt Sophie Calle das Photo eines Vorraums mit zwei leeren
Sesseln. Dieses Motiv des leeren Stuhls erscheint noch einmal bildfüllend,
als Myriam V. von Pierre D. erzählt und Sophie den Lederfauteuil zeigt, in
dem Pierre D. immer gesessen hat.

Auch Pierre D. wird, je länger von ihm die Rede ist, zunehmend ein
Abwesender, ein Unwirklicher, ja fast schon ein Untoter und Wiedergänger.
Er sei eine Wolke in Hosen, lässt Sophie Calle (die übrigens bei Myriam V.
längst Pierres Platz im Fauteuil eingenommen hat) Marianne B., eine
andere Bekannte, Majakovsky zitieren und von Pierre D. sagen, sein Leben
sei rein klar, enthalte nichts Verwerfliches, was auf keinen Lebenden zu-
treffen kann. Dazu sahen die Leser von *Libération* das Bild eines Mannes am
Fenster, wie in einem derealisierten Transit-Raum zwischen Fensterglas und
Tüllvorhang, an einem Übergang. Schliesslich Sylvie B., die von Pierre
erzählt, er wäre fähig zu verschwinden, ohne eine Spur zu hinterlassen, und
von einem Text berichtet, den ihr Pierre D. angeblich gezeigt hat, einen
selbstverfassten Text zu einer Darstellung der Pyramiden, wo er seine
ägyptologischen Sehnsüchte enthüllt, wie er unberührte Gräber entdecken
wollte und warum er heute als Filmdrehbuchschreiber nicht das Gefühl
habe, den Beruf verfehlt zu haben, denn: «... ob Mumienhülle oder
Filmband, haben sie nicht beide die Aufgabe, die Bilder des Körpers zu
konservieren?»

Pierre D.s symbolisches Sterben ist unaufhaltsam. Er habe, so Pascal, seit
dem Tod seiner Mutter bereits als junger Mann weisse Haare, ja, zeige
Anzeichen eines «frühzeitigen Alterungsprozesses». Zweimal taucht das
Motiv der Grabsteine auf, einmal auf dem Friedhof von V., wo Sophie Calle
ein Grab photographiert, das sie in Pierre D.s Adressbuch verzeichnet findet. Die Inschrift ist verwischt, gelöscht. Es ist der Grabstein *(La pierre!),* den
die Künstlerin Sophie Calle gewissermassen symbolisch für Pierre D.
bestimmt hat.

SOPHIE CALLE, SUITE VÉNITIENNE,
Collection Ecrits sur l'image, Editions de
l'Etoile, Paris 1983.

Wie kein anderes Medium täuschen Photographien über ihren Wirklichkeitsbezug hinweg. Erst seit der Digitalisierung, das heisst der völligen technischen Manipulierbarkeit von photographischen Bildern, wird dieser Tatbestand (der natürlich auch für alle auf die Photographie folgenden Medien paradigmatisch ist) gleichsam evident. Photographien sind immer Stories, nie Abbilder, nie blosser nüchterner Report, sondern immer von emotionalen Absichten getränkte Kolportagen. Photographien sind apparatisch genormte Wunschbilder, ihr Stoff besteht aus fragmentarischer Wirklichkeit. In diesem Sinne sind Sophie Calles mit ausführlichen Legenden versehene Photographien wunderbar essentielle Lichtbilder, reine, apparatische Projektion. Sophie Calle projiziert Pierre D.s Namensschriftzug auf den fremden Grabstein, bis er dort ebenso wirklich «erscheint», wie auf der Seite 10 der *Libération* vom 28. September 1983, wenn ein gewisser Pierre Baudry in einem ziemlich empörten, ja verletzten Antwortschreiben behauptet, eben jener Pierre D. zu sein…

Und Sophie imaginiert Henri B. in den von Melancholie und Motiven romantischen Verfalls überwucherten venezianischen Friedhof hinein, bis er dort so abwesend/anwesend ist, wie auf jenen heimlichen Schnappschüssen, auf denen er – angeblich – zu «sehen» ist, immer von hinten und aus jener Distanz der heimlichen Überwachung, die Sophie Calle zu ihrer ebenso einfachen wie zwingenden (und deshalb genialen) Lösung des künstlerisch-photographischen Distanzproblems benutzt hat. Diese, ihre Distanz zum künstlerischen – meist männlichen – Objekt der Begierde ist so existentiell-notwendig und zugleich praktisch, wie bei einem Dompteur, der die Erkenntnisse der Verhaltenslehre über Flucht- und Angriffsdistanz für die Dressur seiner wilden Raubtiere nutzt. Verwischte Grabinschriften bedeuten die unerträgliche Verdichtung, die Apotheose von Abwesenheit, denn Grabinschriften (Grabstätten sind Geburtsstätten der Schrift) müssen Genaueres erzählen über diese Absenzen von Leben; die Inschrift nennt einen Namen und berichtet, dass da ein Leben war, wo und wann es begann und endete.

Grabsteine markieren Orte der Vollendung und sind selbst gewissermassen vollendete Orte: primäre und endgültige Schrift – und Bildträger, Orte der vollendeten Imagination, vor allem dort, wo sich auf einem Grabmal eine Photographie findet (neben dem Photoalbum einer der wenigen Orte, wo Photos von Menschen tatsächlich auf richtige Art ihre letzte Ruhe finden!), oder dort eben, wo jemand einen Grabstein photographiert, was in beiden Fällen die Grabinschrift als Matrix aller photographischen Legenden offenbart.

Bei Photos von Grabsteinen verschwindet – ebenso zwingend und elegant wie die Distanzfrage beim Überwachen – ein photographisches Kardinalproblem: die Bildlegende. Das Photo eines Grabsteins (und ausschliesslich aus solchen besteht LES TOMBES, eine Arbeit Calles von 1991) ist gewissermassen eine perfekte Photographie: Ihre Legende ist Teil des Bildes und bespricht, ja benennt das photographische Wesen: die Abbildung des Abwesenden.

PATRICK FREY

Tombstones, Inscriptions, Photographs, Captions: The Hyperfiction of Life and Death

Works of art, especially when they appear to be immediate and true to life (an a priori assumption of photography), have an inexorable finality that is not for but rather against life, a coldness, a cruelty that goes hand-in-hand with their faculty for dissecting or freezing life.

In 1980, Sophie Calle spent months shadowing strangers in the streets of Paris, not because they interested her, as she said herself, but because of the pleasurable excitement of secret activity. Having photographed them without their knowledge, she would let them disappear from sight and look for new, unwitting subjects. It so happened one evening that she was introduced to one of her victims, Henri B. On learning that he would travel to Venice, she decided to follow him. That decision resulted in SUITE VENITIENNE, a report that is as hyperreal as it is hyperfictional, consisting of written passages, photographs, and maps tracing the routes of pursuit. Henri B.'s ordinary existence becomes strange and mysterious not because Sophie Calle came across tidbits revealing that the journey was more than a mere vacation trip to Venice; no, it is rather her own secret existence, which becomes the mystery of Henri B.'s life. Sophie Calle is the shadow that falls on his life. On the eighth day of her search, after she has finally caught sight of him, seen him through the eye of the camera, and lost him again after an hour, she notes down that at their first brief encounter she learned only that he loved cemeteries. Thus, she proceeds to visit the Jewish cemetery at the Lido and takes two pictures of crumbling tombstones. Henri B. is not there. She writes, "He should have been here. I was counting on him so heavily."

All art reaches beyond the living, beyond the real, to the dead; the art of death as an antidote to death-as-disappearance, to vanishing without a trace.

ON THE MOTIF OF ABSENCE IN TWO EARLY WORKS BY SOPHIE CALLE

For months I followed strangers on the street. For the pleasure of following them, not because they particularly interested me. I photographed them without their knowledge, took note of their movements, then finally lost sight of them and forgot them.

At the end of January 1979, on the streets of Paris, I followed a man whom I lost sight of a few minutes later in the crowd. That very evening quite by chance, he was introduced to me at an opening. During the course of our conversation, he told me he was planning an imminent trip to Venice. I decided then to attach myself to his steps and to introduce myself into his life.

PATRICK FREY is a performer, critic, and publisher in Zurich.

SOPHIE CALLE, *L'HOMME AU CARNET,*
(THE MAN WITH THE ADDRESS BOOK /
DER MANN MIT DEM ADRESSBUCH),
Libération, August 2 to September 4, 1983,
30 photos and text in daily newspaper /
30 Photos und Text in Tageszeitung.

Paris. End of June. Street of Martyrs. I find an address book. I pick it up, make a photocopy of it and send it back anonymously to its owner. His name is Pierre D. I will ask people listed in the address book to talk to me about him. Every day, through them, I will get closer to him.
■
Paris. Ende Juni. Rue des Martyrs. Ich finde ein Adressbuch. Ich hebe es auf, mache eine Photokopie davon und schicke es anonym an seinen Besitzer zurück. Er heisst Pierre D. Ich werde Leute, die im Adressbuch aufgeführt sind, fragen, mit mir über ihn zu sprechen. Jeden Tag werde ich durch sie ihm etwas näherkommen.

Art as the attempt to exorcise death, to ban it in the midst of life and thus to escape it. Art—and most intensely, the art of photography—is always art of the tombstone. Tombstones are primarily art-things. They stand as petrified primeval artistic gestures at a site of transition, where the tributary of each life flows into the great collective current. Their presence stands for an absent person, for the fact of absence.

When Sophie Calle found Pierre D.'s address book on the Rue des Martyrs in June 1983, she decided to move in on him by talking to the people listed in his address book and to publish the intelligence thus acquired in the daily newspaper *Libération* for the duration of one month. The very name of the street where she found the address book presages the fate that Pierre D.'s identity would undergo in the course of her undertaking. The first time she calls him, his answering machine speaks the truth, "I am absent. I am not here." Sophie Calle links these words with the photograph of a reception room and two empty armchairs. The motif of the empty chair reappears when Myriam V. talks about Pierre D. and the leather armchair in which he used to sit when he came to see her. This time the armchair in Calle's photograph fills the entire picture space. The more people talk about him, the more absent this Pierre D. becomes, an unreal being, almost like one of the living dead or a zombie. He is a cloud in trousers, says Sophie Calle (who has long since taken Pierre's place in Myriam V.'s armchair), quoting another friend, Marianne B., who was quoting Mayakovsky to describe Pierre, adding that his life contained nothing reprehensible, that it was pure, limpid—a condition that could never apply to a living person. In connection with Marianne B.'s remarks, the readers of *Libération* see a picture of a man at a window, as if in a derealized space of transit and transition between window pane and curtains. Finally Sylvie B. declares that it is typical of Pierre to disappear without a trace and tells Calle about a text Pierre supposedly showed her that he wrote himself, reflections on a picture of the Pyramids, in which he reveals his infatuation with Egyptology, his desire to discover untouched graves, and why, as a scriptwriter, he does not have the feeling that he has missed his calling because "... whether mummies or film footage, don't they both have the task of conserving images of the body?"

Pierre D.'s symbolic dying is relentless. His hair, according to Pascal, turned white upon the death of his mother when he was still a young man, and he soon showed signs of premature aging.

Twice the motif of the tombstone occurs, once in the cemetery of V., where Sophie Calle photographs a grave that Pierre D. noted in his address book. The inscription is blurred, wiped out. It is the gravestone *(La pierre!)* that artist Sophie Calle has chosen—symbolically—for Pierre D.

Like no other medium, photographs fake the fact of their relation to reality. Only since the advent of digitalization, that is, the ability to manipulate photographed images at will, has this circumstance become obvious (although it is, of course, a paradigmatic feature of all postphotographic media). Photographs are always stories; they do not represent, they do not report, they do not impart disinterested detachment; instead they gossip,

Libération, Thursday August 29, 1983

Thursday
Anne E. 7.00–8.00 p.m.

She lives with Charles C. It is her turn to be questioned about Pierre. She tells me that he stops by at their place when he goes to see his father who lives on the first floor.

"He is a strange character. Full of possibilities that he does not exploit. His mind is always filled with ideas. He asks people what they think about them because he always needs advice, and then he does not follow through." She also says: "He's a little boy." Anne remembers when Pierre had spent several days at Gordes with them. During the night, she and Charles had heard a disturbing noise. They woke Pierre up to ask him if he had noticed anything strange. He was very angry to have been awakened in the middle of the night. Raving mad even. A bit rude.

No, Anne does not know if he was wearing pyjamas or not, but she is sure that he did not sleep in the nude although it was very hot.

Other impressions about Pierre? "He loves food. He always finishes everything on his plate. It is not hunger, but rather a certain behavior. Another typical thing, the day after an encounter or a dinner, he calls you to thank you, to say how nice it was. When he arrives at a person's house, he makes excuses. During the first thirty seconds, you feel that he does not know what to do with himself. He performs a kind of rather obsequious ceremonial: 'Excuse me…,' 'You're sure I'm not disturbing you?' When he leaves a message on the answering machine, it is always very confused. He is not good at condensing ideas. He has to call back several times."

I ask Anne if there are any objects that belong to Pierre in her house? No. For ten years they had a painting that he painted hanging on the wall. It was 20 x 24". It was very abstract, in brown and russet tones; it was on loan, and they returned it. Recently, Pierre forgot a fancy ball-point pen, but he had already gotten it back. He had also made some coffee liqueur for them, but they had finished it. Before I leave, Anne and Charles show me the windows of Pierre's father's apartment that you can see from their terrace. The metal curtain is closed since he is in the country.

In the hallway of the building, by slipping my hand into the mailbox I can check that the mail is piling up.

Libération, Donnerstag, 29. August, 1983

Donnerstag
Anne E. 19.00-20.00 Uhr

Sie lebt mit Charles C. Sie ist an der Reihe, über Pierre befragt zu werden. Sie erzählt mir, dass er bei ihnen vorbeikommt, wenn er seinen Vater besucht, der im Erdgeschoss wohnt.

«Er ist ein merkwürdiger Typ. Voller Möglichkeiten, die er nicht ausnutzt. Sein Kopf ist immer voller Ideen. Er fragt Leute, was sie von ihnen halten, da er immer Rat braucht, und dann befolgt er ihn nicht.» Sie sagt weiterhin: «Er ist ein kleiner Junge.» Anne erinnert sich daran, wie Pierre einige Tage mit ihnen in Gordes verbrachte. Mitten in der Nacht hörten Charles und sie ein beunruhigendes Geräusch. Sie weckten Pierre auf und fragten ihn, ob auch er etwas Merkwürdiges gehört hätte. Er war sehr verärgert, mitten in der Nacht aufgeweckt zu werden. Sogar fuchsteufelswild. Ziemlich grob.

Nein, Anne wisse nicht, ob er einen Schlafanzug getragen hatte oder nicht, aber sie sei sicher, dass er nicht nackt schlief, obwohl es sehr heiss war.

Andere Impressionen von Pierre? «Er isst gern. Er isst immer seinen Teller leer. Es ist kein Hunger, sondern eine Verhaltensweise. Eine andere typische Sache, am Tag nach einer Begegnung oder einem Essen ruft er dich an, um sich zu bedanken und zu sagen, wie schön es gewesen war. Wenn er bei jemandem eintritt, entschuldigt er sich. In den ersten dreissig Sekunden hat man das Gefühl, dass er nicht weiss, was er mit sich anfangen soll. Er vollführt ein ziemlich unterwürfiges Ritual: «Entschuldigt mich…,» «Seid ihr sicher, dass ich euch nicht störe?» Wenn er auf dem Telefonbeantworter eine Nachricht hinterlässt, so ist sie immer etwas konfus. Ideen zusammenzufassen ist nicht seine Stärke. Er muss einige Male zurückrufen.»

Ich frage Anne, ob es in ihrer Wohnung Gegenstände gäbe, die Pierre gehören? Nein. Zehn Jahre lang wäre ein Bild, das er gemalt hatte, an der Wand gehangen. Es war 51 x 61 cm. Es war sehr abstrakt, in Braun- und Rosttönen; es war eine Leihgabe, und sie hätten es zurückgegeben. Vor kurzem hätte Pierre einen teuren Kugelschreiber vergessen, aber er hätte ihn schon wieder zurück. Er hätte für sie Kaffeelikör gemacht, aber sie hätten ihn schon getrunken. Bevor ich gehe, zeigen mir Anne und Charles die Fenster der Wohnung von Pierres Vater, die man von ihrer Terrasse sehen kann. Die Rolläden sind heruntergelassen, da er auf dem Land ist.

Im Foyer des Gebäudes lasse ich meine Hand in den Briefkasten gleiten und merke, wie sich darin die Post stapelt.

they are drenched in emotional intent. Photographs are apparatically standardized dream pictures, their content consists of fragments of reality. In this sense, Sophie Calle's elaborately captioned photographs are marvellously essential; they are apparatic projections. Sophie Calle projects the letters of Pierre D.'s name onto someone else's tombstone until its appearance there is as "real" as the letter published on the tenth page of the September 28, 1983 issue of *Libération,* in which a certain Pierre Baudry writes an indignant, in fact, extremely hurt letter claiming that he is Pierre D.

And Sophie Calle spirits Henri B. into that Venetian cemetery rampant with melancholy and the motifs of romantic decay until he is as absent/present there as he is in the secret snapshots where he can—supposedly—be "seen," always from the back and at the discreet distance dictated by secret pursuit, a deceptively simple, compelling (and ingenious) device, employed by Sophie Calle to solve the artistic/photographic dilemma of distance.

Distance from her artistic—usually male—object of desire is as much an existential and practical necessity for her as it is for a tamer who exploits the laws of distance in escape-and-attack behavior to train his wild animals.

Weathered inscriptions on tombstones signify unbearable compression, the apotheosis of absence, because tombstone inscriptions (the tomb is the birthplace of writing) must provide more precise information about these absent lives; the inscription gives a name, reports the fact of a life, where and when it began and ended.

Gravestones mark the locus of finality and are themselves finalized places: first and final vehicles of letter and image, places of finalized imagination, even more so when a photograph graces the tombstone (which, like the photo album, is one of the few loci where photographs of people actually find an appropriate resting place!) or, as in Sophie Calle's work, when someone takes a picture of a tombstone. In both cases the inscription functions as the matrix of the photographic caption per se.

Photographs of tombstones eliminate this cardinal issue in photography—the caption—in a manner as compelling and elegant as Calle's solution to the problem of distance and surveillance. A picture of a tombstone (which is the exclusive subject matter of LES TOMBES, 1991) is in a sense the perfect photograph. Its caption is part of the picture and discusses, indeed names, the photographic being: the representation of the absent person.

(Translation: Catherine Schelbert)

L'HOMME AU CARNET *A PARTIR DE DEMAIN DANS LIBERATION*

Le carnet de Sophie Calle

C'est maintenant une habitude. Chaque été, durant un mois, une demi-page de *Libération* attend la livraison quotidienne d'un photographe. Un espace autonome réservé à l'image, pour le feuilleton d'un auteur qui, souvent, emploie davantage les visions que les démonstrations. Ce fut le cas avec Raymond Depardon qui nous expédiait le New York sa correspondance, puis avec François Hers qui nous proposait un Paris baroque, architectural, graphique et presque totalement déserté.

Tout cela se situait, avec des modalités et des auteurs particuliers, dans la lignée directe du reportage. Qu'il ait été intimiste ou plus intellectuel pour la première ouverture d'un quotidien à ce statut du photographe relevait de ce choix. Cet été, nous continuons avec une autre forme de publication au jour le jour. Avec, une fois de plus, le désir de faire apparaître dans un quotidien des types d'images et des statuts que l'information ignore. Nous aurions pu puiser tel ou tel travail remarquable de reporters sur un pays, continuer les balades personnelles de grande qualité graphique. Nous aurions eu un peu le sentiment de nous répéter et, surtout, de ne pas avancer dans la multiplication des formes d'images que doit véhiculer un quotidien.

Une autre forme de « reportage », donc, pour l'été 1983. Un feuilleton réalisé par une artiste bien particulière qui se nomme Sophie Calle. Une artiste qui travaille avec les mots et les images, suivant des obsessions, des fantasmes, inventant des histoires et nous étonnant plus d'une fois des narrations qu'elle suscite. Son premier travail connu — elle n'a pour l'instant pas révélé ses carnets, véritables mines

de chroniques étonnantes et passionnelles -s'intitulait *les Dormeurs.* Sophie Calle avait demandé à des gens qu'elle ne connaissait pas de se succéder dans son lit durant huit heures d'affilée. Toutes les heures, la photographe opérait et, durant l'expérience, prenait des notes sur chacun de ses patients ou intervenants. L'expérience commençant au premier avril, ajoutons pour l'anecdote que le poisson rouge acheté par Sophie Calle pour l'occasion et proposé en cadeau à chacun des occupants temporaires du lit qui la refusèrent se suicida le dernier jour en sautant du bocal.

Deuxième travail, exposé à Beaubourg, un autoportrait pas comme les autres. Pour une exposition consacrée à ce thème, Sophie Calle fut invitée. Elle décida de se faire suivre durant une semaine par un détective privé et exposa le résultat de l'enquête le concernant.

Mais c'est cette année, avec la publication de son livre *Suite vénitienne* (1), que Sophie Calle a largement présenté son travail. Apprenant qu'un homme qu'elle avait suivi dans la rue partait pour Venise, elle décide de l'y rejoindre et de l'espionner, de le retrouver, de le suivre, de connaître ses moindres faits et gestes. Elle y parvint, puis se fait repérer et réussit à rentrer à Paris par un train différent de celui de son « modèle » qu'elle immortalise une dernière fois où sa arrivée à la Gare de Lyon. Avec ce livre, Sophie Calle proposait un type particulier de récit, utilisant souvent la photographie comme une forme de preuve, mais qui existe davantage par la relation entre le texte et les images que par la force de chacun des éléments. Beaucoup de photos ne présentent pas d'intérêt graphique particulier et le texte, de facture simple et claire, fait de notes scrupuleuses

et de quelques réflexions personnelles. Mais l'histoire est passionnelle, le récit s'invente entre les photographies et les mots, pétri d'une tension entre deux formes de narrations parallèles.

Avec sa dernière exposition à la galerie Chantal Crousel, Sophie Calle proposait une autre étape, policière - voyeuse et constat -. Engagée dans un grand hôtel de Venise comme femme de chambre, Sophie Calle a enregistré, noté, mis en forme ce que des détails lui disaient de la vie et de la personnalité des clients de l'hôtel dont elle préparait les chambres. Curiosité et

romanesque, attention au détail, passion de l'enquête, terrible portrait d'inconnus qui vous font penser que vous avez eu de la chance de ne pas tomber sur cette femme de chambre d'un autre un peu spécial qui cache son Leica et son carnet de notes sous la serpillière.

Pour notre feuilleton de l'été, Sophie Calle a réalisé une nouvelle histoire. Une histoire de carnet d'adresses. Une histoire toute simple, en fait. Un jour de fin juin, elle découvre un carnet d'adresses perdu par son propriétaire. Elle le ramasse, le photocopie et le renvoie immédiatement à celui dont le nom figure sur la page de garde. Puis elle décide d'appeler des numéros contenus dans le carnet. But de l'opération : faire le portrait d'un individu à travers ce que ses proches — ou supposés tels puisqu'ils sont dans son carnet — disent de lui, confient de lui. Un parti de portrait par personnes interposées, un jeu de puzzle laissant une large place au hasard pour enquêter sur un propriétaire de carnet d'adresses au-dessus de tout soupçon.

Pour construire, liant images et textes, un récit. Un portrait par touches et par épisodes, la découverte d'un inconnu dont nous ne saurons peut-être jamais qui il est vraiment. Ce portrait sera aussi le récit de sa constitution par bribes, avec les échecs et les émotions, les découvertes, les banalités, les contradictions.

Sophie Calle a donc trouvé un carnet d'adresses perdu. C'est devenu une histoire. Un récit. Une aventure ordinaire, au coin de la rue, qui pourrait bien nous arriver pour peu que nous le vouliions. Ça commence demain.

Christian CAUJOLLE

(1) Éditions de l'Étoile, post-face de Jean Baudrillard.

ROBERT BECK

Paranoia by the dashboard light: *SOPHIE CALLE'S AND GREGORY SHEPHARD'S* DOUBLE BLIND

I remember standing at my grandmother's grave with my father and grandfather looking down at the dates on her stone when my grandfather said, "You know, Jimmy, your mother used to sleep around." My father didn't answer, as if he'd heard it all before. We just got in the car and left. Looking back now, I understand that conversation was older than all of us. It hadn't changed.

GREGORY SHEPHARD

Years ago my father told me I had bad breath. He made me an appointment with a generalist. When I arrived, I realized it was a psychoanalyst. I could not believe my father had sent me to one, knowing his allergy to them. My first comment to the doctor was "There must be some mistake. My father sent me to see a generalist because he said I had bad breath." And the man replied, "You do everything your father tells you to do?" I became his patient.

SOPHIE CALLE

DOUBLE BLIND is the story of two artists, Sophie Calle and Gregory Shephard, who drive cross country at cross purposes—her aim is to marry him, his aim is to make a movie. Armed with small-format video camcorders, the two take aim at each other, and somehow manage to make a movie of their marriage. From courtship through climax to dénouement, meandering from New York to Oakland via Las Vegas in his Cadillac convertible, the couple is continually at odds. The difference between his story and hers is the story the tape has to tell, which places DOUBLE BLIND in somewhat of a narrative double bind. Struggling to negotiate the sexual difference of these two very uneasy riders—who do not drive so much as they are driven in flights towards opposing fantasies—DOUBLE BLIND dramatizes just how compulsory heterosexuality is.[1]

The shot/reverse-shot, a traditional cinematic editing technique used to integrate two opposing perspectives, provided the artists with a practical way with which to unify hours of video material shot from their differing points of view. Conventionally, this cinematic device sutures a world authored by a single director. In DOUBLE BLIND it must do double-time, stitching together the wildly discordant perspectives of two antagonistic authors into a unified whole. Both want to enunciate a narrative of a fantasy that persists, an image of themselves as desirable to the other—hers of womanliness in wedlock, his of manliness in moviemaking. As the organizing principle

---

ROBERT BECK is an artist living in New York.

of the tape, the shot/reverse-shot metaphorically exemplifies the couple's opposing desires, representing the struggle for narrative authorship that endlessly wages between them.

With each author participating in the production of the video—both as subject behind the camcorder and as object before it—the male/female binary, at least as it is maintained in mainstream cinematic narrative, is destabilized here. His gaze does not hit the side of her face but the lens of her camcorder, which she trains on him in objection to her own objectification. This is exemplified in a scene in which the two confront one another, camcorder to camcorder, like

SOPHIE CALLE / GREG SHEPHARD
DOUBLE BLIND, 1992
Video, color, sound; 76 min
Production: Bohen Foundation
Postproduction: San Francisco Art Space
Cut: Michael Penhallow
Distribution: Electronic Arts Intermix, New York

a pair of cyclops spawned by SONY. Simultaneously recorded and recording, they each strangely mirror the other in their shot/reverse-shot battle. Here sexual difference does not neatly fold into one—the masculine. And because both look and are looked at, male/female does not conveniently correspond to active/passive. As for the old Lacanian "being vs. having" charade, she may or may not be the image, he may or may not have it.

Symptomatic of this near breakdown, and enhanced by the shot/reverse-shot system, is the latent paranoia the couple experiences at points along the way—as Gregory whispers, "I'm glad she can't hear my mind." The more he withholds "it" ("No sex last night" is her resigned refrain), the further Sophie probes ("You're constantly searching through and turning up evidence of things; invasion of privacy, which you specialize in" is his defense). As the cherished dichotomy of male/female teeters, the artists scramble to secure it, reinforcing other dualisms throughout the tape.

While the coast-to-coast world outside the car is frozen in still images of so many generic roadside sites, the lovers' dashboard romance expands inside in real-time, relative to the claustrophobic universe

Ich dachte, er würde mich filmen, nicht den Wagen.

fiction. These binarisms all but disappear on the occasion of the couple's wedding in Las Vegas at a drive-through chapel. This is the "primal scene" of DOUBLE BLIND, the couple's desired destination. With the convertible roof down, cameras fixed at a distance, and the artists pronounced man and wife, interior opens onto exterior, shot/reverse-shot gives way to an establishing one, and thought becomes action with the words, "I do." If only for a moment, the marriage unifies the discordant narratives, dispels doubt, and abolishes the artists' mutual ambivalence. With the ring she is wed to her fantasy "that a man wanted me enough to marry me." And his filmmaking fantasy is framed with the establishing shot— a camera angle that in narrative cinema connotes "objectivity." When the groom kisses the bride, the artists acknowledge the narrative fulfillment provided by the scene, sealing it with a superimposed red heart—love American style.

When Sophie comments over a still of Gregory carrying her across the threshold of a storybook cottage, "This is how it all began," the cause of DOUBLE BLIND as an effect of the countless romantic narratives that precede it becomes clear. With unhappiness following the couple's happily-ever-after so closely, the tape exposes normative gender as the ruse that it is—promised by the ritual of marriage yet never inhabitable as husband and wife. Accordingly, gender accumulates "authenticity" through its repetition as a performance. Therefore, despite the artists' best efforts, neither he nor she can "be" a gender; they can only "do" one through repeat performances.[2] This may be why their roadway romance is refracted through an endless succession of personal narratives—memories, anecdotes, stories, fantasies, reveries—all of which "naturalize" sexual difference.

In the classic cinematic narrative, woman often stands as the sign of sexual difference, fetishized as the other for a masculine gaze, an "objectivity" which consolidates his identity. DOUBLE BLIND does not overlook the significance of Sophie Calle's willful participation in rehearsing this narrative as a reality. Indivisible from the romantic fantasy, misogyny and masochism are re-presented here as everyday experiences, sanctioned by the institution of marriage. As Gregory says, "Just the fact that we were married...

they inhabit there. As perhaps the most drastic division of narrative cohesion, the seamlessness of the soundtrack is split between his thoughts and hers, whispered in betrayal of their exchanged words and actions. Reading from diaries logged daily throughout the trip, or spoken spontaneously in often mean-spirited retorts, their conflicting voice-over commentaries ultimately contest the verisimilitude of their life together through a viewfinder. Each fights for his or her story as fact, the other's as fiction.

The gendered bifurcation of the narrative also contests the tape's easy classification as one genre or the other. Is it a road movie—a man's flight from social conformity to a place outside the law—or a melodrama—"a woman's film" of life at home within the law? Inverting the codes of the traditional road movie, the artists' flight is not an escape from a suffocating social order but one moving towards it via marriage. And, with sexual difference portrayed as a protracted conflict between the protagonists, a woman's place is clearly no longer in the home. If a genre has a gender, then as a melodramatic road movie, DOUBLE BLIND is a genre-bender.

Road movie/melodrama, shot/reverse-shot, inside/outside, static/moving, thoughts/actions, fact/

Er schaut sein Auto an, als würde er
seiner Frau bei der Geburt ihres Kindes zuschauen.

Es bleiben mir nur noch zwei Tage,
um mir eine gute Erinnerung an diese Reise zu verschaffen.

made me want to take you. And not for one second did I want to ask, or need to ask, or feel I should ask. I just felt I wanted to take you. I'm getting an erection just thinking about it." And as she responds, though only to herself, "That's the first thing marriage has given me." In DOUBLE BLIND, the question raised by Calle's pursuit of the romantic promise offered by the classic cinematic narrative may be understood not as Freud's "What does she want?" but, as Parveen Adams has stated, "How can she want?"[3]

Making a mockery of the artist's anxious passive/aggressive attempts to do otherwise, DOUBLE BLIND problematizes being/having from male/female through the simultaneous presentation of its directors' dynamically opposing points of view. Poking holes in the romantic narrative at the level of cinematic enunciation, the artists denaturalize gender uniformity, which they respond to reciprocally at the level of fantasy. Stranded without the classic cinematic narrative compass of male/female, the spectator's identification must be redirected along the routes of active/passive. The title DOUBLE BLIND may suggest, psychoanalytically, in its metaphorical reference to a blindness experienced by both artists,

that the passage through the original (Oedipal) drama to the sexual difference of its dénouement may not be so dissimilar for boy and girl. Again the question, "What does she want?", is here mirrored by a subsequent one, "What does he want?" Gregory's ambiguous answer in the end, "To try and tell an honest story," hints at the "dishonesty" of DOUBLE BLIND, its dramatic failure to fortify identity on the foundation of heterosexual norms. Repeating the narrative means repeating the role—once more with feeling. Both illusive and elusive, "being" is the affect of "doing" gender, an encore performance in the compulsion to repeat. After all, as Gregory muses somewhere along the way, "It's good to have these destinations until you get there, and then what?"

1) Monique Wittig, "The Straight Mind." Reprinted in Out There: Marginalization and Contemporary Culture, New York and Cambridge, MA, The New Museum of Contemporary Art and M.I.T. Press, 1990.
2) "... the 'unity' of a gender is the effect of a regulatory practice that seeks to regulate gender identity uniform through a compulsory heterosexuality." In: Judith Butler, Gender Trouble, New York, Routledge, Chapman & Hall, 1990.
3) Parveen Adams, "The Three (Dis)Graces," unpublished paper, 1992.

ROBERT BECK

Paranoia hinterm Arma-
turenbrett: *SOPHIE CALLES*
UND GREGORY SHEPHARDS
DOUBLE BLIND

«Ich erinnere mich, wie ich mit meinem Vater und Grossvater am Grab meiner Grossmutter stand und die Inschrift auf ihrem Grabstein las, als mein Grossvater sagte: ‹Weisst du, Jimmy, deine Mutter ging mit jedem ins Bett.› Mein Vater antwortete nicht, so, als hätte er das alles schon mal gehört. Wir stiegen einfach in den Wagen und fuhren los. Wenn ich jetzt daran zurückdenke, begreife ich, dass dieses Gespräch älter war als wir alle. Es hatte sich nicht verändert.»

GREGORY SHEPHARD

«Vor Jahren sagte mein Vater zu mir, ich hätte Mundgeruch. Er vereinbarte für mich einen Termin bei einem praktischen Arzt. Als ich dort ankam, merkte ich, dass es ein Psychoanalytiker war. Ich konnte nicht glauben, dass mein Vater mich dorthin geschickt hatte, wo ich doch wusste, wie allergisch er gegen sie war. Meine erste Bemerkung zu dem Arzt war: ‹Da muss ein Missverständnis vorliegen. Mein Vater hat mich zu einem praktischen Arzt geschickt, weil er sagte, ich hätte Mundgeruch›. Und der Mann erwiderte: ‹Tun Sie alles, was Ihr Vater Ihnen sagt?› Ich wurde seine Patientin.»

SOPHIE CALLE

DOUBLE BLIND ist die Geschichte zweier Künstler, Sophie Calle und Gregory Shephard, die kreuz und quer durch die USA fahren und dabei entgegengesetzte Ziele verfolgen – ihr Ziel ist es, ihn zu heiraten, sein Ziel dagegen, einen Film zu machen. Mit kleinformatigen Video-Camcordern ausgerüstet, legen die beiden aufeinander an, und irgendwie gelingt es ihnen, einen Film über ihre Heirat zu drehen. Das Paar liegt ununterbrochen im Streit – von der Zeit der jungen Liebe über den Höhepunkt bis zur Auflösung –, während es in seinem Cadillac Kabriolett (auf verschlungenen Wegen) von New York via Las Vegas nach Oakland irrt. Der Unterschied zwischen seiner Geschichte und ihrer ist die Geschichte, die der Film erzählen soll; dadurch gerät DOUBLE BLIND in eine Art erzählerische Doppelbindung (Schizophrenogene Interaktion, in der widersprüchliche Informationen aufeinandertreffen. Anm. d. Red.). In dem Bemühen, den Geschlechtsunterschied zwischen den beiden ausgesprochen verkrampften Reisenden, diesen *un-Easy* Riders, zu überwinden – die weniger fahren, als dass sie zur Flucht in entgegengesetzte Phantasien getrieben werden –, thematisiert DOUBLE BLIND gerade den Zwangscharakter der Heterosexualität.[1] Das Verfahren Aufnahme/Gegenaufnahme, eine traditionelle

---

ROBERT BECK ist Künstler und lebt in New York.

Schnittechnik beim Film, die benutzt wird, um zwei entgegengesetzte Perspektiven zu integrieren, war für die Künstler eine praktische Möglichkeit, viele Stunden Videomaterial, die von ihren unterschiedlichen Standpunkten aus aufgenommen waren, zu verbinden. Üblicherweise wird mit diesem Kunstgriff im Film eine Welt zusammengeschnitten, die ein Regisseur allein entworfen hat. In DOUBLE BLIND ist verdoppelte Zeit zu bewältigen, die sich heftig widersprechenden Perspektiven zweier antagonistischer Autoren müssen zu einem einheitlichen Ganzen zusammengeflickt werden. Beiden geht es um die erzählerische Darstellung einer überdauernden Phantasie, eines Bildes von sich selbst, wie es dem jeweils anderen als begehrenswert erscheinen soll – ihres der Weiblichkeit in der Ehe, seines der Männlichkeit des Filmemachens. Das Prinzip Aufnahme/Gegenaufnahme, nach dem der Film aufgebaut ist, veranschaulicht die entgegengesetzten Wünsche des Paares und stellt den Kampf um die erzählerische Autorschaft dar, der endlos zwischen ihnen tobt.

Beide Autoren sind an der Produktion des Videos beteiligt – sowohl als Subjekt hinter dem Camcorder als auch als Objekt davor; dadurch wird hier der Dualismus männlich/weiblich, zumindest so, wie er im Kino dargestellt und aufrechterhalten wird, aus dem Gleichgewicht gebracht. Sein Blick trifft nicht auf ihr Profil, sondern auf das Objektiv ihres Camcorders, den sie als Protest gegen ihre eigene Vergegenständlichung auf ihn richtet. Das wird in einer Szene vorgeführt, in der die beiden sich gegenüberstehen, Camcorder gegen Camcorder, wie ein von SONY gezüchtetes Zyklopenpaar. Gleichzeitig aufgenommen und aufnehmend, ist in der Aufnahme/Gegenaufnahme-Schlacht jeder auf seltsame Art und Weise der Spiegel des anderen. Hier fächert sich die Geschlechterdifferenz für einmal nicht zusammen

SOPHIE CALLE / GREG SHEPHARD
DOUBLE BLIND, 1992
Video, Farbe, Ton; 76 min
Produktion: Bohen Foundation
Nachproduktion: San Francisco Art Space
Schnitt: Michael Penhallow
Verleih: Electronic Arts Intermix, New York

An diesem Morgen, als ich aufwachte, sagte ich zu ihm,
lass uns weggehen von Vegas, und er flüsterte:

zu einem Geschlecht – dem männlichen. Und weil beide sehen und gesehen werden, gibt es hier keine praktische Entsprechung zwischen männlich/weiblich und aktiv/passiv. Was die alte Lacansche Scharade «sein vs. haben» anbetrifft: vielleicht ist sie das Bild, vielleicht auch nicht, vielleicht hat er es, vielleicht auch nicht.

Die Paranoia, die das Paar in manchen Augenblicken seiner Reise erlebt, ist symptomatisch für den Beinahe-Zusammenbruch und wird noch durch die Aufnahme/Gegenaufnahme-Technik verstärkt – so flüstert Gregory: «Ich bin froh, dass sie meine Gedanken nicht hören kann.» Je mehr er ihr «es» entzieht («Kein Sex letzte Nacht», lautet ihr resignierter Refrain), um so mehr dringt Sophie Calle in ihn («Ununterbrochen durchsuchst du und förderst Beweismaterial zutage; Eingriff in die Privatsphäre, darauf bist du spezialisiert», lautet seine Verteidigung). Weil die bequeme Zweiteilung männlich/weiblich ins Wanken gerät, bemühen sich die Künstler, sie abzufedern, und bringen den ganzen Film hindurch andere Gegensätze (wieder) zur Geltung.

Während die Welt ausserhalb des Wagens, von der Ost- bis zur Westküste, in Standphotos so vieler allgemein-typischer Orte entlang des Weges erstarrt, entwickelt sich die Armaturenbrettromanze der Liebenden im Wagen in der Realzeit ihres klaustrophobischen Universums. In der vielleicht drastischsten Aufspaltung des erzählerischen Zusammenhangs teilt

sich die sonst nahtlose Tonspur in seine und ihre Gedanken, geflüsterte Treubrüche ihrer Worte und Taten. Ihre kontroversen Kommentare – vorgelesen aus ihren täglich geführten Reisetagebüchern oder in meist boshaften Entgegnungen spontan dahingesagt – zweifeln letztendlich die Wahrhaftigkeit ihres gemeinsamen Lebens im Bildsucher an. Jede/r kämpft darum, ihre/seine Geschichte als Wahrheit, die der/des anderen als Fiktion darzustellen.

Die durch die Geschlechterdifferenz geteilte Erzählung stellt auch die problemlose Zuordnung des Films zu dem einen oder anderen Genre in Frage. Handelt es sich um ein *Road-Movie* – ein Mann flieht aus der gesellschaftlichen Konformität und stellt sich ausserhalb des Gesetzes – oder um ein Melodrama – «einen Frauenfilm» über das häusliche Leben im Rahmen des Gesetzes? In Umkehrung der Regeln des traditionellen *Road-Movies* ist die Flucht der Künstler kein Entrinnen aus einer erdrückenden Gesellschaftsordnung, sondern mittels Heirat gerade eine Bewegung darauf zu. Weil die Geschlechterdifferenz als langwieriger Konflikt zwischen den Protagonisten geschildert wird, wird deutlich, dass der Platz einer Frau nicht mehr im Haus ist. Wenn man einem Genre ein Geschlecht zuordnen kann, dann ist DOUBLE BLIND als melodramatisches Road-Movie so etwas wie ein Genre-Zwitter.

Road-Movie/Melodrama, Aufnahme/Gegenaufnahme, innen/aussen, statisch/beweglich, Gedanken/

Taten, Wahrheit/Fiktion. Diese Dualismen verschwinden jedoch anlässlich der Hochzeit des Paares in einer *Drive-in*-Auto-Kapelle in Las Vegas. Das ist die «Schlüsselszene» in DOUBLE BLIND: das ersehnte Reiseziel des Paares. Durch das offene Verdeck, die in einem bestimmten Abstand fest angebrachten Kameras und die zu «Mann und Frau» erklärten Künstler öffnet sich das Innen dem Aussen, Aufnahme/Gegenaufnahme weichen einer Gesamtaufnahme, und mit dem Jawort wird der Gedanke zur Tat. Wenn auch nur für einen Augenblick: die Heirat vereinigt die sich widersprechenden Erzählungen, zerstreut die Zweifel und hebt die Ambivalenz der Künstler auf. Durch den Ring heiratet sie ihre Phantasie, «dass ein Mann sie genügend begehrt, um sie zu heiraten». Und seine Filmemacher-Phantasie wird durch die Gesamtaufnahme ausgedrückt – durch einen Kamerawinkel, der im Erzählkino gleichbedeutend ist mit «Objektivität». Als der Bräutigam die Braut küsst, erkennen die Künstler den in der Szene angelegten Höhepunkt an und besiegeln ihn mit einem sie überlagernden roten Herzen – Liebe auf amerikanisch.

Wenn Sophie zu einem Standphoto von Gregory, der sie über die Schwelle eines märchenhaften Häuschens trägt, kommentiert: «So fing alles an», dann wird deutlich, dass die Ursache für DOUBLE BLIND in der Wirkung der zahllosen, dem Film vorausgegangenen Liebesgeschichten liegt. Durch das Unglück, das so bald auf das Versprechen ungetrübten Glücks folgt, entlarvt der Film die präskriptive Geschlechtszugehörigkeit als das, was sie ist – ein Trick: im Heiratsritual wird etwas versprochen, was für Mann und Frau doch nie zu verwirklichen ist. Folglich steigt die «Authentizität» der Geschlechtsrolle durch ihre wiederholte Ausübung. Trotz aller Anstrengungen der Künstler kann deshalb weder er noch sie ein Geschlecht «sein»; sie können nur durch wiederholte Ausübung eins «tun».[2] Vielleicht ist das der Grund, warum ihre Landstrassen-Romanze durch eine endlose Folge von persönlichen Erzählungen gebrochen wird – Erinnerungen, Anekdoten, Geschichten, Phantasien, Tagträumereien –, die alle die Geschlechterdifferenz «als natürlich erklären».

In der klassischen Darstellung im Film steht die Frau als das Symbol für die Geschlechterdifferenz

und wird als das andere (Geschlecht) zum Fetisch
für den männlichen Blick, für eine «Objektivität»,
die seine Identität konsolidiert. DOUBLE BLIND
übersieht nicht die Bedeutung von Sophie Calles
bewusster Beteiligung beim Einüben dieser Darstellung als Realität. Frauenfeindlichkeit und Masochis-
mus sind untrennbar mit der romantischen Phantasie verbunden und werden hier als alltägliche, von
der Institution Ehe sanktionierte Erfahrungen dargestellt. Wie Gregory sagt: «Allein die Tatsache, dass
wir verheiratet waren..., weckte in mir das Verlangen, dich zu nehmen. Und nicht einen Augenblick
lang hatte ich den Wunsch, dich zu fragen, ich hatte
es weder nötig zu fragen, noch hatte ich das Gefühl,
ich sollte fragen. Ich fühlte einfach, dass ich dich
nehmen wollte. Ich kriege eine Erektion, wenn ich
nur daran denke.» Und wie sie, wenn auch nur zu
sich selbst, darauf erwidert: «Das ist das erste, was die
Ehe mir gebracht hat.» Die Frage, die sich durch
Sophie Calles Streben nach dem romantischen Versprechen, das von den klassischen Erzählungen des
Kinos vorgegeben wird, in DOUBLE BLIND stellt,
lautet weniger «Was will sie?», sondern vielmehr, wie
Parveen Adams es formuliert hat, «Wie kann sie
wollen?».[3]

DOUBLE BLIND macht sich lustig über die eifrigen
passiven/aggressiven Bemühungen der Künstler, es
anders zu machen, und problematisiert durch die

gleichzeitige Präsentation der dynamisch entgegengesetzten Standpunkte seiner Regisseure den Unterschied von sein/haben zu männlich/weiblich. Auf
der Ebene des filmischen Ausdrucks durchlöchern
die Künstler die romantische Darstellung, auf der
Ebene der Phantasie reagieren sie wechselseitig auf
die Geschlechterübereinstimmung männlich/weib-
lich und verfremden sie. Ohne den Kompass, den
die herkömmliche Kino-Erzählung des Männli-
chen/Weiblichen abgibt, muss die Identifizierung
des Zuschauers auf die Landkarte des Aktiven/Passi-
ven verwiesen werden. In seinem metaphorischen
Verweis auf eine von beiden Künstlern erfahrene
Blindheit mag der Filmtitel, psychoanalytisch betrachtet, darauf verweisen, dass für Jungen und
Mädchen das Erleben des ursprünglichen (ödipa-
len) Dramas bis zu seiner geschlechtsspezifischen
Auflösung vielleicht nicht so unterschiedlich ist.
Hier wird die Frage «Was will sie?» in einer nach-
folgenden «Was will er?» widergespiegelt. Gregorys
zweideutige Antwort am Schluss: «Versuchen, eine
ehrliche Geschichte zu erzählen», deutet auf die
«Unehrlichkeit» von DOUBLE BLIND, das dramati-
sche Misslingen seines Versuchs, Identität auf der
Grundlage der heterosexuellen Geschlechtsrollen zu
stärken. Die Erzählung zu wiederholen bedeutet, die
Rolle zu wiederholen – noch einmal mit Gefühl.
Gleichzeitig illusorisch und schwer fassbar ist im Sein
der Hang, Geschlecht zu «tun», eine nochmalige
Ausübung unter dem Zwang zur Wiederholung.
Schliesslich sagt Gregory irgendwo unterwegs grüb-
lerisch: «Es ist gut, diese Reiseziele zu haben, bis
man dort ankommt, und was dann?»

(Übersetzung: Bela Wohl)

1) Monique Wittig, «The Straight Mind», Nachdruck in *Out
There*: *Marginalization and Contemporary Culture*, New York, N.Y.,
and Cambridge, MA: The New Museum of Contemporary Art
and Massachusetts Institute of Technology, 1990.
2) «... die ‹Einheit› der Geschlechter ist die Wirkung einer
regulativen Praxis, die die Identität der Geschlechter durch
eine erzwungene Heterosexualität gleichzumachen sucht.» in:
Judith Butler, *Gender Trouble*, New York, Routledge, Chapman &
Hall, Inc., 1990.
3) Parveen Adams, «The Three (Dis)Graces», unveröffentlicht,
1992.

KIRBY GOOKIN

Dimensions variable: Liz Larner

Nestled in a velvety bed of yellow-dyed agar and buttermilk, an open-petaled pink orchid cradling a copper penny: Such is the image of Liz Larner's ORCHID, BUTTERMILK, PENNY as it appeared in her first show, *Room 9, Tropicana Hotel*, in Los Angeles in 1987. Part of her series, *Cultures*, ORCHID, BUTTERMILK, PENNY is a bacterial accumulation grown in a petri dish. In time, bacterial effusions built up around the decaying flower, the curdling buttermilk, and the oily residue of fingerprints left on the penny. The "machinations of the bacteria's metabolism" created a "kind of action painting, producing its own culture."[1] As the bacteria grew and mixed with the agar, a cosmos of different colored bubbles billowed like phosphenes shimmering against our closed eyelids.

Larner's *Cultures* are, literally, living organisms encapsulated in a scientific terrarium of contemporary culture. A photograph taken one week, two weeks, and three months later captures three completely different pictures of the same work. In the first, we see the ebullient hues of growing bacteria; in the last two, the rotted browns of the decomposed flower drained of life. Each moment in between appears in a different guise. Like nature, one must

view the *Cultures* phenomenologically. They are forever transforming, producing new residues, and engendering infinite potential pictures. Confronting them, one finds oneself recalling Goethe's observations on the Laocoön, "A true work of art will always have something of infinity in it to our minds, as well as a work of nature. We contemplate it, but it cannot be thoroughly understood, nor its essence nor its merit be clearly defined by words."[2]

The work of art's physical transformation is an inbuilt characteristic of Larner's project. Whether organic or inorganic, her sculptures always retain a quality of animation. As Larner experiments with diverse materials, often pitting one against another, the resulting works are inherently volatile. In some, this volatility may only be implied, as in USED TO DO THE JOB (1987) where all of the components necessary to build an explosive device are embedded in a wax cube; in others, it is an integral factor of the composition that the final presentation or "completion" be dependent on the participation of the owner, curator, or viewer. BALL SYSTEM (1988) comprises a seemingly complex array of components (spheres of different materials, stainless steel wire racks, collapsible crate) with no instructions as to how they are to be presented. NO M, NO D, ONLY S & B (1990) is similarly amorphous: three weighted patchwork leather sacks like bean bags, their surface

KIRBY GOOKIN is, among other things, waiting for Samuel Beckett.

easily impressionable, their form limp and malleable. A changing installation, each formation of this work is unique, never repeatable.

Instead of closing her art down into predictable systems with limits, Larner has taken every opportunity to open it up, allowing for adaptation rather than preservation, growth in place of stasis. Her art exists in a world of *Panta Rhei* where nothing is ever fixed; even works that had once been considered complete are never forced into frozen submission within the strictures of the conservationist's or preservationist's agenda. In two similarly constructed wall hangings, twenty-seven plaster spheres—alluding to the vertebrae of a human spine—were encased in soft gum-rubber sheeting, forming giant pregnant pods. After eighteen months the lye in the plaster ruptured, gutting the rubber casing. Rather than deny entropy by repairing the tear, Larner accepted the limitations of the work's material fabrication and its ultimate impermanence and swaddled the entire configuration in a blanket of lead, creating a "fallout shelter" to hold the balls firmly inside their rubber envelope. So, what was originally PURE GUM RUBBER SHEETING, PLASTER, PLYWOOD, STEEL (1989) is today GONE.

Stepping outside the pseudo-objective discourse of criticism to look at Larner's work as it is recorded photographically, one can catch a glimpse of her world view in reflection. Traditionally, photography has accentuated the classical tenets of a sculpture's ontology. From Leonardo da Vinci to Gotthold Lessing, the "immutable permanence" of sculpture, its "stasis" and compositional "unity," has been continually asserted. In part, these are qualities "of its material limitations," but more importantly, they define how a sculpture was intended to be perceived by the viewer. Classical norms dictated that the "eye must be able to take in at one glance" the "harmonious effects of [a sculpture's] various parts."[3]

The objectivity of the camera's monocular lens seems invented to reify the standard conception of sculpture. The singular vantage point characterizes the standard photographic norm for reproducing sculpture, even sculpture that was composed to defy singular viewpoints, as in the work of Rodin. As late as 1970, Rudolf Wittkower regretted that, "despite the enormously growing literature on Rodin, no attempt has been made, as far as I know, to do justice to Rodin and show his works or at least some of them from many sides."[4] By emphasizing a vantage point that could be apprehended in a "single glance," the classical canon of sculpture not only stresses that a work must remain static but also renounces the notion of the spectator's spatial mobility and his/her temporal experience of it. Casting its gaze on sculpture, the camera's omniscient, monocular lens is ultimately panoptic (due to its hyperrationalized taxonomic control over its subject).[5]

Monocular unity is antithetical to the spatial and temporal flux that characterizes Larner's artistic project. In fact, her works subvert the very panoptic attitudes of the positivist, unified viewpoint that fixes the drift of meaning in a work of art, as in the webbed vortex of stainless steel chains arranged for CHAIN PERSPECTIVE REFLECTED (1990). With a lattice of chains stretched across the expanse of the room in a configuration that constructs a false perspective of receding frames toward one end of the gallery, Larner has created a singular view. Yet one's experience of the perspectival space fractures any sense of singularity or unity normally associated with one-point perspective: although the illusion is successfully rendered, the arrangement of components actually negates the convention as the diminished space between receding planes is reversed. Approaching the installation's center by the path along which our line of vision leads us, we eventually become entangled in a web of chain-link. Our movements are hampered. Forced to turn back, we discover that our reflection is cast upon the side walls in a series of mirror fragments. We see ourselves scattered across the wall, segmented and dismembered in a series of rectangular frames that refract our bodies in chained bondage.

While an installation founded on the paradigm of one-point perspective seems conducive to photographic reproduction, CHAIN PERSPECTIVE REFLECTED actually undermines the camera's singular view. The most potent focal point is inside the web, where the lateral axis of our reflected bodies intersects with the perspectival axis forced by the chain. Here, at the installation's center, perceptual vectors collide, both drawing us inward and repelling us centrifugally. These forces create a tension incompatible with photography's imposition of the hallucinogenic effects of unity and completeness. Larner's installation heightens the spectator's bodily awareness, as she/ he is caught at a certain point in space in a particular moment in time.

As with her mutable and living objects, Larner's installations extend in space and time. Each time a work such as CHAIN PERSPECTIVE REFLECTED is installed anew, it is significantly reinvented, thus extending the life of the original while simultaneously creating a completely new work. FORCED PERSPECTIVE (REVERSED, REFLECTED, EXTENDED) (1990–1992) is the result of applying the same principle of a forced perspective chain-link web framed by mirrors to a new situation that Larner specifically chose for its multiple, rather than single, viewing point. While many of the resulting decisions were determined by the site (how to accommodate different heights and widths of rooms, and so on), the work was also transformed in order to create a different spatial relation with the viewer. FORCED PERSPECTIVE (REVERSED, REFLECTED, EXTENDED) establishes a more aggressive recession of space than its previous incarnation by creating a blunter, more confrontational chain-link barrier than that effected in its earlier state. The mirrors are reconfigured so that they turn at a slight angle toward the viewer. As we approach the perspectival vanishing point, our image is cast across the wall in a pixilated manner against a filmic succession of square mirrors. The spatial recession is a machine activated by the viewer's temporal passage. But Larner goes one step further in this reinstallation: In the larger space, it is more massive and looming, its structural tension so great as to cause stress fractures in the supporting wall and warps in the metal beams on the other side of the wall, holding in balance passive strain and imminent collapse. The horizontally stretched chains pierce through the perimeter wall into the

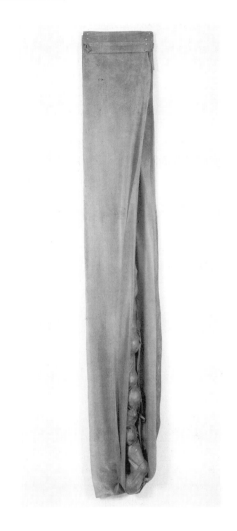

adjoining room, invading the spaces beyond the perspectival view of the mirrors and chains. Extending the chains of pictorial convention beyond the limits of our immediate perception, FORCED PERSPECTIVE (REVERSED, REFLECTED, EXTENDED) enforces the fact that the dictates of convention permeate every aspect of our lives and are larger than the frames of our apprehension.

In her reinstallation of BIRD IN SPACE (1992), Larner again extended the work's life into new spatial and temporal dimensions. In its first manifestation she plotted out the spatial shape of Brancusi's 1923 sculpture in a grid, enlarging and digitizing it in a

web of knotted nylon cord. From its central expanse, the lateral extensions reached upward to the corners of the ceiling while the rest funneled downward to the floor, converging on a weighted base. The final configuration formed a soaring archway of delicately spun white cord that bridged the gallery, dematerializing the iconic solid vertical sculpture into a penetrable horizontal expanse. In order to accommodate the higher ceilings and wider floorspan for the work's subsequent reinstallation in a much larger environment, Larner added an extension to each strand of the cord so it would fit into the new space. The attaching loop of the new extension employs metal fixtures different from those used on the original span. Addition is thus implied through extension, demonstrating in a single metonymic detail the history of the piece and its ability to adapt to a new environment or situation. BIRD IN SPACE is subsequently documented by a series of photographic details of the appendage, a metonymy of the installation and its extension into space and time.

UNTITLED, (UNIDENTIFIED) (1991) follows a similar history of installment and reinstallment. In each incarnation, the word "unidentified" appears projected in huge bold black letters against the four walls of a square room. In addition to the text, there is a reflective entity that in some way mirrors and refracts the environment and the spectator's experience within it. From these simple components a diverse variety of perceptual effects is created in each location. In the first two installations, the letters were contorted to accentuate the corners of the room. Then the word was rotated 45 degrees so that the enlarged letters fell in the middle of each wall, expanding the rectangular space by creating four additional corners. In each case, the legibility of the word is countered by its spatial configuration.

In the work's most recent incarnation DDEE-FIIINNTU (1992) (an alphabetical anagram for un-identified), the text, rather than being on the wall, was painted on movable screens that slid and pivoted according to individual whim. Hence, Larner's UNIDENTIFIED goes through a series of increasingly complex permutations that render the text less and less discernible, therefore subverting the traditional correspondence between legibility and meaning. The mirroring of the spectator and distorted text creates a focal point, a paradigm of the wholly absorbent camera lens collapsed into a black hole. Thus in each variation the word remains forever illegible, forever unidentifiable.

Larner embraces the forces that time plays on art and employs it as part of her craft. Our phenomenological experience of her art is dependent on its context (spatial, cultural, socio-ecological) and its temporality. Larner's works depart from the tradition of nineteenth century sculpture or Minimalist apodictic objects (complete, static, and highly photogenic) that project the delusion of their self-sufficiency from the spectator. Instead of being frozen in the discrete moments of "before" and "after," her objects and installations are forever ticking in "the clockless nowever."

1) From a conversation with the artist, February 14, 1993. Note: the painterly effect is even more pronounced in the other cultures which are made by laying different layers of colored agar (most commonly red, yellow, and blue). Here, the bacteria literally mixes the various layers of colored media as it grows.
2) Johann Wolfgang von Goethe, "Observations on the Laocoön," Monthly Magazine, vii, 1799: 349. (Reprinted in Gert Schiff, German Essays on Art History, Continuum, New York, 1988, p. 41).
3) These quotes are taken from Gotthold Ephraim Lessing's Laocoön: An Essay on the Limits of Painting and Poetry (1766), transl. E.A. McCormick, The Johns Hopkins University Press, Baltimore, MD, 1984, pp. 20, 19, 104 respectively. A casual reading through the writings of the major theorists of sculpture and Renaissance and Neo-Classical art in general yields numerous similar observations, as in the writings of Leonardo, Vasari, Winckelmann, Goethe, Hildebrand, Pater, and even more recently in the criticism surrounding Minimalism. Winckelmann in particular announces an exceptionally strong ethical position when stating that "everything which we cannot survey at once, … loses some portion of its greatness."
4) Heinrich Wölfflin, Principles of Art History, (1915), Dover, New York, 1950, p. 54; Adolph Hildebrand, Problem of Form (1893), G.E. Stechert, New York, 1905, p. 95; Rudolf Wittkower, Sculpture: Processes and Principles, Harper and Row, New York, 1977, p. 234.
5) As with Jeremy Bentham's prison designed as a Panopticon, 1790.

KIRBY GOOKIN

Dimensionen variabel: Liz Larner

Eine rosa Orchidee mit geöffneten Blütenblättern, die in ein samtiges Bett aus gelbgefärbtem Nährboden und Buttermilch geschmiegt ist und einen Kupferpenny umfängt: dieses Bild bot Liz Larners Objekt ORCHID, BUTTERMILK, PENNY (Orchidee, Buttermilch, Penny), als es in ihrer ersten Ausstellung *Room 9, Tropicana Hotel* (Zimmer 9, Hotel Tropicana) im Jahre 1987 in Los Angeles gezeigt wurde. ORCHID, BUTTERMILK, PENNY, Teil ihrer Serie *Cultures* (Kulturen), ist eine Bakterienkultur, die aus den aufgezählten Objekten besteht und in einer Petrischale (flache Deckelschale zur Bakterienzüchtung nach R. J. Petri, Anm. d. Ü.) gezüchtet wird. Im Lauf der Zeit breiteten sich die Bakterien über die verwesende Blume, die geronnene Buttermilch und die fettigen Überreste von Fingerabdrücken auf dem Penny aus. Aus den «Umtrieben des Bakterienstoffwechsels» entstand eine «Art Action Painting, die ihre eigene Kultur hervorbrachte.»[1] Während sich die Bakterien entwickelten und mit dem Nährboden vermischten, türmte sich ein Kosmos verschiedenfarbiger Blasen auf, wie Lichterscheinungen, die durch unsere geschlossenen Augenlider schimmern.

Larners *Cultures* sind im wahrsten Sinne des Wortes lebendig, lebende Organismen, eingeschlossen in einem wissenschaftlichen Terrarium zeitgenössischer Kultur. Ein Photo, das eine Woche, zwei Wochen und drei Monate später gemacht wird, fängt drei völlig verschiedene Bilder desselben Werkes ein. Im ersten Bild sehen wir die schwelgenden Farben sich entwickelnder Bakterien; im letzten die vermoderten Brauntöne der verwesten, leblosen Blume: jeder Augenblick dazwischen zeigt ein anderes Erscheinungsbild. Wie die Natur, so muss man auch die *Cultures* phänomenologisch betrachten. Sie verwandeln sich unaufhörlich, bringen neue Rückstände hervor und erzeugen unendlich viele Möglichkeiten neuer Bilder. Beim Betrachten ihrer Werke fühlt man sich an Goethes Bemerkungen über Laokoon erinnert: «Ein echtes Kunstwerk bleibt, wie ein Naturwerk, für unseren Verstand immer unendlich; es wird angeschaut, empfunden; es wirkt, es kann aber nicht eigentlich erkannt, viel weniger sein Wesen, sein Verdienst mit Worten ausgesprochen werden.»[2]

Ein Merkmal, das Larners Projekte auszeichnet, ist die physische Verwandlung des Kunstwerkes. Ihre Skulpturen, ob organisch oder anorganisch, haben immer die Beschaffenheit von etwas Lebendigem. Da Larner mit unterschiedlichen Materialien experimentiert und häufig das eine gegen das andere ausspielt, sind die daraus resultierenden Werke von Natur aus unbeständig. Diese Unbeständigkeit ist

KIRBY GOOKIN wartet, unter anderem, auf Samuel Beckett.

vielleicht nur angedeutet, wie z. B. in USED TO DO THE JOB (Gewohnt, die Arbeit zu erledigen) (1987), worin alle Elemente, die zum Bau eines Sprengsatzes benötigt werden, in einen Würfel aus Wachs eingebettet sind; in anderen Werken ist es ein implizites Moment der Komposition, dass ihre endgültige Erscheinung oder «Vollendung» von der Mitwirkung des Besitzers, Konservators oder Betrachters abhängt. BALL SYSTEM (Ballsystem) (1988) besteht aus einer scheinbar komplizierten Anhäufung von Elementen (Kugeln aus verschiedenen Materialien, Drahtgestelle aus rostfreiem Stahl, zusammenklappbare Kisten), ohne dass Instruktionen für ihre Anordnung gegeben werden. NO M, NO D, ONLY S & B (Kein M, kein D, nur S&B) (1990) ist ähnlich amorph: drei schlaffe, schmiegsame, mit Gewichten beladene Patchwork-Lederbeutel mit leicht eindrückbarer Oberfläche, die mit Bohnen gefüllten Säckchen ähneln. Wie bei einer sich verändernden Installation ist ihre endgültige Anordnung nie wiederholbar.

Anstatt ihre Kunst in vorhersagbare, begrenzte Systeme einzuschliessen, hat Larner jede Gelegenheit genutzt, um sie zu öffnen, um eher Anpassung als Erhaltung zuzulassen, Entwicklung an Stelle von Stasis. Ihre Kunst existiert in einer Welt des *panta rhei* (griech.: alles fliesst), in der niemals etwas festgelegt ist; selbst Werke, die einmal als vollständig betrachtet wurden, werden nicht den strengen Kriterien der Erhalter oder Bewahrer rigoros unterworfen. In zwei ähnlich aufgebauten Wandgehängen wurden siebenundzwanzig Gipskugeln – in Anspielung auf die Rückenwirbel einer normalen menschlichen Wirbelsäule – von einer Verkleidung aus weichem Kautschukgummi umschlossen, so dass sie riesige, deutlich vorstehende Ausbuchtungen bildeten. Nach achtzehn Monaten bekam die Gipslauge Risse, wodurch das Innere der Gummiummantelung zerstört wurde. Anstatt die Entropie zu leugnen und den Riss zu reparieren, akzeptierte Larner die Grenzen der bei der Herstellung des Werkes verwendeten Materialien und ihre grundlegende Unbeständigkeit und umwickelte das ganze Gebilde mit einer Bleihül-

le, um so einen «Ausfallschutz» zu schaffen, der die Kugeln in ihrer Gummiumhüllung festhielt. So ist aus dem ursprünglichen PURE GUM RUBBER SHEETING, PLASTER, PLYWOOD, STEEL (reine Kautschukgummi-Verkleidung, Gips, Sperrholz, Stahl) (1989) heute GONE (verschwunden) geworden.

Wenn man den pseudoobjektiven kritischen Diskurs verlässt, um die Photographien zu betrachten, in denen ihr Werk protokolliert ist, erhascht man einen flüchtigen Blick auf eine Widerspiegelung ihrer Weltanschauung. Traditionellerweise betont die Photographie die klassischen Ansichten über die Ontologie einer Skulptur. Von Leonardo da Vinci bis

Gotthold Lessing wurden fortwährend die «unveränderliche Dauer» in der Bildhauerkunst und ihre kompositorische «Einheit» beschworen. Teilweise sind dies Eigenschaften «ihrer materiellen Schranken», doch bedeutsamer ist, dass sie definieren, wie eine Skulptur vom Betrachter wahrgenommen werden soll. Die klassischen Normen schrieben vor, dass [körperliche Schönheit] «aus der übereinstimmenden Wirkung mannigfaltiger Teile (entspringt), die sich auf einmal übersehen lassen.»[3]

Die Objektivität des monokularen Objektivs einer Kamera (Objektiv mit nur einer Linse und folglich nur einer Brennweite, Anm. d. Ü.) scheint erfunden worden zu sein, um den klassischen Begriff der Bildhauerkunst zu veranschaulichen. Bei der Wiedergabe von Skulpturen ist die Photographie normgemäss durch einen einzigen günstigen Standpunkt der Kamera charakterisiert, und zwar selbst bei Skulpturen, die entworfen wurden, um sich solchen einzigen Standpunkten zu widersetzen, wie z. B. die Werke von Rodin. Erst 1970 bedauerte Rudolf Wittkower, dass «trotz der gewaltig angewachsenen Literatur zu Rodin meines Wissens nach kein Versuch unternommen wurde, Rodin gerecht zu werden und seine Werke, oder zumindest einen Teil von ihnen, von mehreren Seiten darzustellen.»[4] Indem der klassische Begriff der Bildhauerkunst Wert auf einen günstigen Standpunkt legt, der mit einem «einzigen Blick» erfasst werden kann, wird nicht nur betont, dass ein Werk statisch bleiben müsse, sondern es wird auch die Vorstellung von der räumlichen Mobilität des Betrachters und von seinem/ihrem zeitlich vorübergehenden Erleben des Werkes verworfen. Das allwissende, monokulare Objektiv der Kamera, die ihr starres Auge auf die Bildhauerkunst richtet, umfasst im Grunde alles mit einem Blick (infolge ihrer hyperrationalisierten, systematisierenden Kontrolle über ihr Subjekt).[5]

Die aus einer einzigen Perspektive resultierende Einheit steht im Gegensatz zu der immerwährenden Veränderung in Raum und Zeit, die Larners künstlerische Projekte kennzeichnet. Faktisch untergraben ihre Werke die besondere, allumfassende Position des positivistischen, vereinheitlichten Standpunktes, der den Bedeutungsfluss eines Kunstwerkes eindämmt und festlegt; dies gilt z. B. für das wie ein Sog wirkende Netz von Ketten aus rostfreiem Stahl in CHAIN PERSPECTIVE REFLECTED (gespiegelte Kettenperspektive) (1990). Mit einem Gitterwerk von Ketten, das sich über die gesamte Ausdehnung des Raumes erstreckt und so angeordnet ist, dass daraus eine vorgetäuschte Perspektive von Rahmen entsteht, die gegen ein Ende der Galerie zurückweichen, hat Larner einen einzigartigen Anblick geschaffen. Doch unser Erleben des perspektivischen Raumes zerschlägt jedes Gefühl von Einzigartigkeit oder Einheit, das normalerweise mit einem einzigen Blickwinkel verbunden ist: Einerseits gelingt die Täuschung, andererseits negiert die Anordnung der Elemente die Konvention, und zwar durch die Umkehrung der kleiner werdenden Räume zwischen den zurückweichenden Ebenen. Wenn wir dem Pfad folgen, auf den unsere Blickrichtung uns vermutlich führen wird, und uns dem Zentrum der Installation nähern, werden wir schliesslich in ein Netz von Kettengliedern verstrickt. Unsere Bewegungen werden behindert. Wir werden zur Umkehr gezwungen und entdecken, dass unser Spiegelbild in einer Reihe von Spiegelstücken an die Seitenwände geworfen wird. Wir sehen uns selbst über die Wand verstreut, zerstückelt und zerrissen in einer Reihe von rechtwinkligen Rahmen, die unsere mit Ketten gefesselten Körper brechen.

Während eine Installation, die sich auf das Paradigma eines einzigen Blickwinkels stützt, für die photographische Wiedergabe geeignet zu sein scheint, untergräbt CHAIN PERSPECTIVE REFLECTED sogar den einzigen Blickwinkel der Kamera. Der zwingendste Blickpunkt befindet sich im Inneren des Netzes, wo sich die Querachse unserer gespiegelten Körper und die durch die Ketten forcierte Blickachse schneiden. Hier, im Zentrum der Installation, kollidieren Wahrnehmungsvektoren, die uns nach innen ziehen und uns gleichzeitig vom Zentrum nach aussen stossen. Diese Kräfte erzeugen eine Spannung, die mit den uns von der Photographie auferlegten, halluzinogenen Effekten von Einheit und Vollständigkeit unvereinbar ist. Larners Installation stei-gert das Körperbewusstsein des Betrachters, da er an einem bestimmten Punkt im Raum und in einem bestimmten Augenblick in der Zeit gefangen ist.

Genau wie ihre mutationsfähigen, lebenden Objekte erweitern sich auch Larners Installationen in Raum und Zeit. Jedesmal, wenn ein Werk wie CHAIN PERSPECTIVE REFLECTED wieder aufgebaut wird, wird es weitgehend neu erfunden, so dass die Lebensdauer des Originals verlängert und gleichzeitig ein völlig neues Werk geschaffen wird. FORCED PERSPECTIVE (REVERSED, REFLECTED, EXTENDED) (Erzwungene Perspektive [verkehrt, gespiegelt, erweitert]) aus den Jahren 1990–1992 resultiert aus dem Bemühen, das gleiche Prinzip – eine erzwungene Perspektive in einem von Spiegeln umrahmten Netz aus Kettengliedern – auf eine neue Situation anzuwenden, die Larner ausdrücklich gewählt hat, weil sie nicht nur einen, sondern mannigfache Standpunkte bietet. Zwar wurden viele der daraus resultierenden Entscheidungen durch den Standort bestimmt (wie z. B. die Anpassung der Installation an verschiedene Höhen und Breiten des Raumes usw.), doch wurde das Werk auch abgewandelt, um ein anderes räumliches Verhältnis zum Betrachter herzustellen. Durch die Schaffung einer eindeutigeren und feindlicheren Sperre als in der früheren Version stellt FORCED PERSPECTIVE (REVERSED, REFLECTED, EXTENDED) ein aggressiveres Zurückweichen des Raumes her als sein Vorläufer. Die Spiegel sind neu konfiguriert und in einem kaum merklichen Winkel zum Betrachter hin geneigt. Während wir uns dem perspektivischen Fluchtpunkt nähern, wird unser Bild leicht verdreht auf eine filmartige Folge rechteckiger Spiegel quer über die Wand geworfen. Das räumliche Zurückweichen ist ein Mechanismus, der aktiviert wird, wenn der Betrachter kurzzeitig den Raum durchschreitet. Doch mit dieser Neuinstallation geht Larner noch einen Schritt weiter: im grösseren Raum ist die Installation wuchtiger und ragt drohender auf; die Spannung in ihrem Gefüge ist so gross, dass die Belastung Bruchstellen in der tragenden Wand und Verkrümmungen der Metallträger auf der Rückseite der Wand verursacht, während das Gleichgewicht zwischen der passiven Dehnung und dem drohenden Zusammenbruch gehalten wird. Die horizontal gestreckten Ketten bohren sich durch die äussere Wand ins Nebenzimmer und dringen so in Räume ein, die jenseits des perspektivischen Blickes auf die Spiegel und Ketten liegen. Indem die Ketten der Konvention bildhaft über die Grenzen unserer unmittelbaren Wahrnehmung hinausgehen, unterstreicht FORCED PERSPECTIVE (REVERSED, REFLECTED, EXTENDED) die Tatsache, dass die Gebote der Konvention alle Aspekte unseres Lebens durchdringen und den Rahmen unseres Vorstellungsvermögens überragen.

In ihrer Neuinstallation von BIRD IN SPACE (Vogel im Raum) (1992) verlängerte Liz Larner die Lebensdauer des Werkes wieder in neue räumliche und zeitliche Dimensionen. In ihrer ersten Version legte sie die Umrisse von Brancusis Skulptur aus dem Jahre 1923 in einem Gitter räumlich fest und vergrösserte und digitalisierte sie in einem Netz aus verknüpften Nylonschnüren. Von der mittleren Ausdehnung aus reichten die seitlichen Verlängerungen bis hinauf in die Ecken der Decke des Raumes, während der Rest unten auf dem Fussboden zusammengeführt wurde und auf einem mit einem Gewicht belasteten Sockel zusammenlief. Die endgültige Anordnung bildete einen emporstrebenden Bogen aus fein gesponnenen, weissen Schnüren, der die Galerie überspannte und die konventionelle, massive vertikale Skulptur in eine durchlässige, horizontale Ausdehnung auflöste. Um die folgende Neuinstallation in einer sehr viel weitläufigeren Umgebung an die grössere Deckenhöhe und Grundfläche anzupassen, verlängerte Larner jeden Schnurstrang, damit er in den neuen Raum passte. Für die Verbindungsschlinge der neuen Schnur werden andere Spannvorrichtungen aus Metall benutzt als für den ursprünglichen Umfang. So ist die Hinzufügung durch die Verlängerung angedeutet und demonstriert in einem einzigen, metonymischen Detail die Geschichte des Kunstwerkes und seine Fähigkeit, sich einer neuen Umgebung oder Situation anzupassen. BIRD IN SPACE (Vogel im Raum) wird daraufhin durch eine Reihe photographischer Detailaufnahmen der Verlängerungen dokumentiert – als *pars pro toto* der Installation und ihres Übergriffs in Raum und Zeit.

Larners Installation UNTITLED (UNIDENTIFIED) (ohne Titel [unidentifiziert]) aus dem Jahre 1991 weist eine ähnliche Geschichte der Aufstellung und Neuaufstellung auf wie vorausgegangene Werke. In jeder neuen Version ist das Werk durch das Wort

LIZ LARNER, DDEEFIIINNTU, 1992,

lacquer, screens, aluminum, four parts, 125 x 142 x 2" each /

Lack, Segelleinen, Aluminium, 4teilig, je 317 x 615 x 5 cm.

«unidentified» gekennzeichnet, das vergrössert und in deutlich hervortretenden, schwarzen Buchstaben auf die vier Wände eines im wesentlichen rechteckigen Raumes projiziert wurde. Zusätzlich zum Text gibt es ein reflektierendes Gebilde, das die Umgebung und das Erleben des Betrachters darin irgendwie spiegelt und bricht. Aus diesen einfachen Elementen entsteht an jedem Standort eine Vielzahl von Wahrnehmungseffekten. Jede Veränderung protokolliert die Erweiterung und Vergrösserung des Werkes. In den ersten beiden Installationen waren die Buchstaben vergrössert und kontrahiert, um die Ecken des Raumes zu betonen. Dann liess man das Wort um 45° (um den Raum) kreisen, so dass die vergrösserten Buchstaben in der Mitte jeder Wand angeordnet waren und so durch die Schaffung von vier zusätzlichen Ecken den rechteckigen Raum erweiterten. In jeder Installation entzog sich das Wort erneut der Lesbarkeit, denn es war räumlich rings um den Betrachter herum angeordnet.

In der jüngsten Version des Werkes, DDEEFIIINN-TU (1992) (Anagramm von «unidentified»), wurde der Text nicht auf der Wand verankert, sondern auf bewegliche Leinwände gemalt, die sowohl gleiten als auch sich um ihre eigene Achse drehen können, je nach Laune der Künstlerin, des Betrachters oder des Galeristen. Folglich durchläuft Larners UNIDENTIFIED eine Reihe von immer komplexeren Vertauschungen, die es zunehmend schwieriger machen, den Text zu erkennen, und die dadurch die traditionelle Übereinstimmung von Lesbarkeit und Bedeutung verraten. Die Spiegelbilder des Betrachters und des entstellten Textes schaffen einen Blickpunkt – ein Gleichnis für das alles aufnehmende, in ein schwarzes Loch versenkte Kameraobjektiv. Daraus ergibt sich, dass das Wort in jeder Variante für immer unleserlich, für immer unidentifizierbar bleibt.

Larner macht sich die Kräfte der Zeit zu eigen, die auf die Kunst einwirken, und nutzt sie als Bestandteil ihres Handwerks. Unsere phänomenologische Erfahrung ihrer Kunst ist abhängig von ihrem Kontext (räumlich, kulturell und sozio-ökologisch) und von ihrer Zeitbedingtheit. Larners Werke gehen zurück auf die Tradition der Bildhauerei im neunzehnten Jahrhundert oder auf minimalistische, apodiktische Objekte (vollständig, statisch und höchst photogen), die dem Irrtum Ausdruck verleihen, sie existierten unabhängig vom Betrachter. Anstatt in den für sich allein stehenden Augenblicken des «Davor» und «Danach» zu erstarren, existieren Larners Objekte und Installationen ewig im «zeitlosen Jetzt-und-Immer».

(Übersetzung: Bela Wohl)

(PHOTO: NORBERT ARTNER)

1) Aus einem Gespräch mit der Künstlerin am 14.2.1993. Anmerkung: Noch deutlicher ist der Eindruck von etwas Gemaltem bei den anderen Kulturen, die aus verschiedenen Schichten gefärbten Nährbodens (meist rot, gelb und blau) bestehen. Im Laufe ihrer Entwicklung vermischen die Bakterien hier buchstäblich die unterschiedlichen Schichten gefärbter Nährstoffe.

2) Johann Wolfgang Goethe, «Über Laokoon», aus: *Schriften zur Kunst,* Artemis-Verlag, Zürich 1954, S. 162.

3) Diese Zitate stammen aus Gotthold Ephraim Lessing, *Laokoon oder Über die Grenzen der Malerei und Poesie,* Philipp Reclam jun., Stuttgart 1987, S. 22, 23, 115 und 145. Beim beiläufigen Durchlesen der Schriften der bedeutendsten Theoretiker der Bildhauerkunst, der Renaissance und des Neoklassizismus im allgemeinen stösst man auf zahlreiche ähnliche Bemerkungen; in den Schriften von Leonardo, Vasari, Winckelmann, Goethe, Hildebrand und Pater und sogar in jüngerer Zeit in der Kritik des Minimalismus. Besonders Winckelmann vertritt eine aussergewöhnlich starke ethische Position, wenn er feststellt, dass «alles, was wir nicht unmittelbar überschauen können, ... einen Teil seiner Erhabenheit einbüsst.»

4) Heinrich Wölfflin, *Kunstgeschichtliche Grundbegriffe,* Bruckmann, München 1921; Adolf Hildebrand, *Das Problem der Form,* Heitz & Mündel, Strassburg 1910; Rudolf Wittkower, *Sculpture, Processes and Principles,* Harper & Row, New York 1977, S. 234.

5) Wie bei dem von Jeremy Bentham vorgeschlagenen Gefängnisrundbau, der als panoptische Anlage geplant war (1790). (Der Aufseher kann vom Mittelpunkt aus alle Zellen überblicken, Anm.d.Ü.)

129

LÁSZLÓ F. FÖLDÉNYI

Purgatorium der Sinne:

RUDOLF SCHWARZKOGLER

(1940–1969)

Radikal sein ist leicht; schön sein um so schwieriger. Schwarzkogler gelang es, die Schönheit zu verwirklichen. Aus den Aufnahmen seiner bekanntesten Werke, der *Aktionen,* schlägt uns tödliche Schönheit entgegen. In ihnen strahlt der Tod, schwarzweiss. Aber nicht, um seinen eigenen Sieg zu feiern. Im Gegenteil; gefeiert wird der eigene Untergang. Diese Bilder sind tödlich, wozu es leugnen? Wir müssen uns überwinden, um sie länger zu betrachten. Aber sie enthalten auch etwas wie Abgeklärtheit, Schlichtheit, was Zeichen des Lebens ist. In ihnen geistert eine Art kristallklare, nahezu engelhafte Unschuld. Dadurch erinnern die Aktionen auch an einen Ritus. An ein Opfer, bei dem ein Mensch geopfert wird, um sich auf diese Weise auch des Todes zu entledigen. Schwarzkogler liefert sich in diesen Bildern dem Tode aus, um uns dann vom anderen Ufer des Todes zu erscheinen, lebendiger als je. Kein Wunder, dass er die Aktionen aufgab, nachdem er innerhalb eines Jahres (1965–66) sechs solche arrangiert hatte, um in den restlichen drei Jahren seines Lebens – den

LÁSZLÓ F. FÖLDÉNYI ist Dozent für Literaturwissenschaft an der Universität Budapest. Er ist Autor eines Buches über Melancholie (1988). Im Herbst 1993 wird von ihm *Caspar David Friedrich: Die Nachtseite der Malerei* bei Matthes & Seitz, München, erscheinen.

Tod nunmehr hinter sich wissend – dem Geheimnis der neuen, selbst das Leben übertreffenden Lebendigkeit nachzuspüren. Die Konzentration des Geistes, die den Aktions-Photos entströmt, war auf die endgültige Ausschaltung des Todes gerichtet. Schwarzkogler mochte auf ein intensives, selbst den Tod meisterndes Leben gestossen sein. Die Schönheit dieses Lebens überstrahlt die Photoaufnahmen der Aktionen noch rückwirkend. Es ist eine Schönheit, die den Menschen nicht nur ästhetisch, sondern auch existentiell einfängt.

«Ich habe verschiedene erlebnisse gehabt, es macht mir jedoch mühe, sie zeitlich zu ordnen», schrieb er 1969. Die Lebenswerkausstellung im Museum moderner Kunst Stiftung Ludwig Wien, in der die Werke chronologisch geordnet sind, hilft dem Besucher, sich im Labyrinth der Gemälde, Entwürfe, Photos, Heftseiten, Manifeste und Tagebuchaufzeichnungen zurechtzufinden. Dennoch suggeriert die längst fällige Ausstellung, dass Schwarzkogler der Zeit vermutlich keine übermässige Bedeutung beimass. Die Zeit war für ihn wohl nur ein irdischer Abdruck der Ewigkeit. Sein Lebenswerk weckt den Eindruck, als sei eine einzige innere, seelische Feuerkugel in die Bruchstücke von «Werken» zersprungen. Er war ein Romantiker; er fühlte sich

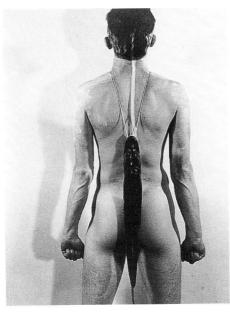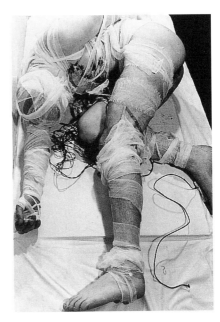

RUDOLF SCHWARZKOGLER, 3. AKTION, 1965. (PHOTOS: L. HOFFENREICH)

hingezogen zum Bruchstückhaften, was in diesem Fall Ausdruck nicht irdischen Mangels, sondern himmlischer Totalität ist. Der Ausstellungsbesucher kann Schwarzkoglers Schaffen durch die Zeit folgen. Auf diesem Weg aber bestätigt sich sein Verdacht, dass das, was diese Werke wie ein Magnet an sich zieht – der Tod also –, selbst nicht Teil der Zeit ist. Es ist jenseits der Zeit, wie auch die Schönheit, die sich Schwarzkogler noch zu Lebzeiten aneignete.

Jetzt, da Schwarzkoglers gesamtes Lebenswerk zum erstenmal umfassend zu sehen ist, wird man gewahr, dass ihn vor allem die Vollkommenheit beschäftigte – die Art und Weise, wie Totalität zu erreichen ist. In den Dienst dessen stellte er seine Kunst. Er achtete weniger auf die fertigen Kunstwerke als vielmehr auf die Umstände ihrer Erschaffung. Daran vielleicht liegt es auch, dass das Lebenswerk zwar ausserordentlich intensiv wirkt, aber quantitativ nicht sonderlich umfangreich ist. Was entstand – ob Gemälde, Photos oder flüchtige Skizzen –, bezeugt eindeutig, dass Schwarzkogler gleich zu Beginn aus den herkömmlichen Rahmen der Kunst heraustrat. Er wollte kein «Aktionist» sein, wollte also nicht die Grenzen der Kunst weiten, um sich hernach einen Platz innerhalb der Kunst zu sichern. Schwarzkogler war ein Mystiker – im ursprünglichen Sinn des Wor-

tes. Zum Künstler machte ihn nicht, dass er Kunst machen wollte, sondern dass er so tief, so kompromisslos nach intensivem Durchleben der Wirklichkeit strebte, dass dies Spuren der Vollkommenheit an jeder seiner Gesten hinterliess.

Mögen sie noch so verschieden sein, mir fiel beim Betrachten der Ausstellung Marcel Duchamp ein. Sein kalter Blick, der sich so unvoreingenommen auf die Dinge richtet, dass sie zu schwitzen beginnen. Danach strebte auch Schwarzkogler: er wollte die sinnliche Wirklichkeit erfahren, ohne jede Vermittlung, den Schleier der Begriffe von ihr reissend. Er wollte sehen, wie nur ein Tier, ein Säugling, ein Geisteskranker oder Gott sehen kann. Danach versuchte er das so Erlebte mit seinem menschlichen Wissen, seinen Erfahrungen in Einklang zu bringen. Er wollte sich, in der Hoffnung auf eine nicht alltägliche Bereicherung, enthüllen. Kurz, er trachtete nach dem Unmöglichen, danach, ohne Unterlass sich selbst zu übertreffen. Nach einer Obduktion seiner selbst, die für ihn die grundlegendste Lebenserfahrung war. «KUNST NACH INNEN: DIE WIRKLICHE MALEREI», schrieb er. Dies ist eine Malerei der inneren Wahrnehmung. Eine Sichtbarmachung des Unsichtbaren. Oder umgekehrt: ein Versuch, unter den Bedingungen das zu entdecken, was in ihnen

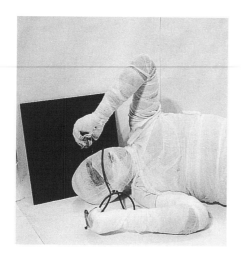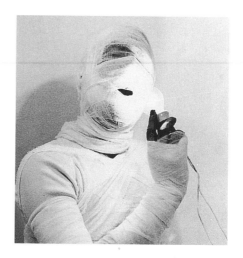

RUDOLF SCHWARZKOGLER, 6. AKTION, 1966. (PHOTOS: M. EPP)

das Unbedingte ist. Es ist das, was Novalis als Romantisieren bezeichnete. Ihn beschäftigte die Alchimie der Sinne. Nicht das Abbilden, sondern das Abbauen der Dinge.

«Es ist ... notwendig, in der kunstübung alles abbildhafte auszumerzen», notierte er 1968. In diesem Sinn arbeitete er von Anfang an. In seinen frühesten Gemälden bemühte er sich, reine Farbenverhältnisse zu schaffen, die von Malewitsch geforderte plastische Sensibilität sichtbar zu machen. Er suchte das Gleichgewicht, ohne welches ein Gemälde nicht gelingen kann, das allein aber aus keinem einzigen Element des Bildes extrahierbar ist. Man könnte durchaus sagen, Schwarzkogler habe weniger die sinnliche Seite der Malerei beschäftigt als vielmehr ihre Theologie. Auch als Maler war er in erster Linie Mystiker, ein besessener Erforscher der unfassbaren Ordnung. Er wollte die sichtbare Welt abbauen, um aus den vorgefundenen unsichtbaren Verhältnissen eine neue Struktur zu erschaffen.

Der menschliche Körper ist ein hierzu ebenso geeigneter Gegenstand wie die Leinwand des Malers. Wenn er den menschlichen Körper «verwendete», interessierten ihn die in diesem verborgenen Möglichkeiten weniger als die Voraussetzungen des lebendigen Körpers selbst: die Wurzel des Lebens

also – das, was sinngemäss mit dem Leben nicht identifizierbar ist. Danach in erster Linie und vor allem anderen forschte Schwarzkogler bei seiner Aktion. Im Gegensatz zu den kompakt sinnlichen Aktionen von Günter Brus, Hermann Nitsch und besonders Otto Muehl war ihm nicht die Einmaligkeit und Unwiderruflichkeit des Gestus wichtig, sondern die Struktur der Umstände der Aktion. Er genoss nicht die Sinnlichkeit, er suchte die abstrakte Ordnung. Und wenn wir die Abstraktion erwähnen, dürfen wir nicht vergessen, dass in der frühchristlichen und neuplatonistischen Tradition sie die Voraussetzung für das Finden Gottes war. Abstraktion, Analyse: das ist Eindringen hinter die Materie in der Hoffnung, das Nichtmaterielle zu finden. Schwarzkogler war nicht ein aktionistischer Künstler, sondern ein aktionistischer Theologe.

Seine Aktionen waren – von der ersten, der «Hochzeit», abgesehen – nicht öffentlich. Er veranstaltete sie für sich selbst beziehungsweise für die Linse des Photoapparats. Statt auf den Prozess legte er die Betonung auf die herausgegriffenen Augenblicke. Die Photos von den Aktionen sind Atelieraufnahmen. Sie sind echte Stilleben – Totenstilleben –, und sie widerspiegeln genau Schwarzkoglers Ziel, die Augenblicke der Aktion erstarren zu lassen und so

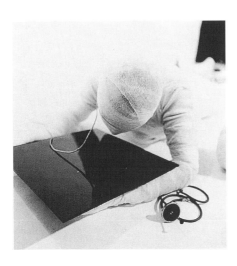

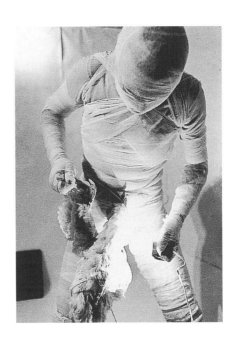

RUDOLF SCHWARZKOGLER, 6. AKTION, 1966. (PHOTOS: M. EPP)

das Leben anzuhalten. In den Aktionen von Nitsch oder Muehl fesseln den Betrachter in erster Linie die ausgeführten Handlungen, und die Aufmerksamkeit gilt den ekstatischen oder abschreckenden Gesten. Die Betonung liegt auf einer Story, einer Ereignisfolge und deren Ausgang. So durchkonstruiert sie sein mögen, bei ihnen ist der Manifest-Inhalt am wichtigsten. Davon sind sie aggressiv, aufdringlich, orgiastisch – im besten Sinn des Wortes. In Schwarzkoglers Aktionen liegt die Betonung auf der Komposition, der reinen Ordnung der sichtbaren Elemente, die aus den Elementen selbst nicht unbedingt resultieren würde. Die herausgreifbaren inhaltlichen Elemente freilich sind ebenso verblüffend und alarmierend wie in den sonstigen Wiener Aktionen: Blendung, Kastration, Todesinjektion, klinische Sterilität, Seziersaalstimmung und Hinrichtung – solche Motive weihen ihn zu einem unverfälschten Wiener Künstler. Und dennoch: vergleicht man die einzelnen Aufnahmen, folgt man nicht so sehr der S T O R Y , der H a n d l u n g und versucht nicht, sie von einem möglichen Abschluss her zu deuten, sondern man beobachtet eher die langsame Fortbewegung der Kompositionen. Das *Orgien Mysterien Theater* von Nitsch entfaltet sich in Raum und Zeit; Schwarzkoglers Aktionen hingegen sind bereits auf den

ersten Aufnahmen «abgeschlossen». Die weiteren Bilder «breiten» den ersten Augenblick nicht in Raum und Zeit «aus», sondern sie sprengen ihn – unter Wahrung seiner zeitlosen und über das Leben hinausreichenden Schönheit – «nach innen». Im Gegensatz zu der Explosion bei Hermann Nitsch ist das Ergebnis eine Implosion. Nicht dionysische Ekstase, wie bei Nitsch und Brus, ist hier bestimmend, sondern die vollkommene ästhetische Ordnung und die stumme Stille. Seine Aktionen spielen in einem Garten Eden; aber nicht am Beginn der Schöpfung, sondern am Ende – dort, wo der Mensch, das Leben einmal durchschritten, wieder unschuldig wird. Die Photos erinnern auch an die Werke von Egon Schiele: ein ins Extreme getriebener Ästhetizismus, der nicht zu übertreffen ist. Noch eine einzige Geste, und alles zerfiele in Nichts.

Die in den Aktionsaufnahmen erkennbare abstrakte Ordnung weist jedoch nicht nur auf künstlerische Parallelen und Vorereignisse hin. Diese Bilder stehen auch den Zeichnungen in den Handbüchern der Alchimisten nahe. Die Zeichnungen im *Donum Dei* oder in der *Sapientia veterum* demonstrieren ebenso Stadien des Eindringens in Materie wie die Aktionen Schwarzkoglers: die *praeparatio*, die *sublimatio*, den *coitus*, die *solutio*, die *generatio*, die *separatio*, die

RUDOLF SCHWARZKOGLER, 4. AKTION, 1965. *(PHOTO: F. CIBULKA)*

coniunctio, die *fixatio* und natürlich die *putrefactio,* wo das sich vereinigende Paar, um ein Kind – um Leben – zeugen zu können, in die schwarze *nigredo* untertauchen und den Tod durchschreiten muss. Auch Schwarzkogler suchte nach der *prima materia,* genau wie seine alchimistischen Vorgänger: nach der Totalität, die den Tod ebenso übertrifft wie das Leben. Das Suchen bedeutet bei ihm Abstraktion von allem, was den Menschen aus der Totalität in die Zerbrochenheit zurückziehen könnte. Überschreitung der weltlichen Grenzen («grenzscheide möglicher wahrnehmung», schreibt er gegen Ende seines Lebens) im Interesse kosmischer Totalität: dem dient die Kunst – einem gesteigerten, intensiven Durchleben des Seins. Deshalb nennt er die Kunst mal «entziehungskur», mal «PURGATORIUM DER SINNE», mal «heilkunst». Die Kunst ist für ihn vor allem anderen eine Quelle neuer Erfahrungen, und dazu glaubt er weder ein Publikum noch vergegenständlichte Kunstwerke zu benötigen. Ähnlich wie Novalis konnte er sagen, der geheimnisvolle Weg führe nach innen, dorthin, wohin man dem anderen nur schwer folgt.

Von diesem Weg blickte er in seinen letzten Jahren nicht mehr zurück. Für seine nun entstandenen Aufzeichnungen, Exzerpte ist eine radikale – mystische – Ausweitung der Kunst bezeichnend. Er hatte, statt der Kunst, ein Lebensritual gefunden. «ich stürze in eine höhle oder: ich will etwas erkennen oder erreichen versuche einzudringen und gerate ausser mir», schrieb er kurz vor seinem Tode in einer Aufzeichnung, in deren tragischen Tiefen die Worte Van Goghs oder Artauds widerhallen. «es ist wie ein schwarzes tuch, das über mich geworfen wird ... ich bin ganz verzückt RIESENGROSS es sind keine grenzen zu erkennen ... meine grosse zehe ist eingefroren.» Und später: «ein teil von mir trennt sich ab.» Hernach: «unvorstellbare traurigkeit.» Aber hierauf: «dabei ist alles klar, ich habe das gefühl ein stern unter sternen zu sein.» Mit seinem Tode erlosch ein Leben; aber das Lebenswerk lässt keinen Zweifel zu, dass das Licht des Sternes nicht erloschen ist.

(Aus dem Ungarischen von Hans Skirecki)

LÁSZLÓ F. FÖLDÉNYI

Purgatory of the Senses:

RUDOLF SCHWARZKOGLER

(1940—1969)

To be radical is easy; to be beautiful is not. Schwarzkogler succeeded in making beauty a reality. The shots of his best known works, the *Aktions,* assault us with their lethal beauty. They are radiant with death in black and white. But not in celebration of death's victory. On the contrary, the object of celebration is death's downfall. It cannot be denied: these pictures are lethal. We have to force ourselves to stay with them. But they exude a serenity, a simplicity that is a sign of life. A kind of crystal clear, near angelic innocence hovers in them, imbuing the Aktions with the quality of a rite. A rite, in which a person is sacrificed as a means of exorcising death. Schwarzkogler throws himself at the mercy of death in these pictures only to reappear very much alive on its opposite shores. No wonder he gave up his Aktions—having presented six within one year (1965–66)—in order to spend the remaining three years of his life, with death now behind him, in pursuit of the secret of this new vitality that was even larger than life. The mental

concentration that emanates from the Aktion photographs was focused on the final exorcism of death. Schwarzkogler may have stumbled upon an intense life that had even mastered death. Today, the photographed Aktions are still luminous with the beauty of this life—a beauty that enthralls not only aesthetically but existentially as well.

"I have had various experiences but it tires me to put them in chronological order," he wrote in 1969. In the exhibition of his lifework at the Museum moderner Kunst Stiftung Ludwig in Vienna, the art is chronologically arranged to help visitors find their way through the labyrinth of paintings, sketches, photographs, pages from notebooks, manifestos, and diary entries. Even so, the long-overdue exhibition suggests that Schwarzkogler did not attach much importance to time. He probably considered numbers a mere earthbound imprint of eternity. His lifework gives the impression as of an inner soul inflamed by one single ball of fire that has burst into fragments of "works." Schwarzkogler was a Romantic; he felt drawn to the fragmentary, an indication, in his case, not of earthly inadequacy but rather of heavenly totality. The artist's works can be traced through time, but in the process our suspicion is

LÁSZLÓ F. FÖLDÉNYI teaches literature at the University of Budapest. He is the author of a book on melancholy (1988) and a study of Caspar David Friedrich to be published in the fall of 1993 by Matthes & Seitz, Munich.

RUDOLF SCHWARZKOGLER, 1. AKTION HOCHZEIT, 1965.
(PHOTO: L. HOFFENREICH / W. KINDLER)

reinforced that what they attract with inexorable magnetism—namely, death—is not part of time. It transcends time, like beauty, which also engaged Schwarzkogler during his lifetime.

The opportunity to view Schwarzkogler's entire lifework for the first time reveals his overriding obsession with perfection, with the manner in which totality may be achieved. His art was devoted to this one objective. The finished artwork was less important to him than the conditions of its creation. This may also explain why his oeuvre, though extraordinarily intense, is relatively small in size. What he did make—be it paintings, photographs, or rough sketches—unmistakably testifies to the fact that Schwarzkogler disdained a conventional frame of reference. He did not want to be an "Aktionist," did not, in other words, want to expand the limits of art in order to secure a place for himself within them. Schwarzkogler was a mystic—in the original sense of the word. He was an artist not by virtue of the fact that he wanted to make art but rather by virtue of the fact that he lived reality with such uncompromising intensity and depth that traces of perfection mark every single one of his gestures.

As different as the two may be, I could not help thinking of Marcel Duchamp while at the exhibition in Vienna: the cold gaze of suspended judgment that he fixes on things until they themselves break out into a cold sweat. Schwarzkogler had the same intent: he wanted to experience an unmediated, unfiltered sensual reality; to strip away its veil of concepts. He wanted to see as only an animal, an infant, a madman, or God can see. The insights thus gained he sought to reconcile with human knowledge and experience. He wanted to unmask himself in the hope of extraordinary enrichment. In short, driven without respite to outdo himself, he aspired to the impossible, to his own post-mortem, which he considered the most fundamental experience in life. "ART TURNED INWARDS: REAL PAINTING," he wrote. His is an art of inner perception. Making the visible invisible. Or conversely: the attempt to discover the unconditional aspect of conditions. It is what Novalis called Romanticizing. His concern was the alchemy of the senses. Not to depict but to decompose things.

"It is … necessary to obliterate all representation in the practice of art," he noted in 1968. This was a lifelong objective. In his earliest paintings he tried to create relations of pure color, to make visual Malevich's call for palpable sensibility. He sought the balance essential to the success of a painting, but not extractable from one single element of the picture alone. Schwarzkogler might be said to have explored not the sensual side of painting but rather its theology. Even as a painter, he was primarily a mystic, obsessed with the exploration of unfathomable order. He wanted to decompose the visible world in order to create a new structure out of the invisible relations thus exposed to view.

The human body is as suitable a support to this end as the painter's canvas. When Schwarzkogler "used" the human body, he was less interested in its hidden potential than in the prerequisites of the living body itself: the root of life, i.e., that which by definition cannot be identified with life. Schwarzkogler's single-minded exploration of these issues defined his Aktions. In contrast to the compact, sensual Aktions of Günter Brus, Hermann Nitsch, and especially Otto Muehl, he did not focus on the uniqueness and irrevocability of the gesture but rather on the structure of the circumstances of the Aktion. He did not delight in sensuality; he was seeking an abstract order. Speaking of abstraction, we must not forget that in early Christianity and Neoplatonic tradition it was a prerequisite for seeking God. Abstraction, analysis, means the attempt to penetrate matter in the hopes of finding nonmatter. Schwarzkogler was not an Aktionist artist; he was an Aktionist theologian.

None of his Aktions—with the exception of his first, the "wedding"—were public. He staged them for himself, or rather for the eye of the camera. The emphasis lay not on process but on isolated moments. The photographs of the Aktions are studio shots. They are genuine still lifes—deathly still lifes—and an exact mirror of Schwarzkogler's wish to freeze moments of the Aktion and thus bring life to a halt. In Nitsch's or Muehl's Aktions, viewers are gripped primarily by the Aktion itself, by the performer's ecstatic or repulsive gestures. The emphasis is on a story, a sequence of events and their outcome. Although thoroughly constructed, it is their content as manifesto that weighs most heavily, that makes them aggressive, obtrusive, and orgiastic—in the truest sense of the word. In Schwarzkogler's Aktions, composition takes center stage, the pure order of visible elements, which is not necessarily an intrinsic feature of the elements themselves. The content of the Aktions is admittedly as shocking and disturbing as in other Viennese Aktions: blinding, castration, lethal injections, clinical sterility, the atmosphere of a dissecting theater, and execution—all motifs involved in an unadulterated Viennese artist's initiation. And yet: on comparing the single shots, we do not follow a storyline, a plot, nor do we try to read a possible conclusion into them; instead we watch and study the slow procession of compositions. Nitsch's *Orgies Mysteries Theater* unfolds in space and time; Schwarzkogler's Aktions are "finished" from the first shot. The pictures that follow do not spread the first moment out in space and time but rather blast it in on itself, while simultaneously preserving its timeless, life-transcending beauty. In contrast to the explosion touched off by Nitsch, Schwarzkogler causes an implosion. Not the Dionysian ecstasy of Nitsch and Brus prevails here

RUDOLF SCHWARZKOGLER, 1. AKTION HOCHZEIT, 1965.
(PHOTO: L. HOFFENREICH / W. KINDLER)

but perfect aesthetic order and mute silence. Schwarzkogler's Aktions take place in a Garden of Eden—not at the beginning of creation but rather at the end, where life has already been lived and innocence regained. The photographs also recall the work of Egon Schiele: aestheticism driven to unsurpassable extremes. Just one more gesture and everything would fall apart, reduced to nothingness.

The abstract order that can be distinguished in Schwarzkogler's photographs evokes not only artistic parallels and previous events; it also shows a resemblance to illustrations in an alchemist's handbook. Like Schwarzkogler's Aktions, the drawings in *Donum Dei* or in *Sapientia veterum* demonstrate stages of penetration into matter: *praeparatio, sublimatio, coitus, solutio, generatio, separatio, coniunctio, fixatio,* and of course *putrefactio,* where the conjoined couple must immerse themselves in black *nigredo* and traverse death in order to conceive a child—to conceive life. Like his alchemist predecessors, Schwarzkogler also sought *prima materia,* a totality that surpasses death as well as life. For him, the quest meant abstraction from everything that could draw humankind away from totality and back to fragmentation.

RUDOLF SCHWARZKOGLER, 1. AKTION HOCHZEIT, 1965. (PHOTO: L. HOFFENREICH / W. KINDLER)

Transgressing profane borders ("borderline of potential perception," he writes towards the end of his life) in the interest of cosmic totality: to live through existence with heightened intensity—that is what serves art. This explains why he variously called art a "cold-turkey cure," a "PURGATORY OF THE SENSES," or the "art of healing." Above all, he considered art a source of new experience, requiring neither a public nor hypostatized works of art. Like Novalis, he could say, the mysterious path leads inwards, to places where it is hard to follow others.

Schwarzkogler never looked back while pursuing this path in the final years before his death. The record he kept of his quest marks a radical—mystical—expansion of art. Instead of art, he had found a ritual for life. "i fall into a cave: i want to recognize or reach, try to penetrate something and end up beside myself," he wrote shortly before he died, expressing himself with a tragic depth that echoes the words of Van Gogh or Artaud. "it is a black cloth that is thrown over me ... i am completely ecstatic GIGANTIC there are no recognizable limits ... my big toe is frozen." Later, "part of me is separating off." Followed by, "inconceivable sorrow." Until he finally writes, "yet everything is clear, i have the feeling i'm a star among stars." A life was extinguished by his death, but his lifework leaves no doubt that the light of the star is still shining bright.

(Translation from the German: Catherine Schelbert)

138

INSERT

RICHMOND

BURTON

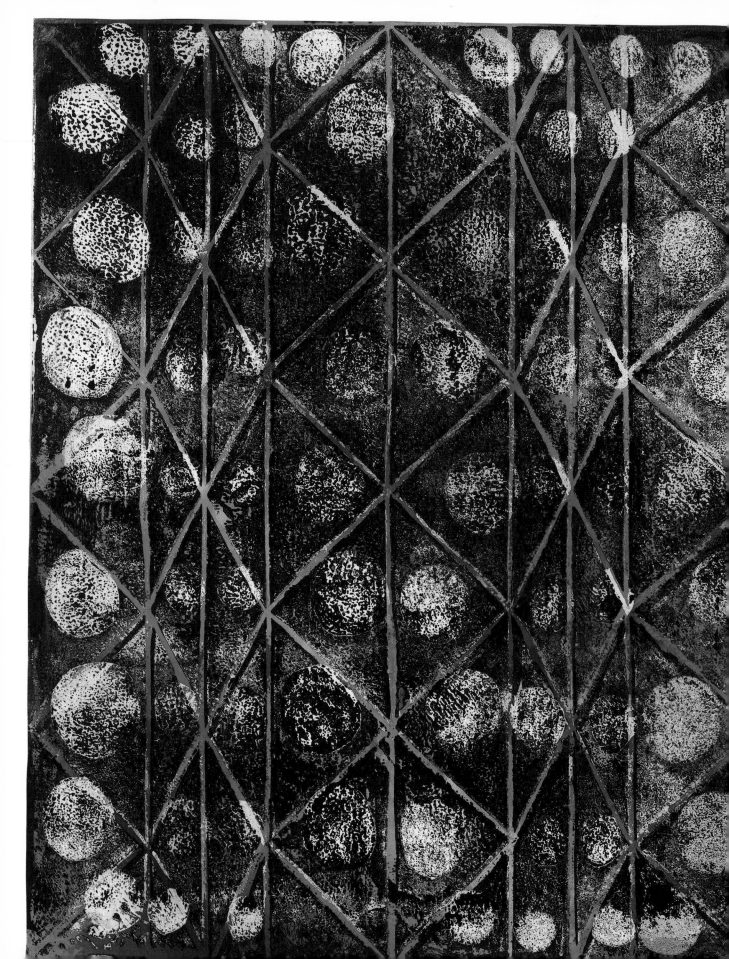

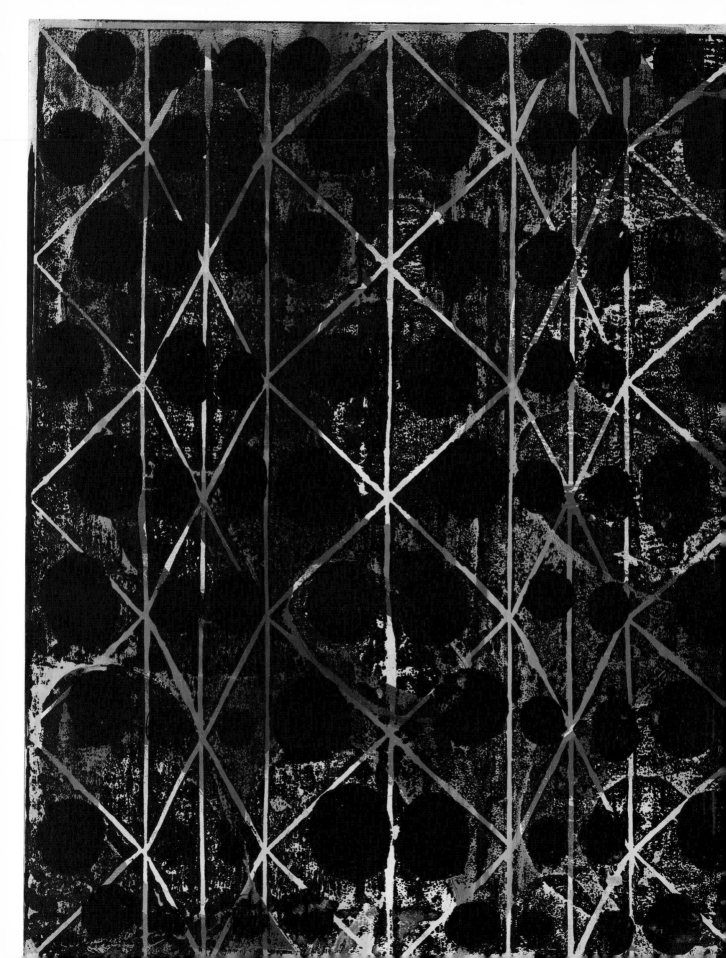

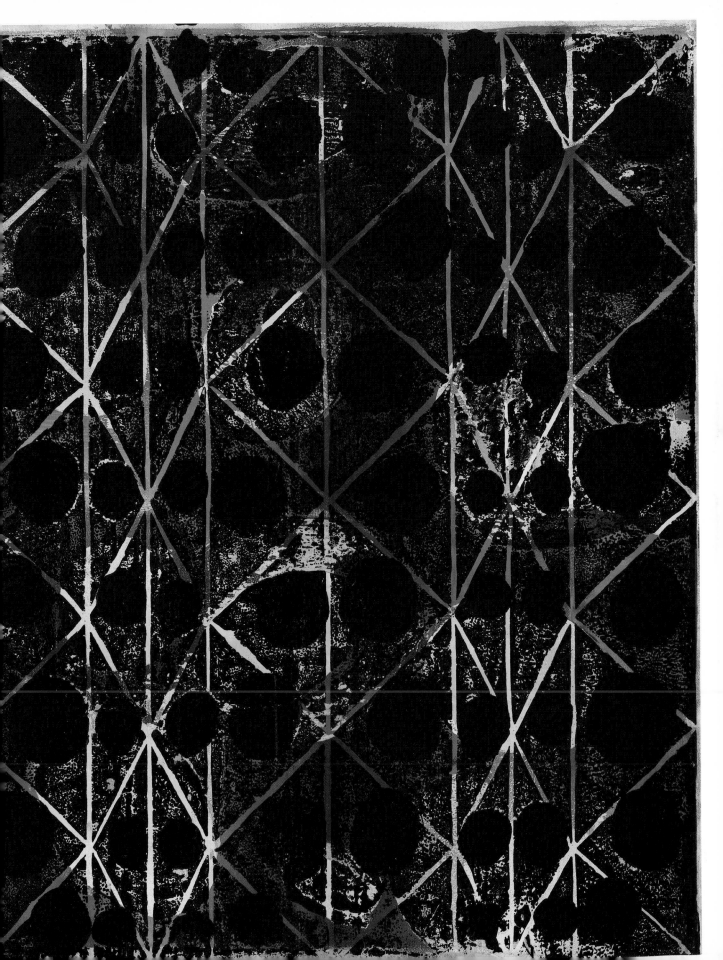

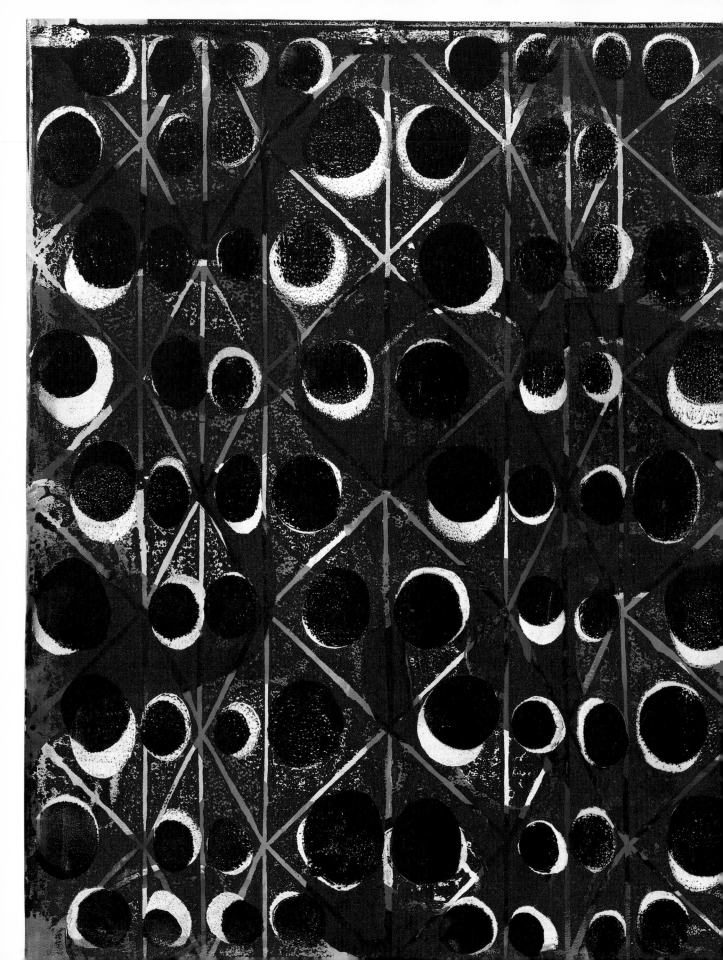

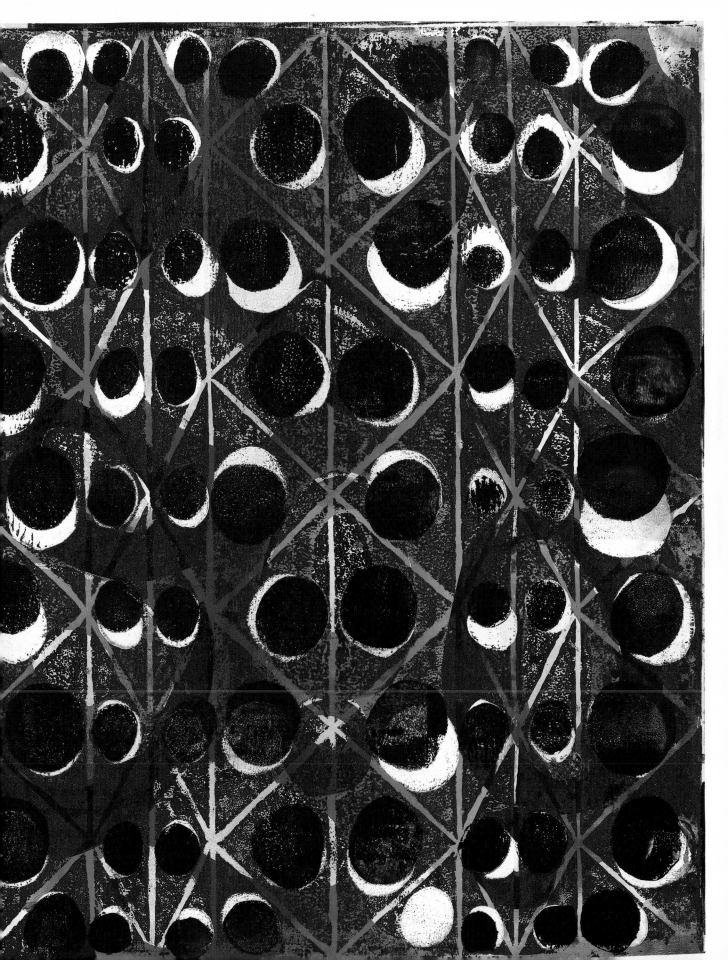

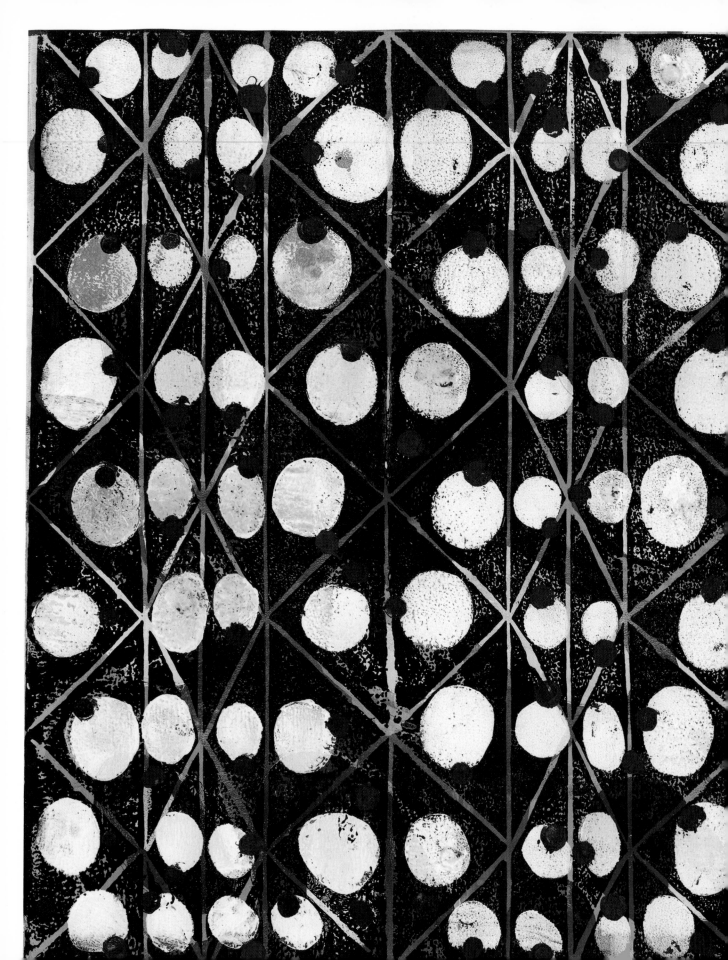

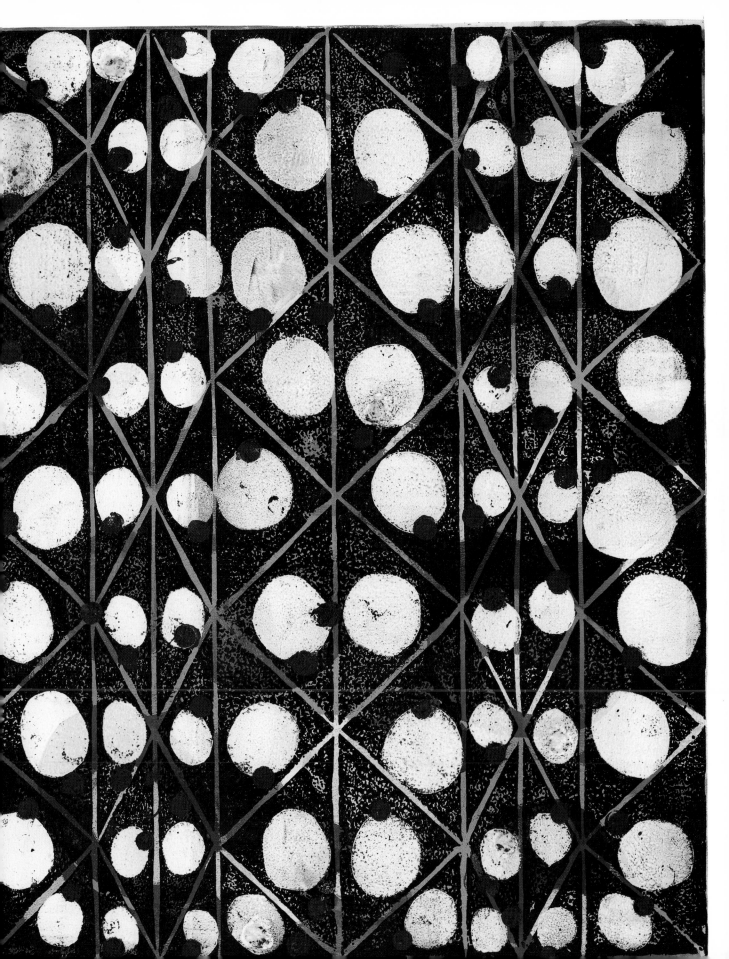

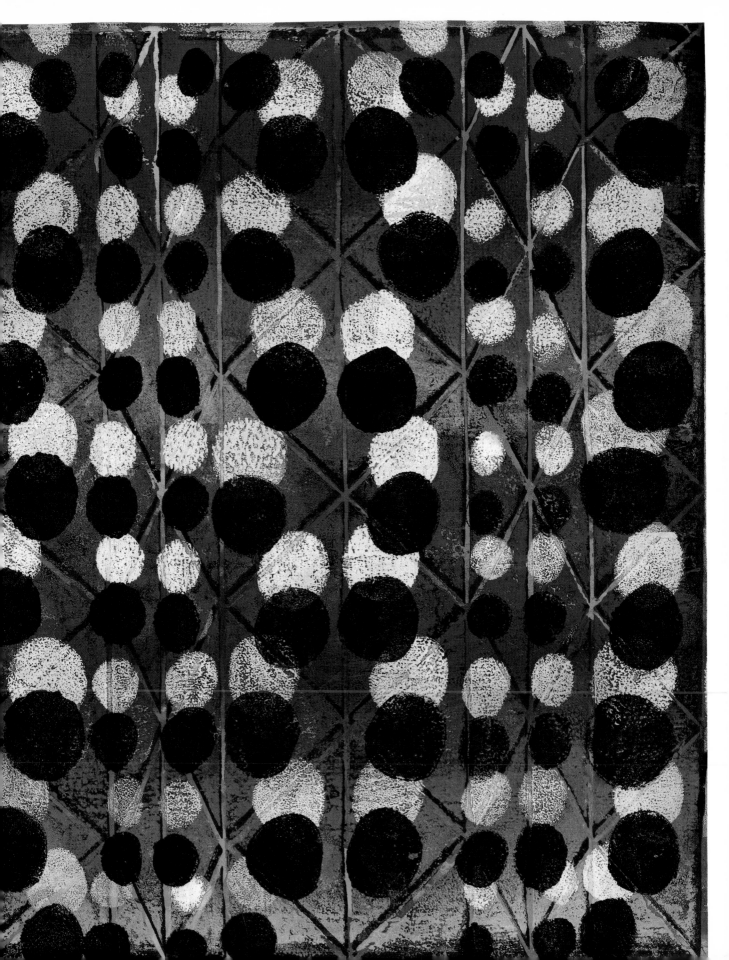

CUMULUS

Aus Europa

IN JEDER AUSGABE VON PARKETT PEILT EINE CUMULUS-WOLKE AUS AME-
RIKA UND EINE AUS EUROPA DIE INTERESSIERTEN KUNSTFREUNDE AN.
SIE TRÄGT PERSÖNLICHE RÜCKBLICKE, BEURTEILUNGEN UND DENK-
WÜRDIGE BEGEGNUNGEN MIT SICH – ALS JEWEILS GANZ EIGENE DAR-
STELLUNG EINER BERUFSMÄSSIGEN AUSEINANDERSETZUNG.

In diesem Heft äussern sich CHRISTOPH TANNERT, *Projektleiter Bildende
Kunst am Künstlerhaus Bethanien, Berlin, und* DAVID RIMANELLI, *Publizist
aus New York.*

Berlin – Fast Forward?

Es gibt wohl gegenwärtig keine deutsche Stadt, die wegen ihres kulturellen
Flairs mehr umstritten wäre als Berlin.
Einerseits kamen im vergangenen Jahr
mehrere hundert junge Leute und
Lebenskünstler aller Couleur, um in
den verschiedensten Projekten und
Initiativen unterzukommen und die
nichtinstitutionalisierte Basis der Stadt
zu verbreitern. Andererseits war das
Geschrei der aus öffentlicher Hand
subventionierten Häuser wegen der
Kürzungen und Sparmassnahmen im
Zuge der deutschen Vereinigung noch
nie so laut und die Zungen der Lokal-
kritiker noch nie so spitz, als es darum
ging, einen lange schwelenden Gene-
rationskonflikt und damit zusammen-
hängende Verteilungskämpfe im Sinne

CHRISTOPH TANNERT

einer Anwartschaft auf bestimmte Räume, Gelder und Posten über die Medi-
en zu verhandeln.

Seit dem Mauerfall versucht die
Stadt aus ihrer Schattenlage heraus-
zukommen und ist doch in vielerlei
Hinsicht nicht über ein Provinzniveau
hinausgelangt. Zwanghaft werkeln die
Kulturpolitiker, um etwas «Haupt-
städtisches» zu etablieren, und fabri-
zieren doch im Ostteil der Stadt nicht
mehr als strukturelles Flickwerk,
während im Westteil der alte Geist
einer Sicherungsmentalität, die alles
beim alten lassen will, Fettlebe feiert.

Doch nichts ist mehr, wie es war,
seit der Westen im Osten liegt. Aus-
weichlösungen werden nicht mehr
geboten. Heiner Müller hat bereits die
Mongolen am Müggelsee zelten sehen.
Darauf hat die Stadt allerdings viel zu
wenig reagiert. Sie hat es versäumt,
sich als Scharnier eines kulturellen
Ost-West-Austauschs zu etablieren. Weder den Nahbereich einer spröden
Gegenkultur der ostdeutschen Lang-

samkeit noch die Veränderungen in
der Ferne, das Herauswachsen Ost-
europas und Asiens aus der kollektiven
Norm hat Berlin im Blick. Die Kontra-
stierung des einen mit dem anderen
noch viel weniger. Es würde sich
z.B. lohnen, nachzudenken über die
Widersprüche zwischen dem neuen
osteuropäischen Ethnozentrismus und
den westeuropäischen und amerikanischen Trends zur kulturellen Mondiali-
sierung (Picasso, Warhol, Koons und
Disneyland *über alles!*). Wohin steuert
Osteuropa? Nach welchen Schablonen
verbildet der Westen die Erwartungen
an den eigenen Wandel? Die Präsentation avancierter Strömungen in der
chinesischen Kunst, Rockmusik und
Literatur, die im Februar 1993 mass-
geblich vom Haus der Kulturen der
Welt getragen wurde, stellt eher eine
konsequente Ausnahme in der Abfolge
verpasster Chancen dar.

Nach wie vor wird in Berlin um das
Für und Wider von «Grossausstellun-
gen» gestritten. Die Neue National-
galerie in der Potsdamer Strasse und
Christos Joachimides als Zeitgeist-

Scout und Gast-Kurator am Martin-Gropius-Bau wetteifern um Rekorde im Besuchertourismus. Eine Provinzposse, möchte man meinen. In Paris oder New York würde niemand auf die Idee kommen, derartige Akte als ungebührlich zu empfinden, im Gegenteil. Aber in Berlin wird nach «Alternativen» gerufen. Am liebsten kämpft man nach pseudodialektischer Methode: «Hochkunst» gegen «nichtetablierte Trendbrecher». Aber 1968 ist längst over, und Kunst lebt heute eher aus ihrer Inexistenz. Es ist wohl wahr, andere deutsche Städte, allen voran Köln, Frankfurt, Düsseldorf, München und Hamburg, haben durch ihre Galerien und Kunstvereine die Entwicklungen der jungen Gegenwartskunst begleitet, oft sogar pointiert, während sich Berlin eher zum Anwalt dessen machte, was ausserhalb aller internationalen Diskurse, aber inmitten einer auf berlinische Traditionen verengten, heimatlichen Perspektive lag nach dem Motto: «Warum in die Ferne schweifen...»

Nur so wird verständlich, warum derzeit massive Kritik auf die Köpfe derer niederprasselt, die der Staatlichen Kunsthalle, den beiden Kunstvereinen und der Berlinischen Galerie vorstehen. Diese Institute haben in den letzten Jahren minutiös den eigenen Nabel umspielt und aus Angst vor dem «unheimlichen Koloss Weltstadt» lieber im Vorgarten der eigenen Sehnsüchte geharkt, als teilzuhaben an den Spannungen zwischen Gestern und Heute. Selbstverständlich gab es auch Lichtblicke, aber das Schmollwinkelfeeling überwog, selten gelang es, Knotenpunkte der Prioritätenverschiebung in der Kunst anzuvisieren. Ich habe das kollektive Engagement des Realismusstudios der Neuen

Gesellschaft für Bildende Kunst bewundert – wohin hat es sich verflüchtigt? Statt Leuchtfeuern kalte Asche.

Wegen dieser und anderer Defizite wird nun der Ruf nach einem Haus, das musterhaft die Reibungsflächen aktueller Kunstentwicklungen in ihren unterschiedlichen kulturellen Sphären sucht und zeigt, immer lauter. Die Schliessung der Staatlichen Kunsthalle alten Stils scheint unvermeidlich. Doch wie weiter? Wegen seiner über 15jährigen Tätigkeit im öffentlichen Dienst ist Dieter Ruckhaberle, Direktor der Kunsthalle, unkündbar. Die vom Kultursenator Roloff-Momin angedachte Fusion zwischen Kunsthalle und Berlinischer Galerie wird jedoch von Jörn Merkert, Direktor der Berlinischen Galerie, kritisch kommentiert. Überdies strebt Jörn Merkert den Umzug der Berlinischen Galerie in das Gebäude des ehemaligen Postfuhrhofs in der Oranienburger Strasse im Ostteil der Stadt, unweit der Museumsinsel und mitten im Herzen des durch seine junge Galerieszene bekanntgewordenen Scheunenviertels, an. Christos Joachimides könnte nach diesem Wechsel die Intendanz des Martin-Gropius-Baus übernehmen. Aber was wird dann aus dem Kunsthallendirektor und seiner Mannschaft? Ruckhaberle ist ein Kämpfer, der für seine Belange prozessieren wird. Fürs erste erhielt er erst einmal eine angemessene Erhöhung des Budgets für das laufende Jahr. War das schon die Abfindung? Vielleicht regelt sich das Problem Kunsthalle aber auch ganz allein. Bereits im Winter 1991/92 drohte die Schliessung der Räume im Bikinihaus am Breitscheidplatz wegen gigantischer Mietsteigerungen. Mittlerweile liegt der Mietpreis für die 2700 m² der Halle bei DM 75,–/m².

Manch einer liebäugelt mit den Ausstellungsräumen am Fernsehturm in Ost-Berlin. Diese schreien geradezu nach einer programmatischen Nutzung. Aber die Angelegenheit Kunsthalle wird erst dann geklärt sein, wenn man sie nicht länger als Sozialmassnahme für ihre Mitarbeiter, sondern im Engagement für das Abstandsverhalten Kunst versteht.

Als Alternative zu den eher konservativen und Berlin-zentrierten Programmen der genannten Häuser bringen sich seit Sommer 1992 die KUNST-WERKE BERLIN E.V., eine Gruppe idealistischer Jungdynamiker mit Hang zum symbolischen Pluralismus ins Gespräch. Es ist ihr Verdienst, als Gegenpol (oder vielleicht auch libertäre Ergänzungsthese zum multikulturellen Cross-Over des Kunsthauses *Tacheles*) ein Beraterteam potenter Berliner Individualisten an sich gebunden zu haben, von denen man sich nun einschneidende Weichenstellungen erhofft. Die bisherigen Ausstellungen und Veranstaltungen von Joan Jonas bis Micha Brendel, Nan Goldin bis Christo, namenlos bis ruhmsüchtig, inszeniert als wuchernder Zellverbund mal hier mal da, waren ein vielbeachteter und kontrovers diskutierter Beginn. Nun wird erwartet, dass der Vorschusslorbeer eingelöst wird. Es wäre dringend nötig, den Berliner Hang zur Selbstbezüglichkeit zu bremsen und über den eigenen Tellerrand hinaus, vernetzter, globalkultureller zu denken.

Nach der Vereinigung der beiden Stadthälften wurde offenbar, wie ähnlich in Ost und West gedacht und unterentwickelt wurde. Die Einseitigkeit der geleisteten Kulturarbeit ist unübersehbar. Die helfende Hand des Staates bzw. der Stadt ermöglichte Künstlern kurzzeitig, aber vergleichsweise fürstlich konditioniert, das Überleben.

Ich plädiere für die «Kulturpflicht» eines jeden Staates. Allerdings muss gefragt werden nach politischem Lobbyismus und den damit im Zusammenhang stehenden Alimentationen, die einem Diktat zeitgenössischer Stimmung nahekommen, den Künsten aber nicht zu einem gehobeneren Qualitätslevel verhelfen. Vor und nach den Farborgien der «Wild Boys» war vieles, was beispielsweise über die Einladungen des Deutschen Akademischen Austauschdienstes nach Berlin kam, spannender, herausfordernder und kompromissloser als die Brutstätten der Heftigkeit zwischen Moritzplatz und Prenzlauer Berg. Nach wie vor nährt sich jedoch eine populistische Aftermoderne von den Brosamen des Establishments, das sich allen Kritikprinzipien gegenüber taub stellt. Wer von den an kultureller Unterschiedlichkeit Interessierten möchte da nicht verzweifeln? Keine Medienakademie in Berlin (ausser der privaten Medienhochschule BILDO), der *Hamburger Bahnhof* als mögliches Zentrum der Kunst nach 1960 weiterhin Baustelle, der Quergeist allerorten in der Warteschleife. Wären da nicht die Galerien und Schauräume von Barbara Weiss, Bruno Brunnet, Franck & Schulte, Gebauer & Günther, Zwinger, Art Acker, Bilderdienst, Botschaft, Anselm Dreher, Fahnemann, Federowskij, Gelbe Musik, Haderek & Fischer, Lukas & Hoffmann, Wewerka, Kapinos oder aber die quicklebendige Art-Guerilla vom Prenzlauer Berg und aus der Stadtmitte, die Déjà-vu-Erlebnisse hätten Berlin noch weiter ins Ödland der Flachware gezerrt. Projekte der Künstlerselbsthilfe oder selbstverwaltete Organisationsstrukturen, wie sie zuhauf in Ost-Berlin

und der DDR aus dem Boden schossen und wieder verblühten, sind Ausdruck einer Notlage und sollten auch als solche gesehen werden. Dass sie als kulturelle Faktoren der Stadt zusätzlich ein bisschen Farbe auf den verzogenen Resonanzboden aufbringen, kann nicht übersehen werden angesichts der Hiobsmeldungen über Ateliernotstand und die Streichung von Arbeitsbeschaffungsmassnahmen im real existierenden System der Mietspekulation. Aber nur die gegenwärtige materielle Zwangslage im Blick zu haben, halte ich für verhängnisvoll, wenn nicht auch gleichzeitig eine Diskussion über das geistige Umfeld und die vorhandenen Erwartungen an Kunst angestrebt wird. Polemik gab es in der Vergangenheit genug, die Chancen, Positionen exemplarisch vorzuführen, wurden vertan. Nach wie vor fehlt Berlin ein Angelpunkt des Seitenblicks, ein Forum der Ungewissheit und natürlich eine Kunstzeitschrift, die die politischen Umbrüche in der Welt und den Paradigmenwechsel in der Kunst begleitet bzw. an elementarer Problemdefinition und Widerspruch selbst beteiligt ist. Die von Matthias Flügge und Michael Freitag in Ost-Berlin herausgegebene *neue bildende kunst* ist freilich auf dem besten Weg, dieses Loch auszufüllen mit Nahrung für die Streithungrigen sowie einem Layout, das den Zeitsprung Ost-West nicht kaschiert, sondern ihn, wie auch die Informationen über Osteuropa, in einen produktiven interkulturellen Erlebnisraum zieht. Berlin kocht in Sachen Kunst noch auf Sparflamme, aber in einer Beziehung glühen die Sensoren: Denn Berlins Underground probiert eine neue Spielart. Nach wie vor sind die durch die Maueröffnung ins Blickfeld einer

amüsierwütigen *Scene* gerückten Häuserruinen, Bunker, Luftschutz- und Kohlenkeller in Ost-Berlin die heissesten Plätze des Nachtlebens. Je gegenwärtiger das Flair des Vergangenen, um so anziehender werden die aus der volkseigenen Erbmasse hervorgegangenen oder sogar NS-Gebäude für die lärmenden Clubber. Der Sound of Berlin und sein visuelles Dekor, die erste deutsche Eigenkreation innerhalb der internationalen Partybewegung, modifiziert seine Stereotypen. Tekkno, bisher von Riesenevents wie der *Love Parade* oder *Mayday* getragen, wird wieder etwas normaler, aber behält seinen samtenen Biss. Der Hype bis hin zur Bizarrerie demonstrationshysterischer «Tekknozid»-Veranstaltungen speckt seinen Bombast ab, aber in der Berührung mit den aktuellen popkulturellen Strömungen ist er zurückgekehrt von der Massenbeglückung zu den Kicks einer differenzierten Gruppenidentität – nun auf enorm verbreiteter Basis. In den Charts der elektronischen Psychotisierung der Gesellschaft durch eine quicklebendige Pop- und Club-Kultur von Soft bis Hardcore liegt Berlin ganz weit vorn, sowohl durch das, was produziert, als auch durch das, was aufgelegt wird.

Die Aufbruchstimmung und der exzessive Aktivismus nach der Maueröffnung hat eine Phase transformatorischer Anpassung an die Realitäten vollzogen. Von der 24stündigen Dancefloor-Panik geht der Trend jetzt in die Langzeitversion einer in sich ruhenden, weniger hart und aggressiv gespielten Trance-Variante. Der Malerei hat das einen Boom post-konzeptueller Malerei beschert.

Unter dieser Verpackung ist also noch Hoffnung. Wenigstens im Dauertanzen sind Berlins Nachtschwärmer olympiaverdächtig.

Berlin – Fast Forward?

CHRISTOPH TANNERT

At the moment, probably no city in Germany boasts a more controversial flair for culture than Berlin. For one thing, several hundred young people of every persuasion flocked into the city last year to work on a variety of projects and programs, thus broadening the noninstitutionalized base of the city. For another, the outcry against budget cuts and curtailment of funds due to reunification has never been so loud, nor the tongues of local critics so scathing as when it came to dealing in the media with the issue of a generation conflict about to boil over and the attendant wrangling over the distribution of space, money, and jobs.

Although the city has been trying to come out of the shadows since the collapse of the wall, it is, in many respects, still mired in provincialism. Cultural pundits and politicians are compulsively frittering away their energies in a frantic effort to establish a "cosmopolitan atmosphere." The result in the eastern half of the city is little more than piecemeal dabs at structural repairs while in the western half the security-blanket mentality of hanging on to the same old tried-and-tested system is enjoying a nonpareil heyday.

However, nothing is what it was since the West moved East. Ersatz solutions are no longer available. Heiner Müller already saw Mongolians camping at Lake Müggel but the city barely took note and thus missed the chance, once again, to act as the linchpin of cultural exchange between East and West. Berlin has adjusted its sights neither to East Germany's unhurried, aloof counterculture next door nor to the distant changes in eastern Europe and Asia as they rise above the collective norm—and even less to contrasting the one with the other. It would, for instance, be well worth thinking about the contradictions between the revival of ethnocentrism in eastern Europe and the west European and American drift towards cultural globalization (Picasso, Warhol, Koons, and Disneyland *über alles!*). Where is eastern Europe heading? Into which molds is the West trying to squeeze its own expectations of change? The presentation of advanced currents in Chinese art, rock, and literature, supported mainly by the House of the Cultures of the World in February 1993, is a striking exception to the succession of missed opportunities.

The pros and cons of "megashows" are still the subject of heated debate in Berlin. The New National Gallery on Potsdamerstrasse and Christos Joachimides as zeitgeist scout and guest curator at the Martin-Gropius-Bau are vying for record numbers of visitors in the flourishing field of art tourism. A provincial farce, to put it mildly. In Paris or New York, no one in his right mind would question the propriety of such efforts. Quite the contrary! In Berlin, however, people are calling for "alternatives," the most popular strategy being to fight for them with pseudo-dialectic arguments: "high art" versus "nonestablished trend-breakers." But '68 has been over for years and art today tends to thrive on its nonexistence. Admittedly, galleries and art associations in other German cities, notably Cologne, Frankfurt, Düsseldorf, Munich, and Hamburg, have kept abreast of developments in recent contemporary art—often even pointedly, while Berlin faithfully espouses developments outside the mainstream of international discourse but within the narrow perspective of traditions native to Berlin, after the motto: why go far afield ...?

Only in this way can one understand why such hefty criticism is raining down on the heads of the Staatliche Kunsthalle, the two Kunstvereins, and the Berlinische Galerie. In recent years, these institutions have conquered their fear of a "terrifying cosmopolis" by meticulously zeroing in on their belly buttons or puttering around in the front yard of their own longings rather than committing themselves to the tensions between yesterday and today.

Despite the occasional, irrepressible ray of hope, the Sulky Sue syndrome still prevails. Rarely has anyone succeeded in changing the sights and shifting the priorities in art. I admire the collective commitment of the Realism Studio of the Neue Gesellschaft für Bildende Kunst (New Association of the Fine Arts) but it seems to have gone up in smoke. Cold embers instead of guiding lights.

These and other shortcomings are fueling the call for an institution that seeks out and shows areas of friction within current developments in the various cultural spheres of the arts. Closing down the old style Staatliche Kunsthalle is apparently inevitable. But what next?

Because of his fifteen years of public service as the director of the Kunsthalle, Dieter Ruckhaberle cannot be asked to step down. On the other hand, the proposed fusion of the Kunsthalle and the Berlinische Galerie, by the minister of culture, Roloff-Momin, has met with criticism from Berlinische Galerie director Jörn Merkert. Besides, Merkert wants to move the gallery east to Oranienburgerstrasse not far from the island of museums and in the heart of the Scheunen quarter known for its burgeoning young galleries. After the move, Christos Joachimides could take charge of the Martin-Gropius-Bau. But then, what will happen to the director of the Kunsthalle and his staff? Ruckhaberle is prepared to go to court to fight for his rights. In the meantime, he has received a budget increase for the current year. Or is that already severance pay? Perhaps the Kunsthalle problem will take care of itself. In the winter of 1991/92, the Bikinihaus on Breitscheidplatz was almost forced to close down because of skyrocketing rents, and the Kunsthalle can barely hold up under the financial strain. Many people have set their sights on the television tower in East Berlin, with spaces that are positively screaming for programmatic utilization.

Whatever the case, the Kunsthalle issue cannot be solved as long as social measures to preserve the staff are pitted against a commitment to the detachment and independence of the arts.

Since the summer of 1992, the KUNST-WERKE BERLIN, a group of young, dynamic idealists with a taste for symbolic pluralism, have made a name for themselves as an alternative to the rather more conservative, Berlin-centered programs of the above-mentioned institutions. They have succeeded in tipping the scales (or perhaps complementing art space *Tacheles*' multicultural crossover) by mandating a team of consultants consisting of potent Berlin individualists who, it is hoped, will set the stage for incisive change. The exhibitions and events organized to date, from Joan Jonas to Micha Brendel, Nan Goldin to Christo, nameless to any-price-glory, staged here, there, and everywhere as a rampant conspiracy of cells, has been a promising, much vaunted, and controversial beginning. Now people expect returns on the advance praise. It is vital to actively discourage Berlin's tendencies towards self-reference; the city's steam has to escape through other valves, above all by thinking in globally intercultural terms.

When the two halves of the city were reunified, their resemblance in terms of mentality and underdevelopment was undeniable, just as the bias in promoting cultural endeavor was evident. The governmental helping hand, be it the state or the city, ensured artists' survival on a short-term basis under relatively royal conditions.

I certainly advocate that every state assume "cultural responsibility," but one must keep an eye on political lobbying and related handouts, which are tantamount to the dictates of the current mood without necessarily raising the level of quality in the arts. Before and after the "Wild Boys" had their color orgies, things were much more exciting, challenging, and uncompromising. Think, for instance, of the contributions that came to Berlin through the invitations of the DAAD, that hotbed of fierce intensity between Moritzplatz and Prenzlauer Berg. Even so, a populist "after-modernity" still feeds on the crumbs tossed out by an Establishment blind to all principles of criticism. Under these circumstances, how can anyone interested in cultural dissent not despair?

In Berlin, no media academy (with the exception of the private institution BILDO); the Hamburger Bahnhof as a possible art center after 1960 still a construction site; and everywhere the monkey-wrench spirit on hold. If it weren't for the galleries and showrooms of Barbara Weiss, Bruno Brunnet, Franck & Schulte, Gebauer & Günther, Zwinger, Art Acker, Bilderdienst, Botschaft, Anselm Dreher, Fahnemann, Federowskij, Gelbe Musik, Haderek & Fischer, Lukas & Hoffmann, Wewerka, Kapinos, or even the lively Art-Guerrillas of Prenzlauer Berg and mid-town, déjà-vu experiences would have continued to drag Berlin further and further into the wastelands of monotony. The myriad self-help artists' projects or self-managed organizational structures that shot up out of nowhere in East Berlin and the GDR only to wither and die indicate a state of emergency that should be treated as such. The fact that they add a bit of color to the warped soundboard of the city cannot be ignored considering the disastrous shortage of studio space and cuts in federally funded positions in the painfully real system of rental speculation, but it would be ruinous to focus only on the current predicament without attempting to explore the spiritual framework and existing expectations of art. There have been enough polemics in the past; the chance to make room for exemplary positions has been passed up. Berlin still lacks the crucial sidelong glance, a forum for uncertainty, and, of course, an art journal that reports on radical political change the world over, on shifting paradigms in art, that is, a journal that is actively involved not only in the elementary definition of the issues at stake but also in the contradictions. The *neue bildende kunst,* edited by Matthias Flügge and Michael Freitag, is doing a valiant job of filling the gap with fuel for argumentative minds and a layout that, instead of concealing the time rift between East and West, places it—along with information on Eastern Europe—in the context of intercultural experience.

Art in Berlin is still only simmering, but in one respect the sensors are red-hot: Berlin's underground has found a new way to play the game. The dilapidated buildings, bunkers, air-raid shelters, and coal cellars, grabbed up by a fun-wild crowd after the wall came down, are still the hottest places in East Berlin's nightlife. The more these buildings embody a flair for the past, as part of the GDR's own heritage or even as Nazi buildings, the more attractive noisy nightclub goers find them. The sound of Berlin and its visual decor, the first creation of Germany's own within the international party movement, is modifying its stereotypes. "Tekkno," music once primarily the domain of mega-events like the *Love Parade* or *Mayday,* is not as wild as it used to be but it still has its velvet sting. The bombastic hype, the bizarrerie of hysterical "Tekkno-cide" extravaganzas, has calmed down a bit, but in contact with trends in current pop culture it has made a comeback. No longer a harbinger of mass euphoria, it now provides the kicks of sophisticated group identification—with an enormously broad base. Berlin's hopping pop and club culture, from soft to hard core, is edging into first place on the charts of the electronic psychotization of society, not only in terms of what is produced but also of what is heard.

The mood of change and the excessive activism that followed hard on the collapse of the wall has undergone a phase of transformative adjustment to realities. The trend is shifting away from 24-hour-dance-floor panic toward a long-term—no longer as hard and aggressive, but rather more stable—trance variety. In the art world, this has prompted a boom in post-conceptual painting.

There is still hope underneath the styling: Berlin's night owls may have Olympic stature after all, at least in the dance marathon.

(Translation: Catherine Schelbert)

CUMULUS

From America

IN EVERY EDITION OF PARKETT, TWO CUMULUS CLOUDS, ONE FROM AMERICA, THE OTHER FROM EUROPE, FLOAT OUT TO AN INTERESTED PUBLIC. THEY CONVEY INDIVIDUAL OPINIONS, ASSESSMENTS, AND MEMORABLE ENCOUNTERS – AS ENTIRELY PERSONAL PRESENTATIONS OF PROFESSIONAL ISSUES.

Our contributors to this issue are <u>DAVID RIMANELLI</u>, a writer living in New York, and <u>CHRISTOPH TANNERT</u>, who is project director of fine arts at the Künstlerhaus Bethanien, Berlin.

"NOBODY WANTS TO SEE A MOVIE WITH MADONNA IN IT"

(Text of a sticker designed by Larry Johnson)

DAVID RIMANELLI

The assertion that we live in a world saturated with the quick-edit images and dissolving voices born of the mass media means almost nothing at this point. Tirelessly weaving discursive webs around the supposed void (of meaning, subjectivity, history) created by the collusion of Hollywood and Madison Avenue leads to a criticism far more hopelessly vitiated than the phantasms that are the avowed objects of its analysis and demystification. The unfortunate fact is that critiques of the mass media usually restate the obvious when they don't simply miss the point. The mass media are obvious in their means and effects; latent no less than manifest content is often dunderheadedly patent. The mass media sometimes even bracket "latent content" as a reamed-out signifier for itself. Part of the minor pleasure that we take in

images of splashing, spilling, and foaming waters inheres in their "latent" sexual content, but you would have to be among the mentally impaired to mistake that content for anything else. So then, what's to critique?

Now some readers are probably already getting impatient with me. You're sweeping with too broad a brush, they'll tetchily complain. Surely the voracious and pervasive spectacles of the mass media deserve—no, require, demand—the serious and sustained critical examination that you so high-handedly dismiss as de trop?

Well, recently I came upon some articles I once clipped from the *Village Voice*, New York's premier tabloid of trendy leftoid lucubration. The sub-

ject: MTV's tenth anniversary and its significance for cultural politics. This is what Mim Udovitch had to say: "Now it seems almost unnecessary to celebrate MTV, since like Walt Whitman, it celebrates itself. And with good reason. Because now, to paraphrase Whitney Houston, no matter what they take from me, they can't take away my MTV." This passage, perhaps not entirely devoid of self-consciousness, evokes familiar techniques of mass media critique—and like such critiques, it has its giddy celebratory side. First, there is the predictable fun to be had in citing high- and low-cultural sources as if no hierarchy existed (Walt Whitman = Whitney Houston). This practice accords with the rather worn (post-) structuralist habit of leveling distinctions in a putatively value-neutral way. It also jibes with a certain brand of well-meaning but spineless cultural politics that doesn't want to see anyone shut out and doesn't want anyone to feel bad: "It's OK, honey, your cultural icon is just as good/valuable/meaningful as mine, and anyone who tells you otherwise is just a mean racist/sexist/classist/homophobic asshole."

The reference to Walt Whitman also provides another, rather more oblique clue to the nature of mass media oriented critique. Udovitch alludes, no doubt sarcastically, to the famous opening lines of Whitman's *Song of Myself*:

> *I celebrate myself,*
> *And what I assume you shall assume,*
> *For every atom belonging to me as good*
> *belongs to you.*

The verb *assume* in the poem's second line has several senses, among them: to don, to take upon oneself, to adopt. These senses accord well with the third line's imagery of sharing or incorporation. But *assume* also means to take for granted or suppose. These various senses or connotations work in concert in a manner that ties in neatly with a belief underlying both the mass media and many of the critiques leveled against them: the belief in a collective consciousness.

The temptation to think in terms of or speculate about a collective consciousness is irresistible, perhaps inevitable, especially if you happen to be a dreary armchair pseud. After all, since everyone in America is intravenously fed off of the TV set, since everyone in America finds the exact image of his or her desire on celluloid, since everyone in America wants to be Madonna's best friend, then it stands to reason that the mass media either possesses extraordinary empathic reserves of knowledge of ordinary citizens' lives, or it functions as an instrument of totalitarian mind control. Maybe it's control through understanding: having tapped the pin-headed collective consciousness, it can all the better manipulate and control it.

Critique which emphasizes a collective consciousness engages in just such games of mystical divination. It wants to answer questions like "Where is the culture now?" and more important, "Where is the culture going?" Maybe these are good questions, but the answers aren't really so easy to come by. For one thing, it is not inconceivable that those answers might only be available to hindsight: a retrospective vantage point of twenty or thirty odd years. Frustrating.

I might add that artists or critics who theoretically or merely habitually assume the existence of a collective consciousness mimic the very processes and functions of the mass media they pretend to demystify or debunk. The entire concerted apparatus of the mass media—movies, television, advertising, newspapers, and magazines—works overtime to divine a collective consciousness that it in fact creates, if only as an image. Even debased cultural products like most of the junk that clutters MTV are not simply reflections but crafted, self-conscious artefacts. Maybe this seems too obvious a point to belabor, especially for those gentle theoreticians among us, but critique of the mass media often takes its objects as a mirror of the American soul and the reality of life today. Hence, for all the third-generation and third-rate (post-)structuralist blather it traffics in, such critique still subscribes at base to old-fashioned ideas of mimesis. I think that at best the sustained critical examination of MTV—my example here, but only one among many—tells us that rock videos mirror the minds of some seventeen-year-old boys. Is that where you want to locate your collective consciousness, or more to the point, your individual consciousness?

The voice behind Larry Johnson's *Untitled (Do You Remember Doris Day?)* belongs to the worlds of the mass media. It speaks of memories, but fictional memories, beyond the compass of recent generations. During the 1970s and '80s the media ushered in a nostalgic '50s fashion. Referring to Doris Day, patent leather shoes, and virgin pins, Johnson alludes to the decade preceding his own historical memory. And yet this text, addressed to its viewers, presupposes these as our collective memories. Sound familiar? Johnson accomplishes a sleight of hand with respect to the phantom of the collective consciousness, because he identifies collective memory with a fictionalizing process of forgetting.

Works like Johnson's abjure the pretense of distance, seeking instead a more covert infiltration—an "inside job," as it were. Too often, self-consciously critical or conceptual art works fail to evince an even rudimentary cleverness. They seem as if they had been cooked up by minds largely oblivious to irony. Hence, an encounter with the most patent sort of irony becomes the occasion for an art work, one which tendentiously "reveals" the obvious. This paradigm of revelation/concealment—the mass media whose procedures conceal insidious intents, the critical art work which brings enlightenment to the benighted—just doesn't work. Art that strives for a genuine critical engagement needs a lighter touch, but a surer hand.

DAVID RIMANELLI

« NIEMAND WILL EINEN FILM MIT MADONNA SEHEN »

(Text eines Aufklebers von Larry Johnson)

Die Feststellung, wir würden in einer Welt leben, die mit schnell geschnittenen Bildern und übergeblendeten Stimmen aus dem Bereich der Massenmedien vollkommen übersättigt ist, hilft uns an diesem Punkt auch nicht weiter. Das unermüdliche Weiterspinnen an einem Endlos-Diskurs um das mutmassliche Vakuum (an Bedeutung/Subjektivität/Geschichte), das seine Existenz einer geheimen Absprache zwischen Hollywood und Madison Avenue verdankt, lässt die Kritik noch unsinniger werden als die Phantasmen, die sie zum Gegenstand ihrer Analyse und Entmystifizierung erwählt hat. Das Übel ist, dass die Kritik an den Massenmedien gewöhnlich nur wiederholt, was sowieso auf der Hand liegt, oder aber an der Sache vorbeiredet. Mittel und Effekte der Massenmedien sind eben leicht durchschaubar. Unausgesprochenes nicht weniger als Offenkundiges wird meist auch von den einfachsten Gemütern begriffen. Gelegentlich setzen die Massenmedien den implizierten Inhalt sogar in Klammern, als ein herausgehobenes, für sich stehendes Zeichen. Ein Teil des Vergnügens, das uns Bilder von spritzendem, übersprudelndem und schäumendem Wasser bereiten, ist auf ihren «latent» sexuellen Inhalt zurückzuführen, aber es wäre ein Zeichen von Dummheit, diesen Inhalt für etwas anderes zu nehmen, als was er ist. Was also noch kritisieren?

Einige Leser mögen inzwischen vielleicht die Geduld mit mir verloren haben und gereizt einwenden: «Viel zu weit ausgeholt.» Doch die gefrässigen, alles verschlingenden Medienspektakel – verdienen, nein, verlangen, schreien sie nicht geradezu nach einer ernsthaften, kritischen Auseinandersetzung, die Sie auf eine so überhebliche Art als überflüssig abtun?

Na schön, kürzlich stiess ich auf ein paar Artikel, die ich aus der *Village Voice* ausgeschnitten hatte, der New Yorker Postille, was trendbewusste, nach links tendierende Berichterstattung anbelangt. Der Gegenstand: das Zehn-Jahre-Jubiläum von MTV und dessen kulturpolitische Bedeutung. Mim Udovitch hatte folgendes dazu zu sagen: «Es scheint gar nicht mehr nötig, MTV zu feiern, da es sich wie Walt Whitman selbst feiert. Und das mit gutem Grund. Denn – um mit Whitney Houston zu sprechen –, ‹was man mir auch nimmt, mein MTV kann mir nicht genommen werden!›» Diese vielleicht etwas befangenen Zeilen evozieren bekannte Verfahrensweisen der Medienkritik – und wie diese Kritik haben sie ihre albern-feierliche Seite. Zunächst einmal ist da die zu erwartende Komik, die sich ergibt, wenn Hochkultur und Trivialkultur unterschiedslos als Quelle für Zitate herhalten müssen, so als gäbe es keinerlei Hierarchie (Walt Whitman = Whitney Houston). Diese Praxis entspricht der überstrapazierten, (post-)strukturalistischen Gewohnheit, Unterschiede in einer angeblich wertneutralen Betrachtungsweise untergehen zu lassen. Gleichzeitig ist sie ein Seitenhieb gegen eine bestimmt gutgemeinte, doch flaue Kulturpolitik, die niemanden ausgrenzen will und die niemandem wehtun möchte: «Ist ja schon gut, deine kulturelle Ikone ist genauso gut/wertvoll/ bedeutungsträchtig wie die meine, und wer dir etwas anderes weismachen will, der ist ein gemeines rassistisches/sexistisches/elitäres/schwulenfeindliches Arschloch.»

Die Bezugnahme auf Walt Whitman enthält ausserdem einen eher indirekten Hinweis auf das Wesen einer auf die Massenmedien ausgerichteten Kritik. Udovitch spielt zweifellos in sarkastischer Absicht auf den berühmten Anfang von Walt Whitmans *Song of Myself* an:

I celebrate myself
And what I assume you shall assume,
For every atom belonging to me as good
belongs to you.
(Ich feiere mich selbst,
Und was ich mir herausnehme,
sollst auch du dir herausnehmen,
Denn jedes Atom, das mir gehört,
gehört ebensogut auch dir.)

Das Verb *assume* in der zweiten Zeile des Gedichts hat mehrere Bedeutungen, u.a.: anlegen, auf sich nehmen, übernehmen. *Assume* bedeutet aber auch: voraussetzen oder mutmassen.

Diese verschiedenen Bedeutungen oder Konnotationen greifen so ineinander, dass sie reibungslos mit dem Glauben zusammengehen, der sowohl den Massenmedien wie auch den vielen Kritiken gemeinsam ist, die sich gegen sie richten: der Glaube an ein kollektives Bewusstsein.

Die Versuchung, über ein kollektives Bewusstsein Betrachtungen oder Spekulationen anzustellen, ist unwiderstehlich, ja vielleicht sogar unvermeidlich, wenn Sie in die Kategorie der langweiligen Möchtegerns im Fernsehsessel fallen. Da schliesslich j e d e r in Amerika am Tropf des Fernsehers hängt, da j e d e r in Amerika seine Wunschträume auf dem Bildschirm realisiert sieht und da j e d e r Madonnas bester Freund sein möchte, kann man daraus nur folgern, dass die Massenmedien entweder über ein ausserordentliches Reservoir an Einfühlungsvermögen und Wissen verfügen müssen, was das Leben der Durchschnittsbürger betrifft, oder dass sie als Instrument totalitärer Kontrolle eingesetzt werden. Vielleicht ist es Kontrolle durch Verstehen: Wenn man das Spatzenhirn des kollektiven Bewusstseins erst einmal angezapft hat, kann man es um so besser manipulieren und kontrollieren.

Eine Kritik, die ein kollektives Bewusstsein in den Mittelpunkt rückt, gibt sich gerne solchen Spielen wie mystischer Erkenntnis hin. Sie möchte Fragen beantworten wie: «Wo steht die Kultur heute?» und noch wichtiger: «In welche Richtung geht die Kultur?» Vielleicht sind das ja auch ganz gute Fragen, sie sind nur nicht gerade einfach zu beantworten. Es könnte nämlich durchaus möglich sein, dass sie sich erst im nachhinein beantworten lassen: von einem Standpunkt aus, der

in zwanzig, dreissig Jahren eingenommen werden kann. Frustrierend.

Hinzu kommt, dass Künstler oder Kritiker, die theoretisch oder vielleicht auch nur aus Gewohnheit an die Existenz eines kollektiven Bewusstseins glauben, genau die Verfahrensweisen und Funktionen der Massenmedien nachahmen, die sie angeblich blossstellen oder entmystifizieren wollen. Der ganze eingespielte Apparat der Massenmedien – Film, Fernsehen, Werbung, Zeitungen und Magazine – sucht ständig einem kollektiven Bewusstsein auf die Schliche zu kommen, das er im Grunde selbst erschafft, wenn auch nur als Bild. Selbst so wertlose kulturelle Produkte wie der Müll, den MTV ausstrahlt, sind keine einfachen Abbilder, sondern sorgfältig ausgearbeitete, sich selbst reflektierende Artefakte. Dieser Punkt mag vielleicht zu banal erscheinen, um überhaupt einen Gedanken daran zu verschwenden, besonders für jene ehrenwerten Theoretiker unter uns. Aber die Kritik der Massenmedien sieht in ihrem Objekt die amerikanische Seele und die Realität unseres heutigen Lebens widergespiegelt. Trotz des drittklassigen, (post-)strukturalistischen Unsinns der dritten Generation gelten für diese Art von Kritik im Grunde noch die altmodischen platonischen Ideen von der Kunst als Mimesis. Ich denke, eine konsequente, kritische Bewertung des MTV – mein Beispiel, das nur eines von vielen ist – lässt uns bestenfalls zu der Erkenntnis gelangen, dass Rock-Videos die Geisteshaltung von ein paar siebzehnjährigen Bengels widerspiegeln. Wollen Sie dort Ihr kollektives, oder genauer, Ihr individuelles Bewusstsein ansiedeln?

Die Stimme hinter Larry Johnsons *Untitled (Do You Remember Doris Day?)* (Ohne Titel [Erinnern Sie sich an

Doris Day?]) gehört der Welt der Massenmedien an. Sie spricht von Erinnerungen, aber von fiktiven Erinnerungen, die ausserhalb der Sphäre der späteren Generationen liegen. Während der 70er und 80er Jahre haben die Medien eine nostalgische 50er-Jahre-Mode propagiert. Wenn Johnson Doris Day, Lackschuhe und virgin pins, Anstecknadeln für «anständige Mädchen» besingt, spielt er auf das Jahrzehnt vor seinem geschichtlichen Erinnerungsvermögen an. Trotzdem setzt der Text bei den Betrachtern diese Dinge als Bestandteil unseres kollektiven Bewusstseins voraus. Klingt irgendwie bekannt? Johnson vollbringt einen Taschenspielertrick, was das Phantom des kollektiven Bewusstseins betrifft, denn er setzt die kollektive Erinnerung mit dem fiktionalisierenden Vergessen gleich.

Werke wie die von Johnson geben den Anspruch auf Distanz auf und streben dabei nach einer verdeckteren Infiltration – ein Insidergeschäft gewissermassen. Bewusst kritische oder konzeptuelle Kunstwerke zeigen leider zu oft nicht die geringste Spur von *Cleverness*. Sie scheinen durchweg von Leuten geschaffen zu sein, die keine Ahnung von Ironie haben. Und deshalb wird die Begegnung mit der simpelsten Form von Ironie zur Gelegenheit für ein Kunstwerk, eines, das tendenziös das Offensichtliche enthüllt. Dieses Paradigma der Verhüllung/ Offenbarung – die Massenmedien, deren Abläufe fiese Absichten verhüllen, die kritischen Kunstwerke, die den Umnachteten Erleuchtung bringen – funktioniert einfach nicht. Kunst, die nach wahrhaft kritischem Engagement strebt, bedarf einer leichteren, aber dafür sichereren Hand.

(Übersetzung: Uta Goridis)

BALKON

ALEXANDER POPPER

DIE ANGEWANDTE KUNST DER TIERZUCHT

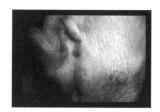

PERSPEKTIVE:

♦ Sie werden Ihre Kuh melken, um ein Produkt der chemischen Industrie zu erhalten.

♦ Langfristig wird man natürlich vom Tier wegkommen müssen, weil es wegen seiner naturbedingten Anfälligkeit für Krankheit und Tod noch immer ein ökonomisches Risiko darstellt.

«273. Zwingt man dich, deine Biographie von dir zu geben, so erzähle jedesmal eine andere. Darauf hingewiesen, zeige dich entrüstet darüber, dass man jene Diskretion, die jeder für sich beanspruchen darf, dir nicht zubilligen will. Man wird deine Phantasie bewundern und deiner Biographie alles zutrauen.» *Walter Serner*

HISTORISCHES: WAS IST WICHTIGER? DAS HUHN ODER DAS EI?

♦ Es war einmal: Einmal waren Haustiere eigene biologische Arten, weil man ihre nahe Verwandtschaft zu wildlebenden Formen nicht erkannte und von der Unveränderlichkeit aller Arten überzeugt war.

♦ Als Beweis suchte man nach Resten vom Urhausschwein und Urhund.

♦ Die Gestaltung lebender Materie war kein Thema: Die individuellen Vorzüge oder Mängel eines Lebewesens waren zufällige, erblich nicht fixierbare Abweichungen von der Norm.

♦ Es ging um Besitz, und wenn irgendwie nach Besonderheiten ausgelesen wurde, ging es um die Kennzeichnung der Lebewesen als Privateigentum.

♦ Schlechte Zeiten für Gestalter.

♦ Als Aufforderung versteht der Gestaltungstrieb im modernen Menschen die Idee von Aristoteles, dass die gesamte Natur einschliesslich des Menschen einen vitalen Impuls zur höheren Manifestation in sich trage.

♦ Veränderung ist denkbar, und zwar nicht als Verfallsgeschichte, sondern als Verbesserung. Die Natur kann nicht nur besessen, sondern auch gestaltet werden.

♦ Der Schöpfer im Menschen spricht den Wesen ihre Unveränderlichkeit ab und sieht die Göttlichkeit von nun an in den Gesetzmässigkeiten, die die Wesen erschaffen: die Eliminierung der schlechten durch die gute Form, das Ersetzen dieser wiederum durch die bessere; Gestaltung als Kampf um Leben und Tod, in dem das Bessere immer das Schlechtere vernichtet.

♦ Der Gestaltungstrieb setzt sich durch.

♦ Der Gott, der einmal knetet und dann brennt, der zerstört und bestraft, ist tot.

• Der andere Gott tötet nicht. Er eliminiert, indem er Neues entstehen lässt, das das Existierende erstickt.

• Da waren die einen, die versuchten, durch das ständige Abschneiden der Schwänze schwanzlose Mäuse oder Hunde zu erzeugen, die hofften, die gute Form durch gute Fütterung und Haltung zu erschaffen.

• Unbefriedigenderweise wurde dennoch kein einziger schwanzloser Hund, keine schwanzlose Maus geboren, warf das fetteste Schwein unter Umständen die magersten Ferkel.

• Und da waren die anderen, die formulierten: Das Huhn ist nur eine Methode des Eis, ein weiteres Ei zu erzeugen.

• Der Erscheinungstyp des Individuums, den man beobachten, besser noch wägen oder messen kann, sei das Ergebnis des Zusammenwirkens der Gesamtheit der erblichen Anlagen des Lebewesens und seiner Umwelt. In diesem Fall spielt die Umwelt nur eine Nebenrolle, weil sie lediglich Voraussetzung dafür ist, dass die Erbanlagen ihre erwünschten Auswirkungen zeigen.

• Der züchterische Gestalter muss bloss Tiere mit verschiedenen Erbanlagen besitzen. Er muss die Tiere nach ihren Erbanlagen bewerten. Danach dürfen sich nur noch Tiere mit den erwünschten Erbanlagen fortpflanzen.

• Die Gestaltung lebender Materie ist also auf die Manipulation ihrer Sexualität fixiert.

• Ziele der Gestaltung ähneln je nach Tierart und Kulturkreis dem Anforderungsprofil an die Gestaltung von Gebrauchsgegenständen, Produktionsmitteln, Proletariern, Kindern, Zierrat.

• Folgt die Form der Funktion, muss das Tier bei der Geburt doppelt so gross sein, mehr Fleisch bilden und schneller sein Mastendgewicht erreichen; zur Erreichung des Mastendgewichtes weniger Futter benötigen und gemäss den Verbraucherwünschen mageres Fleisch erzeugen; die Geschlechtsreife möglichst früh erreichen, um Nachkommen und die Produkte, die damit zusammenhängen, rascher zur Verfügung zu stellen.

• Soll die Form den Betrachter ergreifen, muss das Tier brav, treu, lieb, klug, ehrlich sein. («Am Anfang schuf Gott den Menschen, als er aber sah, wie hilflos der war, schuf er ihm als Gefährten den Hund.»)

• Soll die Form interesseloses Wohlgefallen und meditative Versenkung erzeugen, muss das Tier schön, interessant, beruhigend sein (Fische im Aquarium).

• Gestaltungsziele sind Eigenschaften, die dem Eigentümer des Tieres nützen. Nützlich bzw. verkaufsfördernd sind je nach Marktsegment sowohl funktionelle wie sentimentale als auch ästhetische Ziele.

• Entscheidet die Beschaffenheit der Rohstoffe über die Art der Bearbeitung?

DIE METHODEN, DIE DER ZÜCHTER ANZUWENDEN HAT, SIND IMMER DIE GLEICHEN:

• Man fange Jungtiere und zähme sie.

• Man zäune sie ein, auf dass sie sich ausschliesslich untereinander paaren. Morphologische Veränderungen und Vergrösserung der Formenvielfalt sind die Folge. In der Regel sind die in Gefangenschaft nachgezogenen Tiere kleiner.

• Später wähle man einzelne Tiere aufgrund von Färbung, Form, Fleisch- oder Milchleistung bewusst zur Nachzucht aus.

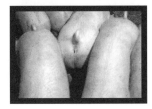

• Man paare die domestizierten kleinen Muttertiere gezielt mit grösseren, vielleicht wilden Vatertieren.

• Schliesslich bejage man die noch verbliebenen Wildtiere solange, bis sie entweder ausgerottet oder in entfernte Rückzugsgebiete vertrieben sind.

• DOMESTIKATION IST EIN GESTALTUNGSVORGANG, DESSEN METHODE

DIE KONTINUIERLICHE ZERSTÖRUNG SOZIALER STRUKTUREN DER TIERGRUPPE IST. (IN MEMORIAM JB. UND SEINER SOZIALEN PLASTIK)

♦ Um Rentiere in Herden zu halten, muss der Rentierzüchter alle Renhirsche nach dem ersten Geschlechtsakt kastrieren.

♦ Nach bestimmten Vorstellungen über erwünschte Körperform und Charaktereigenschaften des Berner Sennenhunds wählte man unter den Hunden der Bauern eine Handvoll aus. Von den Nachkommen dieser Hunde paarte man wieder nur diejenigen, die den Zielvorstellungen entsprachen, alle anderen wurden getötet, geräuchert und geselcht.

DIE GESTALTER

♦ Ohne zu zögern werden wir den Gestalter, der bis ins 19. Jahrhundert ohne wissenschaftliche Handlungsanweisungen Tierzucht nur mit Hilfe seines «ererbten» Geheimwissens, eigener Erfahrung und seiner Intuition betrieb, einen Künstler nennen.

♦ Wir werden kaum einwenden können, dass Kunst in der bürgerlichen Kultur einen zweck- und zwangfreien Raum besetzt. Wir müssten uns sonst mit der Frage konfrontieren, was überhaupt angewandte Kunst sein soll.

♦ Eher werden wir einwenden, dass wir die Verleihung des Prädikats «Kunst» überhaupt nicht an die Verwendung bestimmter Medien oder Methoden binden, weil «Kunst» eine Qualitätsdefinition ist.

♦ Warum unterdrückt dieser Ansatz die Frage nach der Technologie, die Frage nach dem Zusammenhang zwischen Hilfsmitteln und Methoden des Künst-

lers, und der Beschaffenheit des Materials, das er gestalten will?
– Weil die Hilfsmittel und Methoden des Künstlers dessen Ziele und dessen Materialbegriff enthüllen.
– Weil es bestenfalls ein frommer Wunsch ist, dass die Beschaffenheit der Rohstoffe über die Art der Bearbeitung entscheidet.
– Weil wir eher die Beschaffenheit der Rohstoffe bearbeiten, um sie unseren üblichen Gestaltungsmethoden zugänglich zu machen, entscheidet die Art der Bearbeitung über die Beschaffenheit der Rohstoffe.

♦ Die Erfolge praktischer Zuchtarbeit beruhen grossteils auf den Effekten gezielter Inzucht. Dies bewirkt zwar eine Verminderung der Vitalität der Tiere, ist aber die einzige Möglichkeit, um seltene, erwünschte Merkmale schnell zu stabilisieren und möglichst ident zu reproduzieren. Daher werden:
– In der BRD heute drei von vier Kühen künstlich befruchtet. Ein Zuchtbulle besamt auf diese Art pro Jahr durchschnittlich 2000 Kühe.
– Rinderembryonen ausgespült und chirurgisch in Zwischenempfängertiere, sogenannte In-vivo-Systeme, meistens Kaninchen, übertragen, nach einigen Tagen wieder herausgeschnitten und auf die endgültigen Empfängertiere übertragen, die In-vivo-Systeme anschliessend geschlachtet.

♦ Beim Miniaturschwein, Troll, ist der Name durch das Markenzeichen geschützt. Um unkontrollierte Weiterzucht auch praktisch zu verhindern, werden nur weibliche Tiere verkauft.

WERKE: «TAPFER BEI DER OBERFLÄCHE BLEIBEN!»

♦ Der Haustierkörper ist ein buntes Mosaik von Beschleunigtem, Zurückbleibendem, Abirrungen verschiedenster Art. Wachstumsdauer und Intensität sind verändert; Proportionen verschoben.

♦ Der Schädel ist verkürzt und aufgebogen, gleichzeitig sehr viel breiter und höher, die Knochen sehr viel dicker.

♦ Die Haut ist locker, fast schwammig. Gleichzeitig ist die Lederhaut feiner und kompakter.

♦ Haare, Federn, Schuppen, alle Anhangsgebilde sind extrem vermehrt oder gegen Null reduziert. Wolle oder Nacktheit sind die Folge – nackte Hunde, Katzen, Pferde, Schweine.

♦ Die Haut des nackten Schweins ähnelt der menschlichen Haut, so dass Hausschweine heute als Versuchstiere in der Dermatologie Verwendung finden.

♦ Hauspferden wachsen Schnurrbärte, die wie beim Menschen durch starkes Wachstum von Fell, nicht Tasthaaren, über der Oberlippe entstehen.

♦ Die vergrösserte Hautfläche bildet Falten im Gesicht, am Nacken, am Hals, bildet lange, herabhängende Ohren.

♦ Einzelelemente sprengen das Körpergefüge – Schleierschwänze, Teleskopaugen, Hängebäuche. Vergrösserung des Kotelettmuskels, weniger Rückenspeck, weniger Seitenspeck, vier bis sechs Wirbel mehr erzeugen acht bis zwölf Koteletts mehr. Das helle, weiche, fettarme Fleisch ist blass, weich und schrumpft beim Braten.

♦ Hausschweine sind das ganze Jahr über fruchtbar, und die Zahl der Jungen ist durchschnittlich viermal so gross wie bei Wildschweinen. Das Hodengewicht hat sich verdreifacht und bleibt das ganze Jahr konstant.

ZUR GESCHICHTE DES KÜNSTLERS

♦ Nach bestimmten Vorstellungen über erwünschte Körperform und Charaktereigenschaften des Künstlers wählte man unter den Kindern der Bauern eine Handvoll aus. Von den Nachkommen dieser Dilettanten paarte man wieder nur diejenigen, die der Ziel-vorstellung entsprachen, alle anderen wurden getötet, geräuchert und geselcht.

♦ Die Erfolge praktischer Kulturarbeit beruhen grossteils auf den Effekten gezielter Inzucht. Das bewirkt zwar eine Verminderung der Vitalität und Gesundheit der Künstler, ist aber die einzige Möglichkeit, gewisse gewünschte Merkmale schnell zu stabilisieren.

♦ Gestaltungsziele sind Eigenschaften, die dem Künstler nützen. Nützlich bzw. verkaufsfördernd sind je nach Marktsegment sowohl funktionelle wie sentimentale als auch ästhetische Ziele. Die Methoden, die der Künstler anzuwenden hat, sind immer die gleichen: Die Art der Bearbeitung entscheidet über die Beschaffenheit der Rohstoffe.

PERSPEKTIVE:

♦ Sie werden Ihren Künstler melken, um ein Produkt der Kulturindustrie zu erhalten. Langfristig wird man natürlich vom Künstler wegkommen müssen, weil der wegen seiner naturbedingten Anfälligkeit für Krankheit und Tod noch immer ein ökonomisches Risiko darstellt.

Dank an alle meine Freunde, die mich fachlich, praktisch und seelisch unterstützt haben, und meine Familie.

Besonders an: Sepp Auer, Norbert Brunner, Eva Eckert, Alex Ivan, Lukas Kaltenbäck, Ruppert Klima, Oliver Kroy, Claudia Luchesi, Ana Obtresal, Alfred Reisinger, Thomas Ruth, Katrin Stockhammer, Gudrun Wagner, Wolfgang Zinggl.

Herrn Bolzer, Herrn Auer und allen ihren Schweinen.

ALEXANDER POPPER

THE APPLIED ART OF ANIMAL BREEDING

"273. Should you be forced to produce a biography, then tell a different one each time. When this is pointed out to you, show yourself indignant about not being granted the discretion that is every person's due. People will admire your imagination and give your biography free rein."

Walter Serner

APPROACH:

♦ You will milk your cow in order to obtain a product for the chemical industry.

♦ In the long run, animals will, of course, have to be phased out because they are still an economic risk due to their inherent susceptibility to illness and death.

HISTORICAL APPROACH: WHAT IS MORE IMPORTANT? THE HEN OR THE EGG?

♦ Once upon a time, domestic animals were distinct biological species because their close affinity to forms living in the wild went unnoticed and people were persuaded of the immutability of all species.

♦ To prove the point, they tried to find the remains of the primal domestic pig and the primal dog.　▪

• To form living matter was of no interest. The individual merits or shortcomings of a living creature were accidental deviations from the norm and not determined by heredity.

• It was a matter of ownership, and if living beings were selected according to certain qualities, it was only to mark them as private property.

• Dark times for designers.

• Aristotle's idea that the whole of nature, including mankind, contains a vital impulse towards higher manifestations is considered an imperative by the design instinct of modern man.

• Change is conceivable, not as a history of decay but of improvement. Not only can nature be owned, it can also be formed.

• The maker in man does not recognize the immutability of beings and, from now on, sees divinity in the laws governing their creation—the bad form eliminated by the good form, the latter replaced by a better one; design as the struggle of life and death, in which what is better always destroys what is worse.

• The design instinct wins out.

• The God that first kneads and then burns, that destroys and punishes, is dead.

• The other God does not kill. He eliminates by allowing new things to emerge and suppress existing ones.

• There were those who kept cutting off the tails of mice or dogs in the hope of breeding tailless ones, who tried to create good form by means of good feeding and care.

• Unfortunately, not a single tailless dog nor a single tailless mouse was born; the fattest sow could still farrow the puniest piglet.

• There were others who worded it thus: the hen is merely the egg's method of producing another egg.

• The phenotype—that which can be observed, or better yet, weighed and measured—is the result of the combined effect of the living being's entire genetic stock and its environment. In this case, the environment plays a secondary role because it is merely the precondition that enables genes to manifest their desired effects.

• The breedish designer merely has to own animals with different sets of genes. He has to evaluate the animals according to their genetic stock. On that basis, only animals with the desired genes are allowed to reproduce.

• The design of living matter is therefore confined to the manipulation of its sexuality.

• Objectives of design: resemblance—depending on species and cultural context—to the design specifications of objects of daily use, means of production, proletarians, children, decoration.

• If form follows function, the animal has to be twice as big at birth, be meatier, and gain its slaughtering weight faster; require less feed to reach its slaughtering weight and produce leaner meat in keeping with consumer wishes; reach reproductive maturity as early as possible to provide offspring and ancillary products faster.

• If the form is to elicit to the viewer, the animal must be docile, loyal, loving, bright, honest. ("In the beginning God created man, but when He saw how helpless he was, he created the dog as a companion.")

• If the form is to elicit disinterested pleasure and contemplative absorption, the animal must be beautiful, interesting, tranquilizing (fish in aquarium).

• Design objectives are qualities that are useful to the animal's owner. Depending on the market sector, not only functional but also sentimental and aesthetic objectives are useful, i.e. promote sales.

◆ Does the structure of the raw material define the manner of processing?

THE METHODS TO BE EMPLOYED BY THE BREEDER ARE ALWAYS THE SAME:

◆ Capture the young and tame them.

◆ Fence them in so that they mate exclusively among themselves.

◆ Morphologic change and greater variety are the consequence. As a rule, animals raised in captivity are smaller.

◆ Later, choose individual specimens on the basis of coloring, shape, meat or milk production for selective breeding.

◆ Mate small domesticated females with larger, possibly wild males.

◆ Finally, hunt the remaining wild animals until they have either been wiped out or driven to remote hiding places.

◆ DOMESTICATION IS A PROCESS OF DESIGN WHOSE METHOD INVOLVES ONGOING DESTRUCTION OF THE SOCIAL STRUCTURE OF THE ANIMAL GROUP. (IN MEMORIAM JB AND HIS SOCIAL SCULPTURE)

◆ To keep reindeer in herds, the reindeer breeder must castrate all stags after their first mating.

◆ According to specific notions about the desired body shape and personal characteristics of the Bernese mountain dog, a handful of farmers' dogs were selected. From the offspring of these dogs, only those were mated that satisfied the goals; all others were killed, smoked, or cured.

THE DESIGNERS

◆ We will not hesitate to give the name of artist to the designer who bred animals until well into the 19th century without scientific instructions, aided only by his "hereditary" secret knowledge, his own experience, and his intuition.

◆ We can hardly interpose that art in bourgeois culture occupies a niche that is free of purpose and pressure. Otherwise we would have to confront ourselves with the question of what applied art is supposed to be.

◆ Rather we will interpose that rating something as "art" is not tied in to the use of certain media or methods because "art" is defined by quality.

◆ Why does this approach suppress the question of technology, the question of the connection between the artist's means and methods and the structure of the material that he wants to form?
– Because the artist's means and methods expose his goals and his concept of material.
– Because it is at most wishful thinking to suppose that the structure of the raw material defines the manner of processing.
– Since we tend to rework the structure of the raw materials in order to make them conform to our usual methods of design, it is the manner of processing that defines the structure of the raw materials.

◆ The successes of practical breeding rest largely on the effects of controlled inbreeding. Despite the resulting decline in animal vitality, it is the only means of rapidly stabilizing the rare characteristics desired and guaranteeing maximally identical reproduction. Therefore:
– In the GFR today 3 out of 4 cows are artificially inseminated. In this way a breeding bull inseminates an average of 2000 cows per year.
– The embryos are flushed out and surgically implanted in intermediate carriers, so-called in vivo systems (usually rabbits) cut out again after a few days, and implanted in the final carriers; the in vivo systems are then slaughtered.

◆ The name of the miniature pig in Germany, Troll, is protected by registered trademark. To prevent uncontrolled further breeding only females are sold.

WORKS: "STICK BRAVELY TO THE SURFACE!"

◆ The body of the domestic animal is a colorful mosaic of accelerated and devolved features, of all kinds of aberrations. Duration and intensity of growth have been altered; proportions changed.

◆ The skull is shortened and bent upwards, but much wider and higher; the bones are much thicker.

• The skin is loose, almost spongy. At the same time, the hide is finer and more compact.

• Hair, feathers, scales, all appendages are excessively augmented or reduced to almost zero. Wool and nakedness are the consequence—naked dogs, cats, horses, pigs.

• The skin of the naked pig resembles human skin so that domestic pigs are used today as experimental animals in dermatology.

• Domestic horses grow moustaches, which, as in people, are the result of intense hairy growth—not vibrissae—on the upper lip.

• The enlarged skin surface produces folds on the face, nape, and neck, produces low-hanging ears.

• Certain elements break the bounds of the body—goldfish tails, telescope eyes, drooping bellies. Enlargement of the chop muscle, less back fat, less flank fat, 4–6 more vertebrae produce 8–12 more chops. The light, soft, lean meat is pale, soft, and shrinks when fried.

• Domestic pigs are fertile all year round and have litters that are on average four times larger than those of wild pigs. The weight of the testicles has tripled and remains constant all year.

ON THE HISTORY OF THE ARTIST

• According to specific notions about the desired body shape and personal characteristics of the artist, a handful of farmers' children were selected. From the offspring of these dilettantes, only those who satisfied the requirements were mated; all others were killed, smoked, or cured.

• The successes of practical cultural endeavor rest largely on the effects of controlled inbreeding. Despite the resulting decline in vitality and health, it is the only means of rapidly stabilizing certain desired characteristics.

• Design objectives are qualities that are useful to the artist. Depending on the market sector, not only functional but also sentimental and aesthetic objectives are useful, i.e. promote sales. The methods to be employed by the artist are always the same: the manner of processing defines the structure of the raw materials.

APPROACH:

• You will milk your artist in order to obtain a product for the cultural industry. In the long run, the artist will, of course, have to be phased out because he is still an economic risk due to his inherent susceptibility to illness and death.

(Translation: Catherine Schelbert)

My gratitude to all those friends who lent me their scientific, practical, and emotional support, and to my family.

Especially to: Sepp Auer, Norbert Brunner, Eva Eckert, Alex Ivan, Lukas Kaltenbäck, Ruppert Klima, Oliver Kroy, Claudia Luchesi, Ana Obtresal, Alfred Reisinger, Thomas Ruth, Katrin Stockhammer, Gudrun Wagner, Wolfgang Zinggl.

Mr. Bolzer, Mr. Auer, and all of their pigs.

Jede Nummer der Zeitschrift entsteht in Collaboration mit einem Künstler oder einer Künstlerin, die eigens für die Leser von PARKETT einen Originalbeitrag gestalten. Dieses Werk ist in der gesamten Auflage abgebildet und zusätzlich als limitierte und signierte Vorzugsausgabe erhältlich. Preisänderungen vorbehalten. Versandkosten nicht inbegriffen.

EDITIONS FOR PARKETT

Each issue of the magazine is created in collaboration with an artist, who contributes an original work specially made for the readers of PARKETT. The work is reproduced in the regular edition. It is also available in a signed and limited Special Edition. Prices subject to change. Postage is not included.

PARKETT 14

GILBERT & GEORGE, 1987

Photographie auf Karton aufgezogen,
in der Mitte faltbar, 25,5 x 42 cm
Ed. 200, signiert und numeriert, **sFr. 1200.-/**
Photograph, mounted on cardboard
folded in the middle, 10 x 16½", (25,5 x 42 cm).
Ed. 200, signed and numbered, **US$ 950**

Eindringlich und dramatisch spielt das Licht auf den
Gesichtern von Gilbert & George im Photo-Diptychon zum
Aufstellen auf Ihrem Schreibtisch oder Bücherschrank.

Memorabilia from an art world Hall of Fame. A provo-
cative reshoot of the classic wedding photo, the alumni
portrait, the religious diptych, Gilbert & George's stand-up
self-portrait will be an asset to the mantelpiece of any self-
respecting *amateur.*

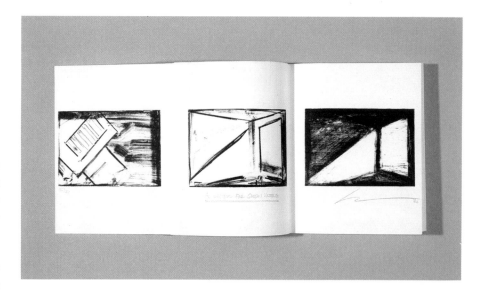

Mit minimalsten Licht- und
Architekturakzenten öffnen sich
traumhafte Bühnenräume, wie
sie nur ein Robert Wilson er-
denken kann.

The director's notebook. This
animated three-part lithograph
is a reminder that every one of
Wilson's dramatic theater works
has its genesis in a powerful,
light-filled drawing.

PARKETT 16

ROBERT WILSON
A LETTER FOR QUEEN VICTORIA

Lithographie auf Rives, 25,5 x 61 cm,
in Parkett eingebunden
Ed. 80, signiert und numeriert, **sFr. 800.-/**
Lithograph on Rives, 10 x 24"
(25,5 x 61 cm), bound in the magazine.
Ed. 80, signed and numbered, **US$ 640**

Wer weiss denn, ob der Himmel oben ist und die Hölle
unten? Sicher ist: Wir befinden uns auf halbem Weg.

Where in the world. Is Heaven up and Hell down, or
vice-versa? In typically cryptic fashion, Ruscha leaves
us in blue limbo, somewhere in-between.

PARKETT 18

EDWARD RUSCHA
HELL 1/2 WAY HEAVEN
Lithographie auf Rives, dreifarbig,
auf Aluminiumplatte gezeichnet,
72,5 x 20,2 cm, in Parkett eingebunden
Ed. 100, signiert und numeriert, **sFr. 1500.-**/
Lithograph on Rives, 10 x 24"
(25,5 x 61 cm), bound in the magazine.
Ed. 80, signed and numbered, **US$ 1200**

Mit dem Prototyp-Medium für Massen-
auflage, dem Offsetdruck, schafft Kippenberger lauter exklusive Originale. Die
80 Sujets – je eines wiederholt sich durch
ein ganzes Buch – stammen aus seiner
privaten Bilderbank.

Art in the age of mechanical reproduction. Unique little books, created by
turning the techniques of offset printing
inside out, each contain a single
photograph from the artist's collection of
naughty snapshots, maddeningly reproduced through every page.

PARKETT 19

MARTIN KIPPENBERGER
80 UNIKAT-BÜCHLEIN
Offsetdruck, 13,2 x 9,5 cm, 260 Seiten,
in Parkett eingelegt.
Ed. 80, signiert und numeriert, **sFr. 1200.-**
80 UNIQUE BOOKS
Printed in offset, 6 x 3 3/4" (13,2 x 9,5 cm),
260 pages, inserted in the magazine. Ed. 80,
signed and numbered, **US$ 960**

Eine poetische Symmetrie oszilliert zwischen Flächigkeit, Stilisierung und Abbild der Natur.

Artificial nature. A deft exercise in Katz's on-going exploration of pictorial flatness and poetic symmetry, this stylized woodcut on the most delicate of papers is a quiet moment of reflection from a preternatural world.

PARKETT 21

ALEX KATZ
SCHWARZER TEICH, 1989
Holzschnitt auf Goyu-Papier, 29,5 x 46 cm
Ed. 100, signiert und numeriert, **sFr. 950.-**
BLACK POND, 1989
Woodcut on Goyu paper,
11⅝ x 18⅛" (29,5 x 46 cm).
Ed. 100, signed and numbered, **US$ 760**

Der Künstler begibt sich auf die Spur von Verdoppelungen, lässt von zwei verschiedenen Händen die zweifache Ausgabe von Newsweek – die nationale und die internationale – abzeichnen.

Double trouble. A perennial obsession with dual identities and symmetry are brought together in a systematic rendering of twin subjects by two detectably different hands. A hand-applied flash of vicious scarlet completes this doubly complex Rorschach test.

PARKETT 24

ALIGHIERO E BOETTI
AUF DEN SPUREN DER GEHEIMNISSE
EINES DOPPELLEBENS, 1990
Lichtdruck (Granolitho), von Hand rot übermalt,
50 x 70 cm, Ed. 100, signiert und numeriert, **sFr. 1200.-**
PROBING THE MYSTERIES
OF A DOUBLE LIFE, 1990
Collotype (Granolitho), overpainted by
hand in red, 19⅝ x 27½" (50 x 70 cm).
Ed. 100, signed and numbered, **US$ 960**

Unken

Krankenwagen

Mühle

Klang- und Geräuschskulpturen, Erinne-
rungsbilder aus dem kollektiven Gedächtnis formen sich aus Ihren Laut-
sprechern heraus.

Music for the eyes. A set of three records,
each pressed with a single ambient sound
from the artist's aural memory—toads
croaking, a watermill churning, a local
ambulance siren wailing—and sealed with
a corresponding emblematic color.

PARKETT 25

KATHARINA FRITSCH
MÜHLE/KRANKENWAGEN/
UNKEN, 1990
Drei Single-Schallplatten
Ed. je 2000, unsigniert, zusammen: **sFr. 45.-**
MILL/AMBULANCE/TOADS, 1990
Set of three single records.
Ed. of 2000 sets, unsigned, for set of three: **US$ 38**

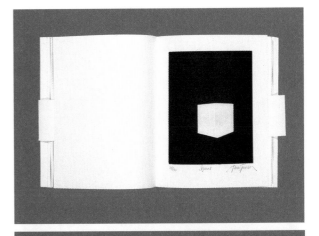

Licht materialisiert sich zu geometrischen Körpern; für einmal nicht in einer
von Turrells Rauminstallationen, sondern in einem traditionsgemäss für
Hell-Dunkeleffekte geschaffenen Medium.

Speed of light. These experimental forays into the medium of etching
yield light as material, not illusion, in the contours of the printed image.

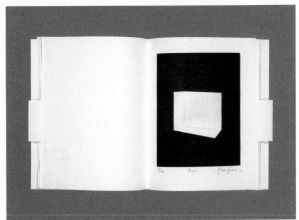

PARKETT 25

JAMES TURRELL, SQUAT, JUKE, CARN, ALTA
Vier Aquatinta-Editionen auf Zerkall 250g, je 25,5 x 21 cm, in Parkett eingebunden,
Ed. je 40 pro Aquatinta, signiert und numeriert, **sFr 1200.-** pro Aquatinta.
SQUAT, JUKE, CARN, ALTA
Four aquatint editions on Zerkall 250g, each 10 x 8¼" (each 25,5 x 21 cm),
bound in the magazine. Ed. of 40 each, signed and numbered, **US$ 960** per print.

Sonderpreis beim Kauf von je einer James Turrell und der Katharina Fritsch-Vorzugsausgabe: **sFr. 950.-**
Special price with purchase of one James Turrell edition and the Katharina Fritsch edition: **US$ 750**

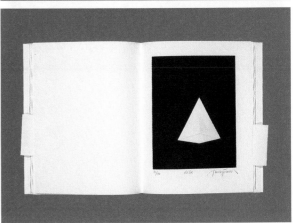

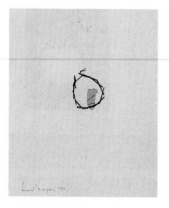 

Die Künstlerin widmet Parkett mit seinem gestickten Schriftzug ein genähtes Flickwerk, das auf viele ihrer künstlerischen und ebenso biographischen Motive anspielt.

A stitch in time. A patched and mended page in a book fuses theory with biography—the sculptor's approach to assemblage as a reparative process and her origins as the child of tapestry-restorers.

PARKETT 27

LOUISE BOURGEOIS

FLICKWERK, 1991

Papier-Objekt aus bedrucktem und handgefärbtem Papier, von Hand gerissen, durchlöchert und mit Faden genäht, 25,5 x 21 cm, in Parkett eingebunden, Ed. 75, signiert und numeriert, **sFr.1800.-**

REPARATION, 1991

Fabrication of printed and handcolored paper, hand-torn, pierced, and sewn with thread, 10 x 8¼" (25,5 x 21 cm), bound in the magazine. Ed. 75, signed and numbered, **US$ 1500**

PARKETT 28

THOMAS RUFF

C-PRINTS, 1991

2 C-Prints (Photos: ESO), je 50 x 50 cm, in Transparenthüllen, astronomische Daten in Siebdruck beidseitig auf Hüllen gedruckt, Ed. je 50, signiert und numeriert, **sFr. 1200.-**

C-PRINTS, 1991

Two c-prints (Photos: ESO), each 19½ x 19½" (each 50 x 50 cm), with astronomic data silk-screened on front and back of transparent wrappers. Ed. of 50 each, signed and numbered, **US$ 900**

Ruffs Sternenhimmel für einmal als Negativprint. Im Zentrum steht ein astronomisch bestimmter Stern.

Milky ways. Phantasmagoric photographs of the night sky and its galaxies are reversed into peppered white fields upon which a single lodestar is pinpointed by its astronomical data.

Sonderpreis beim Kauf von beiden Vorzugsausgaben (Franz Gertsch und Thomas Ruff):**sFr. 1950.-**
Special price with purchase of both editions (Franz Gertsch and Thomas Ruff): **US$ 1450**

FRANZ GERTSCH

CIMA DEL MAR (AUSSCHNITT), 1990/91

Holzschnitt (Kobalt-türkis und ultramarin, halb und halb) auf
Heizoburo Japanpapier, 25,4 x 41,6 cm, gefaltet, nicht eingebunden
Ed. 80, signiert und numeriert, **sFr. 1350.-**

CIMA DEL MAR (DETAIL), 1990/91

Woodcut (cobalt turquoise and ultramarine, half and half) on
Heizoburo Japan paper, 10 x 16⅜" (25,4 x 41,6 cm), folded, not bound
in the magazine. Ed. 80, signed and numbered, **US$ 980**

Detail aus einem über zwei Meter hohen Holzstock,
an dem Franz Gertsch ein Jahr lang gearbeitet hat.

Against the grain. Every point of light on this
minutely described surface corresponds to the
removal of a sliver of wood. This fragment was
taken from a gigantic woodcut measuring more
than 5 x 6 feet (170 x152 cm).

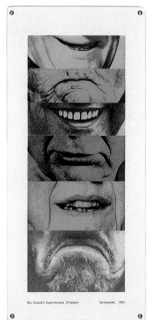

JOHN BALDESSARI

FARBIGER AUSDRUCK, SECHS MAL (EINGEFROREN), 1991

Porzellanemail-Stahlplatte, bedruckt in
achtfarbigem Photorasterprozess, wurde durch
Spezialverfahren resistent gegen
Umwelteinflüsse gemacht, 26,5 x 12 x 0,2 cm
Ed. 75, signiert und numeriert, **sFr 1380.-**

SIX COLORFUL EXPRESSIONS (FROZEN), 1991

Porcelain enamel steel plate, printed
with eight color photographic screen
process, imaged by a proprietary photographic ceramic process, impervious to
environmental influences,
10⁷⁄16 x 4¾ x ⅟16" (26,5 x 12 x 0,2 cm).
Ed. 75, signed and numbered, **US$ 950**

Das Objekt ist so unverwüstlich wie
das wetterfeste Lächeln.

Foul or fair weather friend. This tech-
nically innovated object is guar-
anteed to be as impervious to the
ravages of everyday life as the smile
that defies misfortune.

Sonderpreis beim Kauf von beiden
Vorzugsausgaben: sFr. 2100.-
Special price with purchase of both
editions: US$ 1450

Ein Monster, gedruckt auf feinste
Seide, quillt aus einem Goldrahmen.

The little house of horrors. A silken
greasepaint grotesque rendered in
startling 3-D threatens to burst from its
keepsake frame.

CINDY SHERMAN

OHNE TITEL, 1991

Bedruckte Seide, gepolstert,
in goldfarbenem Holzrahmen,
15 x 11,5 cm (Bild), 21,3 x 17,4 cm (Rahmen)
Ed. 100, signiert und numeriert, **sFr. 1380.-**

UNTITLED, 1991

Printed silk, padded,
in gilded wooden frame, 8⅜" x 6⅞"
(21,3 x 17,4 cm), with frame.
Ed. 100, signed and numbered, **US$ 950**

Das Motiv des Besteckkastens entnahm Polke einer Collage von Max Ernst, der es seinerseits in einem Versandkatalog des 19. Jahrhunderts fand. Polke schickt es auf eine Reise durch Raum, Zeit und Medien.

Fantastic voyage. Reversing his signature process of imitating mechanical reproductive techniques by hand, Polke employs high-tech computer graphics to send an image of a silverware case, pirated via Max Ernst from a 19th century mail order catalogue, on a flight through time, space, and media.

PARKETT 30

SIGMAR POLKE
DR PABSCHT HET Z'SCHPIEZ S'SCHPÄCK-
BSCHTECK Z'SCHPÄT BSCHTEUT, 1980/91
(Schweizerdeutsch: Der Papst hat in Spiez das Speckbesteck zu
spät bestellt) Computer-Reproduktion auf Vinyl, aufgezogen
auf Keilrahmen, 50 x 40 cm, Ed. 100, signiert und numeriert, **sFr. 2900.-/**
(Tongue twister in Swiss-German: The pope ordered the bacon cutlery
in Spiez too late.) Computer reproduction on vinyl, mounted on stretcher,
19⅝ x 15¾" (50 x 40 cm). Ed. 100, signed and numbered, **US$ 2000**

Basketball ist eine der Möglichkeiten für einen Afro-Amerikaner, reich zu werden. So trägt die Photographie des Objet trouvé den Titel Geldbaum.

Readymade magic. A basketball hoop fashioned from the rim of a bicycle tire, embedded in a living tree in a Charleston backyard, testifies to the ingenuity of its anonymous maker.

PARKETT 31

DAVID HAMMONS
GELDBAUM, 1992
Sepia-Print Photographie, 42 x 28 cm
Ed. 70, signiert und numeriert, **sFr. 890.-**
MONEY TREE, 1992
Sepia-Print photograph,
16½ x 11" (42 x 28 cm).
Ed. 70, signed and numbered., **US$ 600**

Die geistige Noblesse und die
Schäbigkeit des Trivialen stellen
den Inhalt eines Goethe-Zitats auf
die Probe.

A tawdry imagination. Intellectual
noblesse combined with thriftstore
fetishism leaves a Goethe quote
wobbling on the brink.

PARKETT 31

MIKE KELLEY
GOETHE-ZITAT, 1992
S/w Photographie und Siebdruck
auf Passepartout in schwarzem Holz-
rahmen mit Acrylglas, 63,5 x 44,5 cm
Ed. 60, signiert und numeriert, **sFr. 1100.-**
GOETHE QUOTE, 1992
B/w photograph with silkscreened
mat in black wooden frame with
plexiglass, 25 x 17½" (63,5 x 44,5 cm).
Ed. 60, signed and numbered, **US$ 790**

Sonderpreis beim Kauf von beiden
Vorzugsausgaben (David Hammons
und Mike Kelley): **sFr. 1600.-**.
Special price with purchase of
both editions (David Hammons and
Mike Kelley): **US$ 1100**

In den 16 cm kleinen Kinderschuhen vereinen sich
Vorstellungen von Niedlichkeit und früher Uniform-
ierung, von Androgynität und Standfestigkeit – als
Bild der Einprobung auf unsere Welt.

A new pair of shoes. Many years ago, Sherrie Levine
found and sold pairs of small shoes in a gallery in New
York. A refined version, handmade in Italy from softest
leather and suede, retraces the artist's first steps.

PARKETT 32

SHERRIE LEVINE
2 SCHUHE, 1992
Ein paar Kinderschuhe, braunes
Leder, je ca. 16 x 6 x 6 cm
Ed. 99, signiert und numeriert, **sFr. 830.-**
2 SHOES, 1992
Pair of shoes, brown leather,
each 6½ x 2½ x 2½" (each 16 x 6 x 6 cm).
Ed. 99, signed and numbered, **US$ 600**

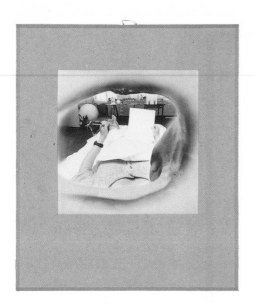

PARKETT 33

Teilen Sie mit Rosemarie Trockel die geheime Perspektive auf ihr Atelier als Hirnsicht durch die linke Augenhöhle.

Mind's eye view. An intimate perspective of the studio that places the viewer inside the secret cave of the artist's left eye.

ROSEMARIE TROCKEL
STUDIO VISIT, 1992
Photogravure in Strohpappe-Passepartout mit Prägedruck, säurefreies Folienfenster, auf Holz montiert mit Aufhänger
Bild: 21 x 21 cm, Rahmen: 38 x 33 x 0,9 cm.
Auflage: 80 Exemplare, numeriert und signiert, **sFr. 850.-**
Gedruckt bei Peter Kneubühler, Zürich.
STUDIO VISIT, 1992
Photoetching and acid-free transparent foil in embossed strawboard matte, mounted on wood with hanger.
Image: 8¼ x 8¼", frame: 15 x 13 x ⅜".
Edition of 80, numbered and signed, **US$ 650**

Die Verwandlung vom Wortbild RUN DOG RUN aus Christopher Wools Malerei zur bildmalerischen Momentaufnahme eines fliehenden schwarzen Hundes.

Word into image. RUN DOG RUN beat a tattoo in an earlier cycle of paintings; here it becomes a fleeting presence captured in a painterly snapshot.

PARKETT 33

CHRISTOPHER WOOL
OHNE TITEL, 1992
Schwarzweissphotographie, 25,4 x 20,3 cm.
Auflage: 70 Exemplare, numeriert und signiert, **sFr. 400.-**
UNTITLED, 1992
Black & white photograph, 10 x 8".
Edition of 70, signed and numbered, **US$ 300**

Sonderpreis beim Kauf von beiden Vorzugsausgaben : **sFr. 950-**.

Special price with purchase of both editions : **US$ 750**

Zwei Gleichnisse zum Leben der Fliege:
«Fliege sein bedeutet, nicht jemand zu sein;
es bedeutet, sich in einem bestimmten
Zustand zu befinden», meint Ilya Kabakov
mit Prochglasko in der Arbeit Zitat.

"To be a fly is not to be a somebody; it
means to be in some condition." Two
parables about existence play on the
ready analogies to be made between the
life of humans and the life of flies.

PARKETT 34

ILYA KABAKOV
ZWEI FREUNDE, 1992
Schachtelobjekt mit Feinrastersiebdruck und 2 Plastikfliegen auf
Museumskarton. Russischer Text auf eingeklebtem Papierband.
Übersetzungen ins Englische und Deutsche. 5 x 11,5 x 14,5 cm.
Auflage: 50, signiert und numeriert, **sFr. 700.-**
TWO FRIENDS, 1992
Silkscreened acid-free cardboard box with two plastic flies and a paper
script (in Russian) attached. English and German translations provided.
2 x 4½ x 5⅝". Edition of 50, signed and numbered, **US$ 520**

ILYA KABAKOV
ZITAT, 1992
Feinrastersiebdruck und Plastikfliege, montiert auf verschiedene
Kartons, gestanzt und bedruckt in Handsatz, mit Plastikfliege in
Holzrahmen mit Acrylglas, 34,6 x 24,3 x 2,5 cm.
Auflage: 50, signiert und numeriert, **sFr. 700.-**
CITATION, 1992
Silkscreened picture and plastic fly mounted on paper and cardboard
in hand-printed passe-partout. Wood frame with acrylic glass.
13⅝ x 9½ x 1". Edition of 50, signed and numbered, **US$ 520**

Greatest hits. Der Meister der Fiktion krönt sich selber mit der höchsten
Auszeichnung der Unterhaltungsindustrie – die goldene Schallplatte –
und fügt ihr ein Muster seiner Erzählkunst bei.

PARKETT 34

Greatest hits. A weaver of fictions awards himself the industry's highest
accolade—a gold record—complete with winning cover design and
haunting "lyrics."

RICHARD PRINCE
GOOD REVOLUTION, 1992
Goldene Schallplatte und graviertes Metallschild auf C-Print, montiert und
gerahmt. Enthält zusätzlich eine beidseitig abspielbare Vinylplatte des Künstlers.
«Good Revolution» (1,46 Min.) und «Don't Belong» (1,46 Min.) arrangiert und
interpretiert von Richard Prince. Aufgenommen und gemischt auf der
Harmonic Ranch von Mark Degliantoni, September 1992. 52 x 41,9 cm.
Auflage: 80, signiert und numeriert, **sFr. 1100.-**
GOOD REVOLUTION, 1992
Presentation gold record with engraved plaque mounted on C-Print, framed.
Includes a playable vinyl record by the artist, recorded both sides.
"Good Revolution" (1:46) and "Don't Belong" (1:46), arranged and
performed by Richard Prince. Recorded and mixed at Harmonic Ranch
by Mark Degliantoni, September 1992, 2½ x 16½".
Edition of 80, signed and numbered, **US$ 820**

Ein Bild mit Gewicht. In weiches, schweres Blei gegossen ist ein Mann flankiert von zwei mannshohen Echsen – Mensch und Tier vereint ohne Furcht und Hierarchie.

Graven image. A triumvirate of a man and two lizards cast in lead—a substance at once elemental and endearing—man coexists with beast, devoid of fear or hierarchy.

PARKETT 36

STEPHAN BALKENHOL
ZWEI ECHSEN MIT MANN, 1993
Dreiteilige Figurengruppe, gegossen in
Bleilegierung durch Giesserei Bärtschi, Aefligen,
Schweiz. Je ca. 30 x 13 x 4 cm, Gewicht je ca. 2kg.
Auflage: 85, signiert und numeriert, **sFr. 1900.-**
TWO LIZARDS AND A MAN, 1993
Group of three cast lead figurines, produced at the
Bärtschi Foundry, Aefligen, Switzerland.
Each figure approx. 11^7/8 x 5^1/8 x 1½",
weighing approx. 4.5 lbs.
Edition: 85, signed and numbered, **US$ 1300**

Eine Seidenkrawatte war das erste von mehreren Kleidungsstücken, die Sophie Calle anonymerweise einem heimlich beobachteten Unbekannten zukommen liess. Die Geschichte dieser imginären Beziehung ist auf der Krawatte niedergeschrieben.

Autobiographical story. A silken tie not only represents the first episode of a story in which a number of tasteful articles of clothing are sent to a badly dressed but attractive man; it also becomes the page on which the story itself is told.

PARKETT 36

SOPHIE CALLE
THE TIE, 1993
Krawatte mit aufgedruckter Kurzgeschichte
"I saw him". Crepe de Chine, braun mit
blauem Text. Hergestellt durch Fabric
Frontline, Zürich. Auflage: 150,
signiert und numeriert, **sFr. 280.-**.
THE TIE, 1993
Pure silk crepe-de-chine man's tie,
printed with an autobiographical story.
Produced by Fabric Frontline, Zurich.
Edition: 150, signed and numbered. **US$ 200**

Sonderpreis beim Kauf beider Vorzugsausgaben: **sFr. 2080.-**
Special price with purchase of both editions: **US$ 1400**

BESTELLKARTE VORZUGSAUSGABEN

Jede Ausgabe von PARKETT entsteht in Zusammenarbeit mit einem Künstler, der eigens für die Leser von PARKETT einen Originalbeitrag in einer limitierten und signierten VORZUGSAUSGABE gestaltet. Dieses Werk ist auch in der Zeitschrift abgebildet.

Die VORZUGSAUSGABE kann mit dieser Bestellkarte in jedem unserer Büros in Zürich, Berlin und New York bestellt werden. Sie erhalten dann Ihre Editionsnummer und eine Rechnung. Sobald wir Ihre Zahlung erhalten haben, schicken wir Ihnen die Vorzugsausgabe. (Lieferung nur solange vorrätig. PARKETT übernimmt keine Verantwortung für etwaige Verzögerungen bei der Herstellung der Vorzugsausgaben.)

Ich bin PARKETT-Abonnent(in) und bestelle folgende VORZUGSAUSGABE(N) numeriert und vom Künstler signiert.

PARKETT Nr.	KÜNSTLER/IN	NAME:
PARKETT Nr.	KÜNSTLER/IN	STRASSE:
PARKETT Nr.	KÜNSTLER/IN	PLZ/STADT:
PARKETT Nr.	KÜNSTLER/IN	LAND:

Schicken Sie diese Bestellkarte an das PARKETT-Büro in Ihrer Nähe:

PARKETT KUNSTZEITSCHRIFT QUELLENSTR. 27 CH-8005 ZÜRICH TEL. 01/2718140 FAX 01/272 43 01
PARKETT KUNSTZEITSCHRIFT MOTZSTR. 30 D-1000 BERLIN 30 TEL.030/211 07 59 FAX 030/211 07 46
PARKETT ART MAGAZINE 636 BROADWAY NEW YORK, NY 10012 TEL.(212) 673-2660 FAX (212)673-2887

SPECIAL EDITIONS ORDER FORM

Each issue of PARKETT is created in collaboration with an artist, who contributes an original work especially made for the readers of PARKETT in the form of a signed limited SPECIAL EDITION. The work is also reproduced in the regular edition of the magazine.

Each SPECIAL EDITION is available by order from any one of our offices in New York, Zurich, and Berlin. Just fill in the details below and send this card to the office nearest you. Once your order has been processed, you will be issued with an invoice and an edition number assigned to you. Upon receipt of payment, you will receive the SPECIAL EDITION. (Please note that supply is subject to availability. Parkett does not assume responsibility for any delays in production of SPECIAL EDITIONS).

As a subscriber to PARKETT, I would like to order the following Special Edition(s), signed and numbered by the artist.

PARKETT No.	ARTIST	NAME:
PARKETT No.	ARTIST	ADDRESS:
PARKETT No.	ARTIST	CITY:
PARKETT No.	ARTIST	STATE/ZIP:

Send this card to the PARKETT office nearest you:

PARKETT ART MAGAZINE 636 BROADWAY NEW YORK, NY 10012 TEL.(212) 673-2660 FAX (212) 673-2887
PARKETT KUNSTZEITSCHRIFT QUELLENSTR. 27 CH-8005 ZÜRICH TEL.01/2718140 FAX 01/272 43 01
PARKETT KUNSTZEITSCHRIFT MOTZSTR. 30 D-1000 BERLIN 30 TEL. 030/211 07 59 FAX 030/211 07 46

PARKETT

BESTELLKARTE ABONNEMENTE

☐ Ich abonniere PARKETT: 1 Jahr (4 Ausgaben) ab Nr._____ sFr. 80.–/DM 108,–, zuzüglich Versandkostenanteil.

NAME: _____

STRASSE: _____

PLZ/STADT: _____

LAND: _____

☐ Ich bestelle folgende noch erhältliche PARKETT-Ausgabe(n) zu je sFr. 25.–/ DM 30,–, zuzüglich Versandkosten:
Nr._____ (Bitte beachten: Nr. 1-10 sind vergriffen.)

☐ Ich zahle mit Visa ☐ Eurocard/Mastercard   Karten Nr.|||||||||||||||||| Gültig bis_____

☐ Mein Scheck über sFr./DM_____ liegt bei. ☐ Bitte schicken Sie mir eine Rechnung.

DATUM   UNTERSCHRIFT   NAME (in Blockschrift)

PARKETT KUNSTZEITSCHRIFT QUELLENSTR. 27 CH-8005 ZÜRICH TEL. 01/271 81 40 FAX 01/272 43 01
PARKETT KUNSTZEITSCHRIFT MOTZSTR. 30 D-1000 BERLIN 30 TEL. 030/211 07 59 FAX 030/211 07 46
PARKETT ART MAGAZINE 636 BROADWAY NEW YORK, NY 10012 TEL. (212) 673-2660 FAX (212) 673-2887

PARKETT

SUBSCRIPTION ORDER FORM

☐ I subscribe to PARKETT ART MAGAZINE starting with issue no._____
1 year (4 issues) USA $63.00 airmail postage included, Europe sFr. 80.- postage not included.

NAME: _____

ADDRESS: _____

CITY: _____

STATE/ZIP: _____

TEL: _____

☐ Please send me PARKETT back-issue(s) no._____ $20.00 each, postage included. (Please note: No. 1-10 are sold out.)

☐ Bill me ☐ Visa ☐ Mastercard   Card Acc. No.|||||||||||||||||| Expiration Date_____

☐ Payment enclosed (US check or money order)

DATE   SIGNATURE   PRINT NAME

PARKETT ART MAGAZINE 636 BROADWAY NEW YORK, NY 10012 TEL. (212) 673-2660 FAX (212) 673-2887
PARKETT KUNSTZEITSCHRIFT QUELLENSTR. 27 CH-8005 ZÜRICH TEL. 01/271 81 40 FAX 01/272 43 01
PARKETT KUNSTZEITSCHRIFT MOTZSTR. 30 D-1000 BERLIN 30 TEL. 030/211 07 59 FAX 030/211 07 46

BISHER ERSCHIENENE NUMMERN / *BACK ISSUES*

COLLABORATIONS

PETER FISCHLI /
DAVID WEISS
PATRICK FREY, GERMANO CELANT,
KAREN MARTA, BERNHARD
JOHANNES BLUME, JEANNE SILVER-
THORNE, SIDRA STICH
INSERT: **LOUISE BOURGEOIS**
MAX WECHSLER: **IMI KNOEBEL**
PAUL GROOT: **MATT MULLICAN**
KATHY HALBREICH:
WOOSTER GROUP

NO. 17

NO. 18

EDWARD RUSCHA
DAVE HICKEY, DENNIS HOPPER,
ALAIN CUEFF, JOHN MILLER,
CHRISTOPHER KNIGHT
INSERT: **BOYD WEBB**
JAN THORN-PRIKKER: **WOLS**
LYNNE COOKE: **TONY CRAGG**
BROOKE ADAMS:
JULIAN SCHNABEL
DER KÜNSTLER ALS EXEM-
PLARISCH LEIDENDER? EINE
UMFRAGE / THE ARTIST AS A
MODEL SUFFERER? AN INQUIRY.

JEFF KOONS · MARTIN
KIPPENBERGER · KLAUS
KERTESS, BURKE & HARE, JEAN-
CHRISTOPHE AMMANN, GLENN
O'BRIEN, DIEDRICH DIEDE-
RICHSEN, PATRICK FREY, MARTIN
PRINZHORN / BICE CURIGER
INSERT: **ANSELM STALDER.** ANNE-
MARIE HÜRLIMANN: **BARBARA
BLOOM.** HANNA HUMELTENBERG:
THOMAS RUFF. FELIX-PHILIPP
INGOLD: **RÉMY ZAUGG.** JAN-THORN
PRIKKER: **GERHARD RICHTER**

NO. 19

NO. 20

TIM ROLLINS + K.O.S.
MARSHALL BERMAN,
TREVOR FAIRBROTHER,
STATEMENTS, DIALOGUE 5
INSERT: **ANDREAS GURSKY**
MICHAEL NASH: **BILL VIOLA**
STEPHEN ELLIS: **ROSS BLECKNER**
KLAUS KERTESS: **TRISHA BROWN**

ALEX KATZ
JOHN RUSSELL, BROOKS ADAMS,
DAVID RIMANELLI, FRANCESCO
CLEMENTE, MICHAEL KRÜGER,
RICHARD FLOOD, PATRICK FREY,
CARL STIGLIANO, BICE CURIGER,
GLENN O'BRIEN
INSERT: **WILLIAM WEGMAN**
LISA LIEBMAN: **ROBERT GOBER**
JACQUELINE BURCKHARDT:
GIULIO ROMANO

NO. 21

NO. 22

CHRISTIAN BOLTANSKI
JEFF WALL
DIDIER SEMIN, GEORGIA MARSH
BÉATRICE PARENT, DAN GRAHAM
JEFF WALL, ARIELLE PÉLENC
INSERT: **CHRISTOPHER WOOL**
DIETER KOEPPLIN:
STEPHAN BALKENHOL
RENATE PUVOGEL:
DAN FLAVIN, DONALD JUDD
WERNER LIPPERT: **VARIOUS SMALL
FIRES IN THE GUTENBERG GALAXY**

RICHARD ARTSCHWAGER
ARTHUR C. DANTO, GEORG
KOHLER, MARIO A. ORLANDO,
JOYCE CAROL OATES, WERNER
OECHSLIN, ALAN LIGHTMAN,
PATRICK McGRATH, DANIEL SOUTIF,
LASZLO F. FÖLDENYI, JEAN STROUSE
INSERT: **DAVID BYRNE**
RENATE PUVOGEL:
ANDRÉ THOMKINS
ULRICH LOOCK: **THOMAS STRUTH**
NANCY SPECTOR: **MEREDITH MONK**

NO. 23

NO. 24

ALIGHIERO E BOETTI
JEAN-CRISTOPHE AMMANN
GIOVAN BATTISTA SALERNO
RAINER CRONE & DAVID MOOS
FRIEDEMANN MALSCH
JEAN-PIERRE BORDAZ
ALAIN CUEFF
INSERT: **CINDY SHERMAN**
SHEENA WAGSTAFF:
SOPHIE CALLE
HERBERT LACHMEYER /
BRIGITTE FELDERER: **FRANZ WEST**
JUTTA KOETHER: **MIKE KELLEY**

KATHARINA FRITSCH
JAMES TURRELL
GARY GARRELS
JULIAN HEYNEN, DAN CAMERON,
JEAN-CHRISTOPHE AMMANN,
DAVE HICKEY, RICHARD FLOOD &
CARL STIGLIANO, TED CASTLE
INSERT: **BEAT STREULI**
PATRICK FREY:
JEAN-FRÉDÉRIC SCHNYDER
DIETER SCHWARZ: **JAMES COLEMAN**
LYNNE COOKE:
RICHARD HAMILTON

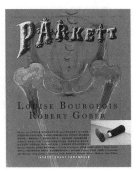

NO. 25

NO. 26

GÜNTHER FÖRG
PHILIP TAAFFE
JOHN CALDWELL, CATHERINE QUELOZ
WILFRIED DICKHOFF
JEFF PERRONE, EDMUND WIHTE
FRANCESCO PELLIZZI
G. ROGER DENSON
INSERT: **PETER GREENAWAY**
BICE CURIGER: **SIGMAR POLKE**
HANS-ULRICH OBRIST:
ROMAN SIGNER
DAVID LEVI STRAUSS:
JOSEPH BEUYS

LOUISE BOURGEOIS
ROBERT GOBER
JOSEF HELFENSTEIN, CHRISTIANE
MEYER-THOSS, MIGNON NIXON,
MANUEL J. BORJA-VILLEL, HARALD
SZEEMANN, NANCY SPECTOR,
NED RIFKIN/THERESIA BUSH/
ROBERT GOBER, GREGG BORDOWITZ
INSERT: **ERNST CARAMELLE**
MARINA WARNER: **BUSH NATURAL**
CLAUDE RITSCHARD:
JOHN M ARMLEDER
HANS-ULRICH OBRIST:
DAVID RABINOWITCH

NO. 27

NO. 28

FRANZ GERTSCH
THOMAS RUFF
HELMUT FRIEDEL, ULRICH LOOCK
I. MICHAEL DANOFF, AMEI WALLACH
RAINER MICHAEL MASON
MARC FREIDUS, JÖRG JOHNEN
TREVOR FAIRBROTHER/NORMAN BRYSON
INSERT: **LIZ LARNER**
JAMES LEWIS: **RICHARD PRINCE**
DAVID HICKEY:
THE INVISIBLE DRAGON/
DER UNSICHTBARE DRACHEN
PAUL TAYLOR: **JAMES ROSENQUIST**

JOHN BALDESSARI
CINDY SHERMAN
HOWARD SINGERMAN, DAVE HICKEY;
THOMAS LAWSON, PATRICK FREY,
JAMES LEWIS, SUSAN DAVIS,
URSULA PIA JAUCH, NORMAN
BRYSON, ELFRIEDE JELINEK,
WILFRIED DICKHOFF, ABIGAIL
SOLOMON-GODEAU, RUDOLF
SCHMITZ, THEODORA VISCHER/
MARIA NORDMAN, CLAUDE
RITSCHARD, INSERT: **NIELE TORONI**

NO. 29

NO. 30

SIGMAR POLKE
THOMAS MCEVILLEY
GARY GARRELS, BICE CURIGER
DAVE HICKEY, LASZLO GLOZER
ROGER DENSON, GABRIELE WIX
INSERT: **GLENN LIGON**
ANNE RORIMER: **MICHAEL ASHER**
LAURA COTTINGHAM: **ANN HAMILTON**
ANDREI KOVALYOV: **FRANCOIS BOUCHER**
EDWARD LEFFINGWELL/LAWRENCE
WEINER

DAVID HAMMONS
MIKE KELLEY
ROBERT FARRIS THOMPSON
IWONA BLAZWICK & EMMA DEXTER
JOHN FARRIS, LYNNE COOKE, LOUISE
NERI, TREVOR FAIRBROTHER,
DIEDRICH DIEDRICHSEN, LANE RELYEA,
BERNARD MARCADÉ, JULIE SYLVESTER
INSERT: **CANDIDA HÖFER**
CLAUDE RITSCHARD: **RÉMY ZAUGG**
JEAN-PIERRE BORDAZ: **IMI KNOEBEL,**
ISA GENZKEN, GERHARD MERZ

NO. 31

NO. 32

IMI KNOEBEL
SHERRIE LEVINE
RUDOLF BUMILLER
RAINER CRONE/DAVID MOOS
LISA LIEBMANN, DANIELA SALVIONI
ERICH FRANZ, HOWARD SINGERMANN
INSERT: **DAMIEN HIRST**
SHEENA WAGSTAFF: **VIJA CELMINS**
JIM LEWIS: **LARRY CLARK**
LIAM GILLICK: **BETHAN HUWS**
THOMAS KELLEIN: **WALTER DE MARIA**

VORSCHAU / *PREVIEW*

NO. 37 SEPTEMBER 1993 COLLABORATION WITH CHARLES RAY AND FRANZ WEST

Garderobe [gardəˈroːbə]

Kleinbörse für Waren, Fragen und Ideen / Exchange of commodities: real and ideal

Wanted: Complete set of PARKETT issues no. 1–10. *Chiffre 3/1*

To order the art historical lowdown on *Picasso and the Age of Iron* exhibition at the Guggenheim:
Rent-a-Guide to the five boys' show pictured standing in front of the show's totem, symbolizing from L to R: Julio Gonzalez (alone), David Smith and Pablo Picasso (dancing), Alberto Giacometti (depressed) with Alexander Calder (mobile).

Bezugnehmend auf das Editorial dieser Ausgabe möchte unsere Photographin Flavia Vogel Ihnen ein weiteres Beispiel aus der Serie *Famose Mäntel in grossen Museen* nicht vorenthalten.

Liebe Grüsse aus Zürich den PARKETT-Lesern in Guatemala.

Eva-Maria-Josef, wir sind Dir gram – Du weisst schon von wem.
K. K. und H. U. O.

Emiliooo,

smettila di

cacciare il gatto!

In reference to our editorial in this issue, photographer Flavia Vogel does not wish to deprive our readers a further sample from her series *Fabulous Coats in Major Museums.*

Pelzparkett-Mantel vor Photoparkett-Bild in der Sigmar Polke-Ausstellung, Kunsthalle Baden-Baden, 1990.
Fur-Parkett coat in front of Photo-Parkett picture at the Sigmar Polke exhibition, Kunsthalle Baden-Baden, 1990.

Der Nabel der Welt, wo sonst, wenn nicht im Appenzell? Hier in der Ortschaft Gais möbliert das Museum Robert Walser in Vitrinenform den Gasthof Hotel Krone. In übersichtlichen Ausstellungen werden vom 4.4. bis 5.5.1993 Dominique Gonzalez-Foerster, im Juni John Miller und später im Sommer Andreas Slominski eine Hommage an den Dichter präsentieren.

Bis Dezember 1993 findet an Bord der Flüge von Austrian Airlines eine Ausstellung von Alighiero Boetti statt.

The navel of the world, where else, if not in Appenzell? Here in the town of Gais, in the Robert Walser Museum Display Case at the entrance of the Krone Hotel, an homage to the writer will be presented by Dominique Gonzalez-Foerster from 4.4. to 5.5.1993 and by John Miller in June, and later this summer by Andreas Slominski.

See the Alighiero Boetti exhibition on bord of the Austrian Airlines flights from January to December 1993.

PARKETT IN BUCHHANDLUNGEN / *BOOKSHOPS*

AUSKUNFT UND ABONNEMENTS / *INFORMATION AND SUBSCRIPTIONS:*

«PARKETT»-VERLAG AG, QUELLENSTRASSE 27, CH-8005 ZÜRICH, TEL. 01/271 81 40, FAX 272 43 01; MOTZSTR. 30, D-1000 BERLIN 30, TEL. 030/211 07 59. FAX 030/211 07 46

PARKETT, 636 BROADWAY, NEW YORK, N.Y. 10012, PHONE (212) 673-2660, FAX 673-2887

SCHWEIZ

VERTRIEB
B + I BUCH UND INFORMATION AG
OBFELDERSTR. 35
8910 AFFOLTERN A. A.

BASEL
BUCHHANDLUNG STAMPA, SPALENBERG 2
BÜCHERSTAND STAMPA, KUNSTHALLE BASEL
W. JAEGGI AG, FREIESTR. 32

BERN
HANS HUBER AG, MARKTGASSE 59
BUCHHANDLUNG STAUFFACHER, NEUENGASSE 25
BUCHHANDLUNG STAUFFACHER
IM KUNSTMUSEUM BERN, HODLERSTR.12

GENÈVE
LIBRAIRIE DESCOMBES, 6, RUE DU VIEUX-COLLÈGE
LIBRAIRIE PAYOT, 5, RUE DE CHANTEPOULET
LIBRAIRIE WEBER, 13, RUE DE MONTHOUX

LAUSANNE
LIBRAIRIE PAYOT, 1, RUE DE BOURG

SCHAFFHAUSEN
BÜCHER-FASS, WEBERGASSE 13

ST. GALLEN
BUCHHANDLUNG COMEDIA, KATHARINENGASSE 20

ZÜRICH
BUCHHANDLUNG ZUM ELSÄSSER, LIMMATQUAI 18
BUCHHANDLUNG CALLIGRAMME, HÄRINGSTR. 4
SCALO BOOKS & LOOKS, WEINBERGSTRASSE 22 A
HEINIMANN & CO, KIRCHGASSE 17
BUCHHANDLUNG HOWEG, WAFFENPLATZSTR. 1
BUCHHANDLUNG AM KUNSTHAUS AG, RÄMISTR. 45
BUCHHANDLUNG KRAUTHAMMER, OBERE ZÄUNE 24
KUNSTKIOSK, LIMMATQUAI 31/HELMHAUS
ORELL FÜSSLI, PELIKANSTR. 10
SEC 52, JOSEFSTR. 52

DEUTSCHLAND

VERTRIEB
KARLHEINZ BIERSACK GmbH
ERNST-SACHS-STR. 6
POSTFACH 5666 + 5206
7750 KONSTANZ

BERLIN
BÜCHERBOGEN, AM SAVIGNYPLATZ
GALERIE 2000, KNESEBECKSTR. 56–58
WASMUTH GmbH & CO., HORDENBERGSTR. 9A
WERNER GmbH, EHRENBERGSTR. 29

BONN
CARL KAYSER, POSTSTR. 16
GALERIE PUDELKO, HEINRICH-VON-KLEIST-STR.

BREMEN
ANTIQUARIAT, BEIM STEINERNEN KREUZ 1
JOHS. STORM, LANGENSTR. 10
KUNSTBUCH, SPITZENKIEL 16/17
B. SIEBRECHT, PANORAMA, VOR DEM STEINTOR 136
KUNST UND BUCH,
AM NEUEN MUSEUM, WESERBURG, TEERHOF 20

BREMERHAVEN
KABINETT FÜR AKTUELLE KUNST, KARLSBURG 4

DÜSSELDORF
M. + R. FRICKE, POSTSTR. 3
WALTHER KÖNIG, HEINRICH-HEINE-ALLEE 15
MÜLLER & TILLMANNS, NEUSTR. 38

FRANKFURT
HUGENDUBEL, STEINWEG 12
KARL MARX BUCHHANDLUNG, JORDANSTR. 11
PETER NAACHER, SCHWEIZERSTR. 57
SCHUMANN & COBET, BÖRSENSTR. 2–4
WALTHER KÖNIG, DOMSTR. 6

HAMBURG
H. VON DER HÖH, GROSSE BLEICHEN 21
SAUTTER UND LACKMANN
ADMIRALITÄTSSTRASSE 71/72
PPS, FELDSTR./ HOCHHAUS

HANNOVER
BUCHHANDLUNG IM SPRENGELMUSEUM
KURT-SCHWITTERS-PLATZ

HEIDELBERG
KUNSTHANDLUNG W. WELKER, HAUPTSTR. 106

KARLSRUHE
KUNSTBUCHHANDLUNG JUST, WALDSTR. 85

KIEL
GALERIE + EDITION KOCH, HOLSTENTÖRNPASSAGE

KÖLN
WALTHER KÖNIG, EHRENSTR. 4

MÜNCHEN
ILKA KÖNIG, AM KOSTTOR 1
H. GOLZ, TÜRKENSTR. 54
L. WERNER, RESIDENZSTR. 18
INT. BAHNHOFSBUCHHANDLUNG, BAHNHOFSPLATZ 2
MAX SUSSMANN GmbH, ARNULFSTR. 1/II
BASIS ANTIQUARIAT, ADALBERTSTR. 43

MÜNSTER
HEINRICH POERTGEN
HERDERSCHE BUCHHANDLUNG, HÖLTENWEG 51

NÜRNBERG
HEINRICH HUGENDUBEL, LUDWIGSPLATZ 1

OSNABRÜCK
H. TH. WENNER GmbH, GROSSE-STR. 69

SAARBRÜCKEN
BOCK & SEIP, FUTTERSTR. 2

STUTTGART
WENDELIN NIEDLICH, SCHMALESTR. 9
GALERIE VALENTIEN, KÖNIGSBAU

TÜBINGEN
HUGO FRICK, NAUKLERSTR. 7

ULM
BUCHHANDLUNG UND GALERIE HOLM
HAFENBAD 11

WUPPERTAL
GRAEFF & HEINRICH, OBERGRÜNEWALDER STR. 13

ÖSTERREICH

VERTRIEB
LECHNER + SOHN, HEIZWERKSTRASSE 10, 1232 WIEN

GRAZ
BUCHHANDLUNG GALERIE
VERLAG DROSCHL, BISCHOFPLATZ 1

INNSBRUCK
PARNASS, SPECKBACHERSTR. 21
WAGNERSCHE UNIVERSITÄTSBUCHHANDLUNG
MUSEUMSTR. 4

LINZ
ALEX STELZER, HAUPTPLATZ 17

WIEN
JUDITH ORTNER, SONNENFELSGASSE 8
SHAKESPEARE & COMPANY
BOOKSELLERS, STEINGASSE 2

HOLLAND

DISTRIBUTION
IDEA BOOKS
NIEUWE HERENGRACHT 11
1011 RK AMSTERDAM

AMSTERDAM
ART BOOK, PRINSENGRACHT 645
ATHENAEUM NIEUWSCENTRUM, SPUI 14–16
NIJHOF & LEE, STAALSTRAAT 13 A
PREMSELA, VAN BAERLESTRAAT 78
SCHELTEMA/HOLKEMA/VERMEULEN, KONIGSPLEIN 20
VALETON & HENSTRA, NES 26
VERBEELDING, UTRECHTSESTRAAT 40

ARNHEM
HIJMAN, GROTE OORD 15
ARNHEMS GEMEENTEMUSEUM, UTRECHTSEWEG 87

EINDHOVEN
MOTTA BERGSTRAAT 35
VAN ABBEMUSEUM, BILDERDIJKLAAN 10

GRONINGEN
SCHOLTENS/WRISTERS, GULDENSTRAAT 20

HENGELO
BROEKHUIS, ENSCHEDESTRAAT 19

MAASTRICHT
ARCADIA, VRIJTHOF 29
TRIBUNE, KAPOENSTRAAT 8
VELDEKE, KLEINE STAAT 14

ROTTERDAM
BOYMANS VAN BEUNINGEN MUSEUM
MATHENESSERLAAN 18–20

THE HAGUE
HAAGS GEMEENTE MUSEUM, STADHOUDERSLAAN 41

UTRECHT
CENTRAAL MUSEUM, AGNIETENSTRAAT 1

BELGIQUE

ANTWERPEN
BRAMANTE, KOEPORTBRUG 4

BRUXELLES
POST-SCRIPTUM, 37 RUE DES ÉPERONNIERS

GENT
COPYRIGHT, JAKOBIJNENSTRAAT 8
INTELLECT, KALANDESTRAAT 1

KORTRIJK
THEORIA, ONZE LIEVE VROUWESTRAAT 22

ESPAÑA

DISTRIBUTIÓN
VIS-A-VIS ART BOOKS
HORNSTRASSE 1
1000 BERLIN 61

BARCELONA
NOA NOA, CENTRE CULTURAL DE LA FUNDACIÒ
CAIXA, PASSEIG DE SANT JOAN, 108
NOA NOA LIBRES D'ART
CENTRE D'ART STA. MONICA
RAMBLA STA. MONICA 7
MADRID
LIBROS ARGENSOLA, DOCTOR MATA, 1
CENTRO REINA SOFIA, STA. ISABEL 52

F R A N C E
DISTRIBUTEUR
HAZAN ÉDITION, 35–37, RUE DE SEINE, 75006 PARIS
AIX-EN-PROVENCE
LIBRAIRIE VENTS DU SUD, 7, RUE MARÉCHAL FOCH
BORDEAUX
LIBRAIRIE DU MUSÉE CAPC, ENTREPÔT LAINÉ
LIBRAIRIE MOLLAT, 9–15, VITAL CARLES
LYON
LIBRAIRIE LE RÉVERBÈRE, 4, RUE NEUVE
PARIS
LA HUNE, 170 BLVD ST-GERMAIN
«FLAMMARION 4», CENTRE GEORGES POMPIDOU
PLATEAU BEAUBOURG
LIBRAIRIE DU MUSEE D'ART MODERNE
9, RUE FERRIÈRE
GALERIE NATIONALE DU JEU DE PAUME
PLACE DE LA CONCORDE
TOULOUSE
LIBRAIRIE OMBRES BLANCHES, 50, RUE GAMBETTA

I T A L I A
MILANO
MILANO LIBRI, VIA G. VERDI 2
MODENA
LOGOS IMPEX
VIA CURTATONA, 5/F, 41010 SAN DAMASO/MODENA
ROMA
· CENTRO DI GALLERIA NAZIONALE
D'ARTE MODERNA, VIA DELLE BELLE ARTI 131
FELTRINELLI, VIA DEL BABUINO 41
GALLERIA PRIMO PIANO, VIA PANISPERNA 203

P O R T U G A L
LISBOA
COMICOS ESPAÇO INTER-MEDIA
RUA TENENTE RAUL CASCAIS 1B

S V E R I G E
STOCKHOLM
BOK & BILD, KULTURHUSET, SERGELSTORG 3
NORDENFLYCHTSVÄGEN 70

G R E A T   B R I T A I N
DISTRIBUTOR
CENTRAL BOOKS, 99, WALLIS RD. LONDON E9 5LN
LONDON
HAYWARD GALLERY BOOKSHOP, SOUTH BANK
ICA BOOKSHOP, NASH HOUSE
12, CARLTON HOUSE TERRACE
LIBERTY, BOOK DEPT., 210 REGENT STREET
NIGEL GREENWOOD BOOK
4, NEW BURLINGTON STREET

USA
DISTRIBUTOR
D. A. P. (DISTRIBUTED ART PUBLISHERS)
636 BROADWAY, RM 1208 NEW YORK, NY 10012
BOSTON, MA
RIZZOLI INTERNATIONAL BOOKSTORES
100 HUNTINGTON AVE.
TRIDENT BOOKSELLERS & CAFE, 338 NEWBURY ST.
BERKELEY, CA
MOE'S BOOKS, 2476 TELEGRAPH
UNIVERSITY ART MUSEUM
2625 DURANT AVE.
BLOOMINGTON, IN
MORGENSTERN BOOKSELLERS, 2650 E. 3RD. ST.
CHICAGO, IL
MUSEUM OF CONTEMPORARY ART
237 EAST ONTARIO ST.
RIZZOLI INTERNATIONAL BOOKSTORES
835N. MICHIGAN AVE.
COLUMBUS, OH
WEXNER CENTER FOR THE ARTS
UNIVERSITY OF OHIO, 30 W. 15TH ST.
LOS ANGELES, CA
ART CATALOGUES, 625 N. ALMONT DR.
MUSEUM OF CONTEMPORARY ART
152 N. CENTRAL AND 250 S. GRAND
BOOK SOUP, 8818 SUNSET BLVD.
RIZZOLI INTERNATIONAL BOOKSTORES
3333 BRITSOL AVE., COSTA MESA
HOUSTON, TX
BRAZOS, 2421 BISSONNET ST.
MUSEUM OF FINE ARTS, 1001 BISSONET
KANSAS CITY, MO
WHISTLER'S BOOKS, WESTPORT SQUARE
427 WESTPORT ROAD
MINNEAPOLIS, MN
WALKER ART CENTER, VINELAND PLACE
NEW YORK, NY
BOOKS AND COMPANY, 939 MADISON AVE.
JAAP RIETMANN, 134 SPRING STREET
MUSEUM OF MODERN ART, 11 W. 53RD ST.
PRINTED MATTER BOOKSTORE AT DIA,
77 WOOSTER ST.
RIZZOLI INTERNATIONAL BOOKSTORES
31 W. 57TH AND 454 WEST BROADWAY
ST. MARK'S BOOKSHOP, 12 ST. MARK'S PLACE
UNTITLED II INC., 680 BROADWAY
WHITNEY MUSEUM OF AMERICAN ART
945 MADSION AVE.
OAK PARK, MI
BOOK BEAT, LTD., 26020 GREENFIELD
PHILADELPHIA, PA
PAUL CAVA GALLERY & FINE ART BOOKS,
22 N. 3RD ST.
SAN FRANCISCO, CA
SAN FRANCISCO MUSEUM OF MODERN ART
BOOKSHOP, VAN NESS AVE. AT MCALLISTER ST.
CITY LIGHTS BOOKSTORE, 2625 DURANT AVE.
JACK HANLEY GALLERY, 41 GRANT AVE.
ARIEL, 2901 LEAVENWORTH ST.
SANTA MONICA, CA
ARCANA, 1229 3RD ST. PROMENADE
HENNESSEY + INGALLS BOOKS
1254 SANTA MONICA MALL
SEATTLE, WA
ELLIOT BAY BOOKS, 1ST AND MAIN ST. S SOUTH
HENRY ART GALLERY BOOKSTORE

UNIVERSITY OF WASHINGTON
WASHINGTON, DC
BOOKWORKS – WPA, 400 7TH ST. NW
NATIONAL GALLERY, 6TH STREET
AND CONSTITUTION AVENUE NW

C A N A D A
MONTREAL
ARTEXTE, 3575 ST. LAURENT
TORONTO
ART METROPOLE, 788 KING STREET WEST
ART GALLERY OF ONTARIO, BOOKSTORE
317 DUNDAS ST. WEST
EDWARDS BOOKS & ART, 356 QUEEN ST. WEST
DAVID MIRVISH BOOKS ON ART, 596 MARKHAM ST.
VANCOUVER
ART GALLERY STORE, 750 HORNBY ST.

A U S T R A L I A
DISTRIBUTORS
MANIC EX-POSEUR, WORLD TRADE CENTER
MELBOURNE 3005
THE ARTS BOOKSHOP, 1067 HIGH STREET
ARMADALE, VICTORIA 3143
VICTORIA
HARTWIGS BOOKSHOP
245 BRUNSWICK STR., VICTORIA 3182

N E W   Z E A L A N D
DISTRIBUTOR
PROPAGANDA, 44 COLLEGE HILL, AUCKLAND

F A R   E A S T
DISTRIBUTION
VIS-A-VIS ART BOOKS, HORNSTRASSE 1
1000 BERLIN 61

H O N G   K O N G
PUBLISHERS MARKETING LTD.
TUNG ON BUILDING, 171, PRINCE EDWARD ROAD
KOWLOON
TAI YIP ART BOOK CENTRE
HONG KONG MUSEUM OF ART
TSIM SHA TSUI, KOWLOON

J A P A N
TOKIO
EUROPA ART GmbH, KAMIOGI 4-16-4, SUGINAMI-KU
ON SUNDAYS, 3-7-6 JUNGUMAE, SHIBUYA-KU
AOYAMA BOOKCENTER, ROPPONGI STORE
MINATO-KU
HAKUO TRADING COMPANY
KOJIMACHI SHINE BLD., 8F, CHIYODA-KU
SANSEIDO BOOKSTORE, 7-11-8 KOHAKU, ADACHI-KU
MY BOOK SERVICE, AOI BLD. 5-8, SARUGAKU-CHO

E X H I B I T I O N S

BASEL

FILIALE BASEL	Kannenfeldstr. 22, Basel	CLAUDIA + JULIA MÜLLER	13.5.–20.6.93
	Tel. 061/692 59 06		
	061/321 09 00		

TONY WÜTHRICH	Vogesenstr. 29, Basel	SIEGFRIED ANZINGER:	
	Tel. 061/321 92 92	MALEREI UND SKULPTUR	13.6.–31.7.93
		VOLKER TANNERT	Sept./Okt. 93

BERN

ERIKA + OTTO	Junkerngasse 39, Bern	SUZAN FRECON	bis 28.5.93
FRIEDRICH	Tel. 031/22 78 03	ALEX HANIMANN	5.6.–17.7.93
		ART BASEL, STAND 214/B16	16.–22.6.93

SUSANNE KULLI	Nydeggstalden 30, Bern	RUDOLF HAAS:	
	Tel. 031/21 06 40	ZEICHNUNGEN UND ASSEMBLAGEN	bis 28.5.93
		ESTHER BÄTTIG:	
		ARBEITEN AUF PAPIER	12.6.–1.7.93

FRANCESCA PIA	Münstergasse 6, Bern	HANS-PETER FELDMANN	21.5.–26.6.93
	Tel./Fax 031/22 73 02	BETTY WOODMAN	27.8.–1.10.93
		IAN ANÜLL	Okt. 93

RAPHAEL T. RIGASSI	Münstergasse 62, Bern	ARNULF RAINER	bis 22.5.93
	Tel./Fax 031/22 69 64	MARTIN DISLER:	
		BILDER UND SKULPTUREN	26.5.– Ende Juli 93

MICHÈLE ZELLER	Kramgasse 20, Bern	GUNNAR MÜLLER	bis 22.5.93
	Tel. 031/22 93 88	LILIANE CSUKA: INSTALLATION	26.5.–26.6.93
		INT. SCHMUCKAUSSTELLUNG	30.6.–24.8.93

E X H I B I T I O N S

GENÈVE

DANIEL VARENNE	8, Rue Toepffer, Genève	*PAINTINGS AND DRAWINGS*
	Tel. 022/789 16 75	*19th AND 20th CENTURY*

ST. GALLEN

WILMA LOCK	Schmidgasse 15, St. Gallen	*INFOLGE RENOVATION DES «HAUSES*
	Tel. 071/22 62 52	*ZUM PELIKAN» AUSSTELLUNGS-UNTER-*
	Fax 071/22 72 66	*BRUCH BIS ZUM BEZUG DER NEUEN*
		RÄUME AN DER BISHERIGEN ADRESSE

ZÜRICH

THOMAS AMMANN FINE ART	Restelbergstr.97, Zürich P.O.Box 922, Tel. 01/252 90 52	*IMPRESSIONISTS & 20th CENTURY MASTERS*	*by appoint-ment only*
ARS FUTURA	Bleicherweg 45, Zürich Tel. 01/201 88 10	*YUKINORI YANAGI*	*4.6.–9.7.93*
GALERIE LELONG	Predigerplatz 10–12, Zürich Tel. 01/251 11 20	*SKULPTUREN*	*Juni/Juli 93*
STORRER GALLERY	Scheuchzerstr. 25, Zürich Tel. 01/362 73 14	*PAUL ROTTERDAM: ZEICHNUNGEN UND RADIERUNGEN*	*April bis Juni 93 by appointment*
ANNEMARIE VERNA	Scheuchzerstr. 35, Eingang Turnersteig, Zürich Tel. 01/361 90 70	*GIULIO PAOLINI DAVID RABINOWITCH/ FRED SANDBACK: SCULPTURE*	*4.5.–3.7.93 6.7.–25.9.93*

INTERNATIONAL CANDIDACY CALL

SIXTH SESSION

Theme: "Center and periphery"

Autumn 1993 - Spring 1994

Professors:
Daniel Buren, Serge Fauchereau, Pontus Hulten, Sarkis

Research center of contemporary art and on the interaction of art with other disciplines, the "Institut des Hautes Etudes en Arts Plastiques" invites 20 young artists, 20 to 30 years old, speaking french to participate to seminaries with internationally renowned personalities.

Each yearly session is divided in two parts of six to eight weeks each on a general research theme.

The artists are chosen at the end of a dual assessment: upon presentation of their portfolio – application form to be asked in writing to the Institute and to send back before June 4th 1993 – followed by an interview with the "Comité Scientifique", June the 28th or the 29th 1993.

Those selected receive a scholarship and have at their disposal a collective studio to pursue their personal work.

Institut des Hautes Etudes en Arts Plastiques
75 rue du Temple, 75003 PARIS, FRANCE
Phone: (1) - 48.87.05.00 – fax: (1) - 48.87.03.88
Association régie par la loi de 1901

The institute is subsided by the City of Paris and receives the generous support of The Georges Pompidou Art and Culture Foundation, Houston.

Der zerbrochene Spiegel

Der zerbrochene Spiegel

‘Alles ist gesagt worden,
aber die Worte ändern
Ihre Bedeutung und
die Bedeutungen ändern
die Worte’

JEAN PAULHAN

Der zerbrochene Spiegel
Positionen zur Malerei

Kuratoren:
Kasper König & Hans-Ulrich Obrist

26. Mai bis 25. Juli 1993
Museumsquartier –
Messepalast Halle B *und*
Kunsthalle Wien

Eine Ausstellung von Wiener Festwochen und
Kunsthalle Wien in Zusammenarbeit mit
dem Museumsquartier.

RUDOLF HAAS

TECHNIQUES MIXTES

Exposition du 6 au 28 mai 1993
Vernissage mercredi 5 mai dès 19 heures

INSTITUT AUTRICHIEN
ÖSTERREICHISCHES KULTURINSTITUT
30, Boulevard des Invalides, 75007 Paris, Tél. (1) 47 05 27 10

IMAGES EFFACÉES

Exposition du 6 juin au 1er août 1993
de 10h - 18h, sf mardi

MUSÉE DES AUGUSTINS, TOULOUSE
21 rue Metz, 31000 Toulouse, Tél. (61) 222 182

KUNST HEUTE

Die von Wilfried Dickhoff herausgegebene Reihe KUNST HEUTE stellt zeitgenössische Künstler im Gespräch über ihre Arbeit, ihre Ideen und Entwicklungen vor. Diese Bände bieten die Möglichkeit, sich aus erster Hand über die Gedankenwelt, die Konzepte und Absichten der jeweiligen Künstler zu informieren.

In der Reihe KUNST HEUTE sind bisher erschienen:

Nr. 1   Joseph Beuys
Nr. 2   Georg Baselitz
Nr. 3   Robert Rauschenberg
Nr. 4   Markus Lüpertz
Nr. 5   Francesco Clemente
Nr. 6   A. R. Penck
Nr. 7   Albert Oehlen
Nr. 8   Walter Dahn

In Vorbereitung:

Nr. 9   Jenny Holzer
Nr. 10   Jiří Dokoupil

In Ihrer Buchhandlung. Jeder Band DM 24,80 / sFr 25.80 / ÖS 194,–

Kiepenheuer & Witsch

SONSBEEK 93

5·6·93 - 26·9·93

ARNHEM (31)85-429044 PGEM / VSB FONDS NL

APRIL - JUNE **THE ARCHITECTURE OF HERZOG & DE MEURON**
PHOTOGRAPHED BY MARGHERITA KRISCHANITZ · BALTHASAR BURKHARD
THOMAS RUFF · HANNAH VILLIGER WITH A VIDEO OF ENRIQUE FONTANILLES

JULY - AUGUST **PEDRO CABRITA REIS · JIMMIE DURHAM · DAVID HAMMONS**
WITH THE COLLABORATION OF THE BELLUARD FESTIVAL '93 AND THE M.H.K. GENT

SEPTEMBER - OCTOBER **ERIC LANZ**

NOVEMBER - DEZEMBER **"THE MUELLER"**
FROM AN IDEA OF JEAN TINGUELY

CENTRE D'ART CONTEMPORAIN KUNSTHALLE

PETITES-RAMES 22 – CH 1700 FRIBOURG SWITZERLAND PHONE 037 / 23 23 51 FAX 037 / 23 15 34

WIENER SECESSION

A-1010 WIEN, FRIEDRICHSTRASSE 12, TEL. 43-1-587 53 07

ERNST CARAMELLE
MATTHIAS HERRMANN
28.5. – 4.7.1993

"OPPOSITIONEN & SCHWESTERNFELDER"
Kurator Sabine Vogel
Penelope Georgiou (A), Edwin Janssen (NL), Martin Krützfeldt (D), minimal club (D),
Kirsten Mosher (USA), Dan Peterman (USA), p.t.t.red (D), Joe Scanlan (USA),
Schäfer & Skene (D), Ralf Weißleder (D), Achim Wollscheid (D)
14.7. – 25.8.1993

BRIGITTE KOWANZ
RONI HORN
8.9. – 17.10.1993

THE KINGDOMS OF ELGALAND-VARGALAND

With effect from the 14th of March 1992, we are annexing and occupying the following territories:
I: All border frontier areas between all countries on earth, and all areas (up to a width of 10 nautical miles) existing outside all countries' territorial waters. We designate these territories our physical territory.
II: Mental and perceptive territories such as the Hypnagogue State (civil), the Escapistic Territory (civil) and the Virtual Room (digital).
On the 27th of May 1992 at 12 noon, we proclaimed the state of Elgaland-Vargaland.

LEIF ELGGREN & CM VON HAUSSWOLFF

29.4. - 6.6. 1993
Official inauguration of the embassy in Stockholm, Sweden
ANDRÉHN SCHIPTJENKO
Kammakargatan 21, S-111 60 Stockholm - ph/fx:+46-8-676 05 15

15.5 - 23.5 1993
Official inauguration of the consulate in Gothenburg, Sweden
MORS MÖSSA
Husargatan 11, S-411 01 Göteborg - ph:+46-31-13 22 82

GENEVIÈVE CADIEUX

MUSÉE D'ART CONTEMPORAIN DE MONTRÉAL
31 MARS – 30 MAI 1993

GALERIE RENÉ BLOUIN

372 OUEST, RUE STE-CATHERINE, CH. 501
MONTRÉAL (QUÉBEC) CANADA H3B 1A2
TÉL.: (514) 393-9969 FAX: (514) 393-4571

BARBARA STEINMAN

"OBJECTS & INSTRUMENTS"

TATE GALLERY, LIVERPOOL
SPRING 1993

IKON GALLERY, BIRMINGHAM
SUMMER 1993

GALERIE RENÉ BLOUIN

372 OUEST, RUE STE-CATHERINE, CH. 501
MONTRÉAL (QUÉBEC) CANADA H3B 1A2
TÉL.: (514) 393-9969 FAX: (514) 393-4571

TONY SMITH

WILLY

30 April-29 May 1993

CHANGING GROUP SHOW

June and July

PAULA COOPER GALLERY

155 Wooster Street New York 10012 212 674.0766 Fax 212 674.1938

Distributed Art Publishers is an international consortium of publishers, museums, galleries, foundations, and artists dedicated to creating enduring art books of the highest quality. Founded by Scalo/Parkett Publishers, Archer Fields Press, and Daniel Power, **D. A. P.** specializes in the marketing and distribution of art, photography and artists' books to bookstores, wholesalers, museum shops, cataloguers, libraries, universities, and individuals throughout the United States, Europe, and Asia.

We welcome your inquiries about our extensive collection of catalogues, monographs, and limited editions, and about our marketing and distribution services.

D.A.P.
Distributed Art Publishers
636 Broadway, Room 1208
New York, New York 10012

Fax: 212-673-2887
Tel: 212-473-5119

BRICE MARDEN
NEW PAINTINGS, DRAWINGS, & ETCHINGS

5 May to 26 June 1993

A fully illustrated catalogue will be published to accompany the exhibition

Matthew Marks Gallery
1018 Madison Avenue · New York 10021 · tel 212 861 9455 · fax 861 9382

RICHMOND BURTON

is represented by

MATTHEW MARKS GALLERY
NEW YORK

NAM JUNE PAIK
«JARDIN ILLUMINÉ»
1. MAI BIS 3. JULI 1993

HARDTURMSTRASSE 127   ZÜRICH

DI–FR 14.00–18.00 UHR   SA 14.00–17.00 UHR

SAMMLUNG HAUSER & WIRTH · ZÜRICH

SONNEGGSTRASSE 84   CH-8006 ZÜRICH   TELEFON 01 / 364 01 41   TELEFAX 01 / 364 01 44

DAVID BAKER

MAY

JAMES WELLING

JUNE

ROBERT FONES
CAROL WAINIO

JULY

S.L. SIMPSON GALLERY

515 Queen Street West
Toronto, Ontario
Canada M5V 2B4
tel: (416) 362-3738
fax: (416) 362-0979

BARBARA GLADSTONE GALLERY

MAY 1993 ━━━━━━━━━━━━━━━━━━━━

RICHARD PRINCE

99 GREENE STREET NEW YORK NY 10012 212 431 3334 FAX 966 9310

GALERÍA JUANA MORDÓ

Villanueva 7, 28001 MADRID, Tel. 435 84 42 - 431 05 28, Fax 5751626

MITSUO MIURA
March -April

JAVIER VALLHONRAT
May - June

YUKINORI YANAGI
4. JUNI - 9. JULI 1993

arsFutura
G A L E R I E

BLEICHERWEG 45 CH-8002 ZÜRICH TELEFON 01-201 88 10 FAX 01-201 88 11

GALERIE **LALLOUZ + WATTERSON**

René Pierre Allain   Sorel Cohen   John McEwen

Gerald Ferguson   Jochen Gerz   Brian Groombridge

Jan Groth   Nicole Jolicoeur   Joan Jonas   Peter Kolisnyk

Naomi London   Anne et Patrick Poirier   Sylvie Readman

Blair Robbins   Keith Sonnier   Nell Tenhaaf   Serge Tousignant

372, Ste-Catherine O., ch. 528, Montréal, (Québec) H3B 1A2   tél. (514) 398-9806   fax. (514) 398-9807

MAI 36 GALERIE

JOHN BALDESSARI
June 9 – July 24, 1993

STEPHAN BALKENHOL   LES LEVINE
IAN ANÜLL   CHRISTOPH RÜTIMANN
THOMAS RUFF   MATT MULLICAN
RÉMY ZAUGG   LAWRENCE WEINER
Art Basel, Halle 12/Stand B 23, June 15 – 21, 1993

Dufourstrasse 137, CH-8034 Zürich, Tel. 01 381 55 35, Fax 381 55 36
Tuesday–Friday 12–18.30 h and Saturday 11–16 h or by appointment

HARDTURM GALERIEN ZÜRICH

hardturmstr. 127
tel. 01 273 25 70
fax 01 273 25 71
Marc Jancou
di – fr 14 – 19 uhr
sa 11 – 16 uhr

CATHY DE MONCHAUX, KAREN KILIMNIK 27. 5. – 17. 7.
ART'24 BASEL 214/D9 15. – 21. 6.
HANNES BRUNNER 20. 8. – 25. 9.

hardturmstr. 127
tel. u. fax 01 271 39 57
Peter Kilchmann
mi – fr 12 – 18 uhr
sa 11 – 16 uhr

SUZANNE LAFONT 23. 4. – 5. 6.
MICHAL ROVNER 11. 6. – 17. 7.

hardturmstr. 124
tel. 01 273 01 12
fax 01 273 01 81
Mark Müller
mi – fr 12 – 18 uhr
sa 11 – 17 uhr

STEFAN GRITSCH 5. 6. – 10. 7.
ART'24 BASEL 214/D15 15. – 21. 6.
SOMMER III – MALEREI 17. 7. – 14. 8.

hardturmstr. 124 a
tel. u. fax 01 273 11 00
Bob van Orsouw
mi – fr 12 – 18.30 uhr
sa 11 – 16 uhr

«ZEICHEN UND MAL»
IN KOOPERATION MIT ROBERT FLECK 4. 6. – 17. 7.
ART'24 BASEL 212/B27 15. – 21. 6.

hardturmstr. 127
tel. u. fax 01 271 39 57
Jamileh Weber
mi – fr 12 – 18 uhr
sa 11 – 16 uhr

ROBERT RAUSCHENBERG, DARRYL POTTORF 16. 4. – 3. 7.
ART'24 BASEL 211/A4 15. – 21. 6.

Jeden letzten Sonntag des Monats Openhaus 12 – 17 uhr

HAIM STEINBACH

Mai - Juni

GALERIE PHILOMENE MAGERS

Maria-Hilf-Strasse 17, 5000 Köln 1, TEL. 0221-318843 Fax: 0221-31867

KUNSTHALLE BERN

1993

3. JULI—15. AUGUST   CANDIDA HÖFER, SHIRLEY WIITASALO

75 JAHRE KUNSTHALLE BERN — 75 SPEZIELLE ANLÄSSE

9. OKTOBER—28. NOVEMBER   BRICE MARDEN

HELVETIAPLATZ 1   CH-3005 BERN   TELEFON 031/43 00 31   TELEFAX 031/44 53 85

Galerie Erika + Otto Friedrich
Junkerngasse 39 CH-3011 Bern
Tel. 031/22 78 03 Fax 21 13 45
16. April–28. Mai Suzan Frecon
5. Juni–17. Juli Alex Hanimann
16. Juni–21. Juni ART Basel, Stand 214/B16

Galerie Francesca Pia
Münstergasse 6 · CH · 3011 Bern
Telefon 031 · 22 73 02 Privat 031 · 22 48 72
21.5.–26.6. Hans-Peter Feldmann
27.8.–1.10. Betty Woodman
Oktober – Ian Anüll

GALERIE LELONG

ZÜRICH

PREDIGERPLATZ 10–12 8001 ZÜRICH TEL. 01 251 11 20

JUNI/JULI

SKULPTUREN

**DESSINS ITALIENS
DE 1980 A 1993**

**EXPOSITION
DU
8 MAI
AU
30 JUIN
1993**

ARIENTI ASCHIERI BOETTI CABIATI CANEVARI CATELANI
CECCOBELLI CHIA CINGOLANI CIRINO CLEMENTE
CUCCHI CUOGHI E CORSELLO DE LORENZO DE MARIA
DELLAVEDOVA DI LERNIA FUSI GALLIANO GARUTTI
GUAITA KAUFMANN KOUNELLIS KOZARIS MARCOVINICIO
MARTEGANI MERZ PALADINO PANCRAZZI PAOLINI
PEROLI PESSOLI PIVI PUSOLE RASMA ROTELLA RUSSO
SALVO SANTARLASCI SGHERRI SILVESTRO

CATALOGUE DISPONIBLE
AVEC TEXTES DES ARTISTES

 GALERIE **ANALIX**
B & L POLLA

39 AVENUE DE LA PRAILLE
CH 1227 CAROUGE GENEVE
TÉL 41 22 342 31 29

FBM studio

FRANZISKA BODMER & BRUNO MANCIA

PHOTOGRAPHERS

SPECIALISTS FOR

ART AND ARTISTS

LUXURY SILKS

ARCHITECTURE

COMPUTER PHOTO RETOUCHING

AND MORE ...

STUDIO

WEBEREISTRASSE 69   CH 8134 ADLISWIL / ZURICH   TEL 01 / 710 31 57   FAX 01 / 710 73 41

7. juni — 17 juli   1993

jeanne dunning   karen kiliminik   susan walder
wendy jacob   angela bulloch   pipilotti rist
sue williams   art party gang

galerie walcheturm walchestr. 6   CH-8006 zürich
tel. 01/ 252 10 96   fax. 01/252 10 97
di-fr 12-18³⁰   sa 11-16

FRONTLINE ZURICH

THE LEADING AVANT-GARDE SPECIALIST FOR LUXURY SILKS

PRESENTS THE LIMITED EDITION OF TIES DESIGNED BY:

MARTIN KIPPENBERGER
WERNER BÜTTNER
HEIMO ZOBERNIG
LUIS CLARAMUNT
MEUSER
ALBERT OEHLEN
GÜNTHER FÖRG
HUBERT KIECOL
JÖRG SCHLICK

BEN VAUTIER
NIKI DE SAINT PHALLE
TADEUSZ MYSLOWSKI

SEIDENSALON

FABRIC FRONTLINE DIENERSTRASSE 16   8004 ZÜRICH   TEL. 01 / 241 64 55

1.

Welche Druckerei arbeitet schneller?

Manchmal kann es nicht genug druck-zuck gehen. Besonders im grafischen Gewerbe, wo der Ausdruck «Termindruck» eindrücklich verdeutlicht, dass der Termin ebenso wichtig wie der Druck ist. Aber was nützt die modernste Fünffarben-Speedmaster-Druckmaschine (Geschwindigkeit: null-kommaplötzlich, Beschleunigung: professionell-schnell, Antrieb: computergenau), wenn sich beim Satz ein Dreckfehler eingeschlichen hat? Der Dreck multipliziert sich – das liegt schliesslich in der Natur des Drucks – ins Zehntausendfache, ja Hunderttausendfache, so dass alles nochmals von vorne beim vertrackten Druckfehler beginnen muss.

Deshalb unterscheidet sich eine Druckerei nicht nur in der Geschwindigkeit des Maschinenparks, sondern in den kleinen und feinen Details von der ersten Kontaktnahme an: 01 928 51 11 verbindet Sie prompt mit dem für Sie richtigen Aussendienstspezialisten, der die weiteren Abläufe Ihres Auftrages exakt an die für Sie richtigen Innendienstspezialisten weiterleitet, für den Satz, die Lithos, das Papier, den Druck, das Stanzen, das Perforieren, das Numerieren, das Sortieren und Zusammentragen, das Binden, Heften oder Kleben, das Ausrüsten, Verpacken und Spedieren. Alles ohne Tempolimite, vorausgesetzt, die Qualität ist perfekt.

Mit einer kleinen Ausnahme: Bei der Spedition halten wir die Geschwindigkeitsbegrenzungen des Strassenverkehrsgesetzes ein.

Zürichsee Druckereien AG

Ein gemeinsames Unternehmen
von Orell Füssli und Zürichsee Medien AG

8712 Stäfa, Postfach, Seestrasse 86, Telefon 01 928 53 03, Fax 01 928 53 10
8700 Küsnacht, Oberwachtstrasse 2, Telefon 01 910 06 00, Fax 01 910 10 24

2.

Welche Druckerei ist für höhere Auflagen geeigneter?

Selbstverständlich ist der Druck von happigen Grossaufträgen wie die «Zürichsee-Zeitung», die farbigen Zeitschriften und Bücher, die komplizierten Mailings und Prospekte, Hauszeitungen und Kataloge nur mit Hilfe modernster Technologie zu bewältigen. Zum Beispiel mit der Fünffarben-Speedmaster-Druckmaschine. Inklusive fünf Farben im gleichen Druckgang. Inklusive Perforation. Inklusive Drucklackierung.

Allerdings genügt High-Tech alleine noch lange nicht für den exklusiven Unterschied am Ende. Denn was ist, wenn die Beratung unvollständig erfolgte? Wenn der Auftrag nicht korrekt weitergeleitet wurde? Wenn Änderungen in letzter Minute nicht nullkommaplötzlich berücksichtigt werden können? – Die fervlixten Vehler multiplizieren sich in Grossauflagenhöhe (und schlagen auf den Magen…).

Deshalb sind Grossauflagen bei uns (bis hin zum ganz kleinen Auftrag) immer mit einer zusätzlichen Auflage verbunden: Professionalität und Perfektion bis ins kleine, feine Detail, für das letztlich keine Maschine, sondern nur Menschen garantieren können: unsere Mitarbeiter. Von der ersten Kontaktnahme an (01 928 51 11) bis hin zum beeindruckenden Happy-End.

Zürichsee Druckereien AG

Ein gemeinsames Unternehmen
von Orell Füssli und Zürichsee Medien AG

8712 Stäfa, Postfach, Seestrasse 86, Telefon 01 928 51 11, Fax 01 928 53 10
8700 Küsnacht, Oberwachtstrasse 2, Telefon 01 910 06 00, Fax 01 910 10 24

ART - AND BOOKFAIRS
1993

Der PARKETT Verlag freut sich, Sie an folgenden Ausstellungsmessen an seinem
Stand begrüssen zu dürfen:

PARKETT Publishers are pleased to welcome you at their booth during the
following fairs and exhibitions:

ART 24´93

Basel	16.–21.6.	1993

FIAC

Paris	9.–17.10.	1993

ART COLOGNE

Köln	11.–17.11.	1993

New: Art 24'93

Basel 16.–21. 6. 1993

Klassiker und neueste Tendenzen an der bedeutendsten internationalen Kunstmesse in Basel. Neue Galerien präsentieren richtungsweisende Projekte. Fotogalerien und internationale Editeure erhalten eigene Sektoren. Ihre Messe Basel.

Your discreet Swiss partner for the storage and transport of works of art.

MAT SECURITAS EXPRESS AG

Kloten-Zürich 01 / 814 16 66 Fax 01 / 814 20 21
Basel   061/271 43 80 Fax 061/271 43 18
Chiasso   091/ 43 75 51 Fax 091/ 43 98 08
Genève   022/343 04 55 Fax 022/343 26 30

RICHARD LONG
MOUNTAINS AND WATERS ·

ORIGINAL DRAWINGS

River Avon Mud on handmade Japanese paper.
Thirty five drawings, each 6 x 9 inches
with artist's stamp, mounted in a folder
with slipcase, accompanied by the book
MOUNTAINS AND WATERS published in
the UK by Anthony d'Offay, in the USA by
George Braziller and in Germany by Oktagon.
Price on application.

ANTHONY d'OFFAY GALLERY LONDON
TEL 071-499 4100 FAX 071-493 4443

Post War &
Contemporary Art

LONDON, 24TH JUNE 1993

Gerhard Richter, *Neger (Nuba)*, signed and titled on the reverse,
oil on canvas, 145 by 200cm, executed in 1964. Estimate: £200,000-250,000

Enquiries: In London, Tobias Meyer, Elena Geuna. *Tel:* (44 71) 408 5400
Sotheby's, 34 - 35 New Bond Street, London W1A 2AA.

Illustrated catalogues are available in our offices and galleries worldwide

SOTHEBY'S
FOUNDED 1744

YDESSA HENDELES
ART FOUNDATION

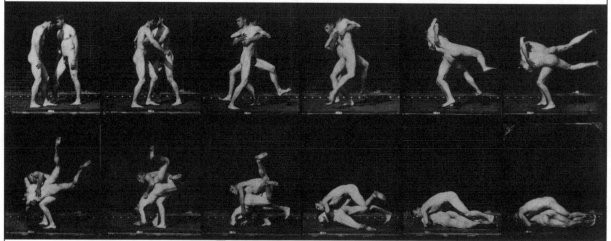

Eadweard Muybridge, *Animal Locomotion, Plate 347*, 1887

EADWEARD MUYBRIDGE

130 collotypes from *Animal Locomotion*, 1887
Panorama of San Francisco from California Hill, 1877

BILL VIOLA

The Arc of Ascent, 1992
Heaven and Earth, 1992

GIULIO PAOLINI

Intervallo (wrestlers), 1985

GARY HILL

Inasmuch As It Is Always Already Taking Place, 1990
Tall Ships, 1992

JAMES COLEMAN

Box (Ahhareturnabout), 1977
Living and Presumed Dead, 1983-85

778 KING STREET WEST, TORONTO, CANADA M5V 1N6

NEW SCULPTURES FOR MIDDELHEIM

Richard Deacon, Isa Genzken,
Harald Klingelhöller, Per Kirkeby,
Bernd Lohaus, Matt Mullican,
Juan Muñoz, Panamarenko,
Thomas Schütte, Didier Vermeiren

OPEN-AIR MUSEUM OF SCULPTURE MIDDELHEIM
FROM JUNE 6

THE SUBLIME VOID
AN EXHIBITION ON THE MEMORY OF THE IMAGINATION

Jean-Marc Bustamante, René Daniëls,
Thierry De Cordier, Lili Dujourie,
Luciano Fabro, Fortuyn/O'Brien,
Robert Gober, Cristina Iglesias,
Niek Kemps, Harald Klingelhöller,
Jannis Kounellis, Juan Muñoz,
John Murphy, Michelangelo Pistoletto,
Gerhard Richter, Thomas Schütte,
Ettore Spalletti, Mitja Tušek, Luc Tuymans,
Jan Vercruysse, Didier Vermeiren,
Jeff Wall, James Welling,
Franz West, Rachel Whiteread

ROYAL MUSEUM OF FINE ARTS
25 JULY - 10 OCTOBER

Cultural capital of Europe

information ANTWERP 93: [32] [3] 226.93.00

THOMAS AMMANN FINE ART AG

IMPRESSIONIST & 20TH CENTURY MASTERS

SELECTED WORKS BY MAJOR ARTISTS

ARP
BALTHUS
BEUYS
BOTERO
CALDER
CHILLIDA
COURBET
ERNST
GIACOMETTI
KLEE
DE KOONING
LAURENS
LEGER
LICHTENSTEIN
MANZU
MATISSE
MIRO
MODIGLIANI
MONDRIAN
MOORE
NEWMAN
OLDENBURG
PICASSO
RENOIR
RICHTER
RODIN
ROTHKO
SEGAL
STILL
TWOMBLY
WARHOL

RESTELBERGSTRASSE 97   CH-8044 ZÜRICH

TEL. (411) 252 90 52   FAX (411) 252 82 45